"Gary Smith has given us a treasure trove of questions about the practical applications of financial economics. Anyone teaching a course on capital markets, corporate finance, or personal finance will find a rich variety of puzzles here, some conceptual, some numerical, and many that remind us how easy it is for pundits to go astray when they fail to think like economists. This book is a superb resource for the teaching of finance."

— **John Y. Campbell**, *Morton L. and Carole S. Olshan Professor of Economics, Harvard University*

"To be successful in finance, it is important to know what you know and to know what you don't know. This book is an invaluable resource to calibrate your expertise. Highly recommended."

— **Campbell R. Harvey**, *Professor, Duke University, 2016 American Finance Association President*

"Coming up with excellent questions for a introductory finance class is quite challenging. Gary Smith has assembled a treasure trove of interesting and thought-provoking questions that can be used as exam questions or as the focus of discussion sections."

— **John Shoven**, *Professor, Stanford University, undergraduate finance teacher for 45 years*

"Gary is brilliant with an uncanny clarity on finance. His incisive commentary on practical finance questions always cuts right to the chase and is so illuminating."

— **Hamilton Helmer**, *author of* 7 Powers *and Co-Founder of Strategy Capital*

"Gary has put together a masterful collection of finance questions emanating from his 50 years of teaching finance courses. Other professors will definitely find them useful in their classes."

— **Brian Nelson**, *Founder and President of Equity Research, Valuentum Securities, Inc.*

"Gary has created an entertaining collection of test questions and answers addressing the most important topics of finance. The questions illustrate common mistakes made by the media and even academics. The answers are entertaining and informative. Every finance student should be required to read this book."

— **Gary Antonacci**, *author of* Dual Momentum Investing: An Innovative Strategy for Higher Returns with Lower Risk

Exercises and Solutions in Finance

This book contains hundreds of engaging, class-tested finance exercises (and detailed solutions) that test student understanding of the material. Many are educational in their own right—for example, delaying social security benefits does not give a safe 8% real return; the correlation between bond and stock returns is not stable, and most measures of company performance regress toward the mean.

Gary Smith is the Fletcher Jones Professor of Economics at Pomona College. He has won two teaching awards and written (or co-authored) more than 100 academic papers and 20 books. His statistical and financial research has been featured in various media, including *The New York Times*, *Wall Street Journal*, *Wired*, *NPR Tech Nation*, NBC Bay Area, CNBC, WYNC, WBBR Bloomberg Radio, *NBC Think*, *Silicon Valley Insider*, *Motley Fool*, *Scientific American*, *Forbes*, *MarketWatch*, MoneyCentral.msn, *NewsWeek*, *Fast Company*, *The Economist*, *MindMatters*, *OZY*, *Slate*, and *BusinessWeek*.

Exercises and Solutions in Finance

Gary Smith

CRC Press
Taylor & Francis Group
Boca Raton London New York

CRC Press is an imprint of the
Taylor & Francis Group, an **informa** business
A CHAPMAN & HALL BOOK

Designed cover image: Gary Smith

First edition published 2026
by CRC Press
2385 NW Executive Center Drive, Suite 320, Boca Raton FL 33431

and by CRC Press
4 Park Square, Milton Park, Abingdon, Oxon, OX14 4RN

CRC Press is an imprint of Taylor & Francis Group, LLC

ISBN: 978-1-041-04838-1 (hbk)
ISBN: 978-1-041-04836-7 (pbk)
ISBN: 978-1-003-63016-6 (ebk)

DOI: 10.1201/9781003630166

Typeset in Palatino
by KnowledgeWorks Global Ltd.

Contents

Introduction

This book contains hundreds of selected finance questions (and solutions) that I have used on midterm and final examination tests in investment and finance classes that I taught for more than 50 years.

Every question has been class-tested. Questions that did not work well or do not seem particularly interesting have been omitted. In recent years, I have been teaching increasingly interactive classes in which randomly chosen teams work on a longer exercise outside of class and give presentations of their conclusions in class. So, I've also included dozens of longer exercises in a special chapter (Chapter 17).

1

Present Value

1.1 The [Motley] Fool School:

> Imagine you're looking at a newfangled invention called the "dollar machine." Once a year, for ten years, it spits out a brand-new dollar bill. How would you value this contraption? .... Let's say you expect a rate of return equal to the stock market's historic rate of about 11 percent growth per year. If so, you might decide to pay just \$3.52 for the machine. \$3.52 invested for ten years earning 11 percent annually becomes \$10 [that is, $\$3.52(1.11)^{10} = \$10$].

Carefully explain why, if you have an 11% required return, you would pay (a) \$3.52, (b) more than \$3.52, or (c) less than \$3.52 for this dollar machine. Do not make any calculations to answer this question.

1.2 In 1988, Congress accused the Federal Home Loan Bank Board of making inconsistent and misleading estimates of the resources needed to clean up the savings and loan (S&L) industry during the next 10 years. In Congressional testimony that summer, Board Chairman M. Danny Wall estimated that the present value (in 1988) of closing or merging 500 sick S&Ls was \$30.9 billion and that the Board expected to collect \$42 billion in revenue during the 10 years 1988–1998, giving it \$12 billion more than it needed. Explain why, in the words of one Senator, the Board's calculations are "comparing apples and oranges" and how Congress could use the very same data and estimate that the bank board's revenue might be inadequate to cover its expenses.

1.3 Firms that market time-share condominiums offer prizes to those who endure a tour and sales pitch. One prize was a \$1000 savings account maturing in 55 years, in return for a \$55 fee for "handling, processing and insurance." What is the implicit annual rate of return for someone who takes this prize?

1.4 "If you pay us \$1,000 a year for 10 years, we will pay you and your heirs \$1,000 a year forever." What is the implicit rate of return on this offer?

Assume that the first \$1,000 payment is due a year from today and that the first \$1,000 received begins 1 year after the tenth \$1,000 payment. You just need to set up the equation that needs to be solved for the implicit return.

1.5 In 2023, it was reported that Otha Anders had been collecting pennies found on the ground or received as change for 45 years and had accumulated enough to fill 15 five-gallon water bottles. When his home

DOI: 10.1201/9781003630166-1

insurance company balked at selling him a home-insurance policy that would insure the pennies, he cashed them in at a friendly bank for $5,136.14, an average collection of $114.14 per year.

> After paying the dental bill, he decided to treat his family to a vacation, and if that wasn't enough he chose to show his gratitude in life and donated whatever was left to his church.

How much would he have had if he had invested $114.14 every year for 45 years at a 5% rate of return? At a 10% rate of return? (For simplicity, assume that he invested $114.14 at the end of every year, beginning 45 years ago.)

1.6 In 2023, Shohei Ohtani signed a 10-year contract with the Los Angeles Dodgers for $700 million; however, in order for the Dodgers to continue spending money on Mookie Betts, Freddie Freeman, and their other stars, Ohtani agreed to defer all but $2 million of his annual salary until after the end of his contract. He would be paid $2 million a year for 10 years, 2024–2033, and then $68 million a year for the next 10 years, 2034–2043. With a 10% discount rate, what was the present value of his contract in 2023? (Assume, for simplicity, that the payments are made annually, beginning 1 year after signing the contract.)

1.7 In the 1980s, it was argued that because some Japanese firms could borrow virtually unlimited amounts interest-free from the government, they should use a 0% required return in evaluating investment projects. Explain why you either agree or disagree.

1.8 You will receive $1,000 twenty years from now. Your annual real required return is 5%, and the annual rate of inflation is 5%. Is the real value of this $1,000 in today's dollars larger than, smaller than, or equal to the present value of this $1,000?

1.9 A Spring 1992 publication by Rensselaer Polytechnic Institute showed a "smart option" in which the family of a student enrolling in the Fall of 1992 could save $4,931 by pre-paying 4 years of tuition with an amount equal to four times the current $15,900 tuition:

Year	Annual Tuition (5% annual increase)	Prepayment Tuition
1992–1993	$15,900	$63,600
1993–1994	16,695	0
1994–1995	17,530	0
1995–1996	18,406	0
	$68,531	$63,600

Explain why this "smart option" may not be so smart.

1.10 In October of 1992, the *Los Angeles Times* reported that the Elliot Wave Institute "recently came up with a prediction that is most controversial, mainly because it is so optimistic. The Dow Jones industrial average will top 100,000 points by the year 2060 in the biggest bull market of all time." At the time, the Dow was at 3150. If the Dow increases from 3150 to 100,000 over this 68-year period, what will be the annual compounded rate of increase?

1.11 A *Wall Street Journal* article claimed that a 9.25% annual interest rate, compounded daily, was more attractive than a 9.40% annual interest rate, compounded quarterly; a reader wrote in to say that his calculations showed just the opposite. Which rate is more attractive?

1.12 In 2008, an Englishman received £200 from an Australian tourist who had borrowed £5 from him 40 years earlier. The Australian calculated the £200 debt as £5 for each year that had gone by since he borrowed £5. If the Englishman had made a £5 investment 40 years ago that was now worth £200, what would be the rate of return?

1.13 In the *Sopranos* television show, Tony Soprano turned down an offer of $225 a square foot for some property he owned, explaining that, "As a businessman, I gotta tell you that in ten years' time that property's gonna be worth twice as much as they're offering." If the realtor had been familiar with the Rule of 72, she could have calmly replied, "That's about X percent a year; not bad, but not as good as an average year in the stock market." What is the value of X?

1.14 In 1996, a *BusinessWeek* story titled *"The Most Bang for Your MBA Buck,"* reported that a professor at the Cincinnati College of Business had ranked business schools by comparing the cost of attending (including the lost wages while attending) with the increase in salary afterward from having an MBA from that school. The schools were ranked by the number of years it took for the cumulation of the higher salaries to payback the cost of business school. For example, at MIT (ranked fifth), the cost of attending was $159,800 and it took slightly more than 5 years for the cumulative additional salary to reach $159,800. What conceptual flaws do you see in a payback calculation such as this?

1.15 Explain the error in management's reasoning: "We are considering the construction of a shopping center. Because we will finance this project by borrowing money from Citibank at 9%, this is the interest rate that we should use to discount the project's cash flow."

1.16 A developer is contemplating a 5-year investment in a skateboard emporium. Since she firmly believes that inflation will average 2% over the next 5 years, she says that 2% is the appropriate rate to use in discounting the projected cash flows. A financial adviser says that her required rate of return should be 4% since she could earn 4% by investing in 5-year Treasury bonds. Explain why both are wrong.

1.17 Explain why this argument is correct or incorrect: "If you and I agree on the cash flow from an investment, then we should use the same required return."

1.18 Explain why you either agree or disagree with this argument: "Your great-grandfather has just died and left you $120,000, which you will invest in a small winery; because this inheritance cost you nothing, your required rate of return is 0%."

1.19 Starting in 1209, the British Treasury paid Oxford University £3.08 every year as compensation for people in the city of Oxford hanging some students who had helped another student murder his mistress. In 1985, the University accepted a one-time payment of £33.08 to settle this obligation. What interest rate was used to determine this settlement?

1.20 You will save X a year for 5 years, beginning a year from today, in order to accumulate sufficient wealth to pay an annual prize of $10,000 a year forever, beginning 6 years from now. If your rate of return is 8%, what is the appropriate value of X?

1.21 Babe Ruth was paid $80,000 in 1931 to play for the New York Yankees; Aaron Judge was paid $40 million in 2024 to play for the Yankees. The consumer price index was 15.2 in 1931 and 314 in 2024. Which of these two salaries is higher in real terms? What would Judge's 2024 salary be if he were paid an amount with the same purchasing power as Ruth's 1931 salary?

1.22 It has been argued that nominal interest rates move up and down with inflation so as to hold real interest rates constant at, say, 2%. If a 5% fall in prices is anticipated, what nominal rate of return will give a 2% real return? How much does a $100 investment have to pay a year from now to give this nominal return? Why will most people be reluctant to make such an investment?

1.23 Vincent Van Gogh sold only one painting during his lifetime, for about $30. In 1987, a Japanese insurance company paid $39.85 million for a sunflower still life Van Gogh painted in 1888, more than three times the highest price paid previously for any work of art. Observers attributed the record price in part to the fact that his other sunflower paintings are all in museums and most likely will never be available for sale. If this painting had been purchased for $30 in 1888 and sold 99 years later for $39.85 million, what would have been the annual rate of return?

1.24 In 2015, *Bloomberg Businessweek* reported that Russians can get loans through an ATM: "The interest rate is 2% a day, which works out to 730% on an annualized basis."

a. How did they get the 730% number?

b. What is the effective annual interest rate, taking into account daily compounding and assuming 365 days in a year?

1.25 When a child loses a baby tooth, an old U.S. tradition is for the tooth to be put under the child's pillow, so that the tooth fairy will leave money for it. A survey by a Northwestern University professor found that the tooth fairy paid an average of 12 cents for a tooth in 1900 and $1 for a tooth in 1987. A Delta Dental 2024 poll found that the average value of a single lost tooth was $5.84. The consumer price index was 8.4 in 1900, 114 in 1987, and 313 in 2024.

a. Did the real value of tooth fairy payments rise or fall over this period?

b. If tooth fairy payments had kept up with inflation between 1900 and 2024, how large should the payment have been in 1987? In 2024?

1.26 Warren Buffett took control of Berkshire Hathaway on May 10, 1965, when Berkshire stock closed at $18 a share; 59 years later, on May 10, 2024, Berkshire closed at $622,000 a share. Berkshire has never paid a dividend. If an investor had bought Berkshire in 1965 for $18 and sold it 59 years later for $622,000, what would her annual rate of return have been?

1.27 The "Beardstown Ladies" (an investment club of grandmothers in Beardstown, Illinois) wrote five best-selling investment guides after reporting that their investment club had made 23.4% a year from 1984 through 1993, while the Dow Jones Industrial Average returned only 15.7% a year. However, it turned out that their 23.4% return was only for 2 years, 1991–1992 and that they had simply compared the value of their portfolio at the beginning and end of the period, without taking into account the annual dues that were added to the portfolio. Once these were taken into account, their annual return from 1984 through 1993 dropped to 9.1%. How would you calculate the annual return for an investment club's portfolio that had regular dues added to the portfolio? Give an explicit equation and define all variables.

1.28 In many state lotteries, the grand prize carries over to the next drawing if there is no winner. In 1992, the Virginia grand prize grew to $27 million. A ticket cost $1 and would win the grand prize if the buyer correctly picked 6 of 44 numbers, 1 to 44, not necessarily in order. An Australian syndicate attempted to purchase all 7,059,052 possible ticket combinations in order to ensure that it would win the lottery. It was only able to buy 5,000,000 tickets, but it did win the $27 million jackpot, paid in 20 annual installments of $1,350,000 beginning immediately. What was the implicit annual rate of return on its investment?

1.29 The Powerball lottery has two drums, one with 69 white balls (numbered 1 to 69) and one with 26 red balls (numbered 1 to 26). A player pays $2 for a ticket and picks 5 white numbers and 1 red number (the Powerball). The player wins the jackpot if their 5 white numbers match the 5 numbers drawn from the white-ball drum (not necessarily in order) and the player's red number matches the one number drawn from the red-ball drum. In the August 23, 2017, Powerball drawing, the stated jackpot was $700 million, with the winner having the choice of taking an immediate prize of $443 million; or 30 annual payments, starting at $10,536 immediately and increasing by 5% each year.

With either option, there is a federal 25% tax on the payout. Which is financially more attractive, the $443 million immediate prize or the 30 annual payments? (Just set up.)

1.30 An October 2021 *New York Times* article titled, *The True Cost of Upgrading Your Phone*, argued that

> Let's talk about buying an iPhone for $1,000. Tim Cook, Apple's chief executive, once compared this eye-popping price tag to buying a cup of coffee a day over a year. No big deal, right?
>
> But financial advisers see this differently. By some estimates, an investment of $1,000 in a retirement account today would balloon to about $17,000 in 30 years.

a. What rate of return did this calculation assume?

b. Do you agree that the true cost of an iPhone is $17,000?

1.31 Suppose that you start work at age 21 and save $10,000 at the end of the first year and 5% more every year thereafter (for example, $10,500 at the end of the second year) and that you earn a 10% annual after-tax return. How much will you have accumulated after 20 years? Just set up.

1.32 In 2018, a financial columnist wrote that since, "1996, [Berkshire Hathaway] stock averages 12.3% annual returns. [An S&P 500 index fund] over the same timeframe averages 9.5%. Granted, Berkshire stock obviously has the better performance, but it's not *that* much better." How much difference would it make to a $10,000 investment made in 1996?

1.33 In a 1988 mail solicitation, the Editor of the Telephone Switch Newsletter wrote

> Get ready for a shocker. A 20% annualized compounded growth rate over the next 10 years would provide you with profits averaging 51.9% per year on your original investment.

He apparently reasoned that $10,000(1.20^{10}) = $61,917 implies a profit of $51,917. This total profit over 10 years was then divided into 10 annual parts: $51,917/10 = $5,191.70, each of which represents a 51.9% return on the original $10,000 investment. Do you think that 20% or 51.9% is a more accurate description of your annual rate of return? Why?

1.34 In March 2022, the Cleveland Browns football team announced that they had restructured their contract with quarterback Deshaun Watson (they had already paid Watson $46 million in 2022) in order to free up $35,868,000 in salary cap space in 2023:

	Original (millions)	Restructured (millions)
2023	$46	$19.125
2024	$46	$63.96
2025	$46	$63.96
2026	$46	$63.96
2027	$0	$8.967

Is the restructured contract more or less financially advantageous for Watson?

1.35 A solicitation from Yale University gave this real-life example of the financial advantages of giving money to Yale: Yale grandparents "contributed $100,000 to a trust which will pay their granddaughter $9,000 a year for ten years, beginning a year after the contribution—a total of $90,000. They were entitled to an immediate income tax charitable contribution of $41,000. Yale will receive the remaining trust assets after ten years." If the grandparents are in a 35% tax bracket, the $41,000 charitable contribution will reduce their taxes by .35($41,000) = $14,350 immediately (assuming the grandparents itemize and there is no alternative minimum tax or other complications). What is the implicit rate of return on this contribution? Just set up.

1.36 A local bank advertised "Daily compounding for highest possible yields." Why does daily compounding increase the effective yield? What kind of compounding would give an even higher yield? How much higher if the quoted annual percentage rate is 5%?

1.37 In 1972, the Census Bureau estimated that a male college graduate could expect to earn a total of $199,000 more between the ages of 22 and 64 than a male with only a high school diploma. In a well-known article titled, "College is a Waste of Time and Money," Carolyn Bird wrote that,

> If a 1972 Princeton-bound high-school graduate had put the $34,181 that his four years of college education would have cost him into a savings bank at 7.5% interest compounded daily, he would have had at age 64 a total of $1,129,000,...more than five times as much as the $199,000 extra the more educated man could expect to earn between 22 and 64.

Identify the logical mistake in this financial comparison. (Ignore the likelihood that the increase in income for a Princeton graduate may be above average.)

1.38 Cameron is 18 years old and considering two career paths:

a. Take a job immediately with an annual income that is initially $50,000 and will grow by 3% a year.

b. Go to college for 4 years, with tuition, room & board, and other expenses totaling $75,000 the first year and increasing by 5% each year; after 4 years of college, take a job with an annual income that is initially $70,000 and will grow by 4% a year.

Which choice is more financially attractive? Ignore taxes, assume that all income and expenses are paid at the beginning of each year, and assume that, either way, Cameron will retire at age 70.

1.39 In December 2006, the *New York Times* reported that 25-year-old David King purchased a burial insurance policy for which he would pay $3 a week until he died, at which point his heirs would be paid $10,000, which can be used to pay for his burial. Mr. King explained that $3 is "not very much" and that if he bought burial insurance when he was older, it would cost more: "Might as well get it while the getting's good." If he dies at age 85, what is the implicit annual rate of return on this policy? Assume that there are 60(52) = 3,120 payments, with the first payment made immediately and the last payment made 1 week before death. (Just set up.)

1.40 In the television series *Entourage*, a legendary Hollywood producer brags that a home he purchased 50 years ago for $140,000 is now worth $13 million. What was the annual rate of increase?

1.41 Here is an excerpt from a letter to the editor of Barron's:

> I read with interest your tale of woe about Caprimex and the IMAC Currency Hedge Fund. In addition to having computer problems, Alex Herbage also cannot do interest arithmetic. An investment that produces a profit of 257% in 6 1/2 years (i.e., $100 grows to $357) has a rate of return of [….] %, not the 39.5% as quoted by Herbage….This calculation goes beyond the limits of reasonably puffery … and is certainly without significance.

a. How was the 39.5% calculated?

b. What is the correct rate of return (which has been omitted from the above excerpt)?

1.42 At age 55, Jones bought a $1 million life insurance policy for $3,000 a year for 15 years, payable annually beginning on the day Jones signed the policy. He did not die during the policy period. How much money would Jones have had after 15 years if, instead of buying the insurance policy, he had invested $3,000 each year, earning a 10% annual return? (Just set up.)

1.43 (True story) A conservative investor kept $40,000 in a locked safe "for emergencies" for 40 years, from 1978 until his death in 2017. If this money had instead been invested in the S&P 500, which had a compounded annual return of 11.94% over this period, what would the value of the investment have been at the end of 2017?

1.44 It was recently reported that Gene Sukie cashed in 1,407,550 pennies that he had collected over the previous 34 years. If he collected an equal number of pennies each year and, on the last day of the year, invested these pennies in stocks that earned a 10% annual return, how much would he have had at the end of 34 years? (You do not need to calculate a numerical value, but you must explicitly show the equation that would be used to calculate a numerical answer.)

1.45 In 2023, a 65-year-old man was offered the following annuity: Pay $100,000 now and receive an annual $7,000 payment, beginning 1 year after the $100,000 payment and continuing until the man's death. If he lives to 80 and receives 15 payments, what is the implicit rate of return?

1.46 In 1988, the president of a community college wrote a letter to *The Wall Street Journal*, arguing that federal aid to college students is a great investment for the government:

> If the average cost of a bachelor's degree is $36,800 and the average additional earnings resulting from it are $640,000, a 30% tax bracket would produce $192,000 in additional taxes from the degree holder. That's over 500% return on investment.

Explain why his calculations are misleading, and, assuming his numbers are correct, show how you would calculate the government return.

1.47 The Academic Management Services Monthly Payment Plan allows college students to pay their tuition and other college charges in 12 equal monthly installments, in place of the two semester charges. For example, if a college's total charges for the 2024–2025 academic year come to $60,000, with $30,000 due on August 7, 2024, and $30,000 due on January 8, 2025—the AMS plan allows the student to pay $5,000 each month, beginning on March 15, 2024, and ending on February 15, 2025. The only fee for this service is a $45 application fee. How can AMS, a private company, afford to offer this plan? (Use logic, not math.)

1.48 A recent baseball contract had a face value of $10,000,000. Every year for 10 years, beginning 21 years from today, the player will be paid $1,000,000 + 3% interest on the balance of the $10,000,000 that has not yet been paid. Thus, the first payment, 21 years from today, is $1,000,000 + 3%(10,000,000) = $1,300,000; the second payment, 22 years from today, is $1,000,000 + 3%($9,000,000) = $1,270,000. What is the present value of this contract? (Just set up.)

1.49 Suppose one mutual fund charges an annual management fee equal to 1.6% of assets, and another fund's annual management fee is .2% of assets. If both funds earn 8% a year before management fees, what will be the difference in an investor's wealth after 20 years?

1.50 In a 2022 spousal-support case, an expert witness testified that a 59-year-old woman who invested $1,000,000 to earn 2.3% a year, with a rate of inflation equal to 2% a year, could spend $41,547 a year in real terms and run out of money in exactly 25 years. Show the formula you would use to make this calculation. (Assume, for simplicity, that spending is annual, beginning 1 year from today.)

Answers

1.1 The Fool looks at $\$3.52(1.11)^{10} = \$10$, but you do not have to wait 10 years to get the $10; you get $1 each year for 10 years, which is better than getting $10 at the end of 10 years. At an 11% required return, the present value of $1 a year for 10 years is $5.89.

1.2 Wall compared a present value to an undiscounted sum of revenue. The present value of a $42 billion cash flow spread over 10 years may be substantially less than $30 billion. For instance, if the $42 billion cash flow is divided evenly, $4.2 billion a year for 10 years, its present value at a 10% required return is only $25.8 billion, which is $5.1 billion less than the $30.9 billion present value of expenses:

$$P = \frac{\$4.2}{(1.10)^1} + \frac{\$4.2}{(1.10)^2} + \ldots + \frac{\$4.2}{(1.10)^{10}}$$
$$= \$25.8$$

It is especially puzzling that a federal bank board would make such an obvious present-value mistake. After aides to the House Banking Committee uncovered this inconsistency in the way revenue and expenses were reported, the committee chairman said, "The miscalculations are serious. They are the result of either gross incompetence or deliberate attempts to mislead and minimize the problem to Congress and the public."

1.3 Using the future value formula, $F = P(1 + R)^n$:

$$\$1000 = \$55(1 + R)^{55} \text{ implies } R = .0666\ (6.66\%).$$

1.4 Equating the present values,

$$\frac{\$1000}{(1+R)^1} + \frac{\$1000}{(1+R)^2} + \ldots + \frac{\$1000}{(1+R)^{10}} = \frac{\$1000}{(1+R)^{11}} + \frac{\$1000}{(1+R)^{12}} + \ldots$$

The solution works out to be R = .0718 (7.18%).

1.5 The 2023 value would have been

$$P = \$114.14(1+R)^{45} + \$114.14(1+R)^{44} + \ldots + \$114.14(1+R)^{1}$$
$$= \$19{,}140 \text{ for } R = .05 \text{ and } \$90{,}261 \text{ for } R = .10$$

1.6 The present value equation is

$$P = \frac{\$2}{(1.10)^1} + \frac{\$2}{(1.10)^2} + \ldots + \frac{\$2}{(1.10)^{10}} + \frac{\$68}{(1.10)^{11}} + \frac{\$68}{(1.10)^{12}} + \ldots + \frac{\$68}{(1.10)^{20}}$$
$$= \$173.38$$

1.7 They still should compare alternative investments—for example, bonds versus machines—and therefore should take interest rates into account, plus risk premiums.

1.8 The real value is obtained by discounting by the rate of inflation:

$$\text{real value} = \frac{\$1{,}000}{1.05^{20}}$$

The present value is obtained by discounting this nominal payment by the nominal required rate of return, which is approximately equal to the real rate plus the rate of inflation: 5% + 5% = 10%:

$$\text{present value} \approx \frac{\$1{,}000}{1.10^{20}}$$

The present value is smaller than the real value.

1.9 Prepaying an expense that is growing by 5% a year is like making an investment with a 5% return. A present value calculation confirms that prepaying tuition that is growing by 5% annually breaks even with a 5% required return (and is disadvantageous with a higher required return).

$$\$63{,}600 = \$15{,}900 + \frac{\$16{,}695}{(1+R)^1} + \frac{\$17{,}530}{(1+R)^2} + \frac{\$18{,}406}{(1+R)^3}$$
$$= \$15{,}900 + \frac{15{,}900(1.05)^1}{(1+R)^1} + \frac{5{,}900(1.05)^2}{(1+R)^2} + \frac{5{,}900(1.05)^3}{(1+R)^3}$$
$$= 4(15{,}1900) = \$63{,}600 \text{ if } R = .05$$

In addition, the student may not stay at RPI for four years.

1.10 Applying the future value formula, the annual rate of growth g works out to be 5.2%:

$$\$3{,}150(1+g)^{68} = \$100{,}000$$

$$1+g = \left(\frac{\$100{,}000}{\$3{,}150}\right)^{1/68}$$

$$g = .052(5.2)$$

1.11 With daily compounding, the effective annual return is $(1 + .0925/365)^{365} = 1.0969$ (9.69%). With quarterly compounding, the effective annual return is $(1 + .0940/4)^4 = 1.0974$ (9.74%). The reader is right.

1.12 Using the future value formula, $F = P(1 + R)^n$: $200 = 5(1 + R)^{40}$ implies $R = .0966$ (9.66%).

1.13 The Rule of 72 is that the number of years it takes to double an investment is approximately equal to 72, divided by the annual rate of return: $n = 72/R$ or $R = 72/n$. Here, $R = 72/10 = 7.2\%$.

1.14 A payback period calculation such as this ignores the time value of money, and it ignores the extra income after the investment is paid back.

1.15 The required rate of return presumably includes a risk premium.

1.16 A 2% inflation doesn't mean she will earn 2% by making an alternative investment. Most people prefer safe government bonds to investing in a risky skateboard emporium. A reasonable required return is the safe return on Treasury bonds plus a risk premium.

1.17 An individual's required return depends on the returns on alternative investments and their aversion to risk and other undesirable characteristics of the investments.

1.18 The required rate of return depends on the rates of return available on alternative investments (which are surely larger than 0%) and the riskiness of the investment.

1.19 Using the perpetuity formula: £33.08 = £3.08/R implies R = .093 (9.3%).

1.20 Setting the present value of the savings equal to the present value of the prizes,

$$\frac{X}{(1.08)^1} + \frac{X}{(1.08)^2} + \ldots + \frac{X}{(1.08)^5} = \frac{\$1,000}{(1.08)^6} + \frac{\$1,000}{(1.08)^7} + \ldots$$

$$= \frac{1}{(1.08)^5}\left(\frac{\$1,000}{(1.08)^1} + \frac{\$1,000}{(1.08)^2} + \ldots\right)$$

$$= \frac{1}{(1.08)^5}\left(\frac{\$1,000}{.08}\right)$$

The solution works out to be X = $21,307.

1.21 Judge was paid far more in real terms, since his salary was 500 times Ruth's salary, and prices increased by only a factor of 20.7. More formally, real income is calculated by deflating nominal income by the price level:

$$\text{Babe Ruth } \$80{,}000 / 15.2 = \$5{,}263$$

$$\text{Aaron Judge: } \$40 \text{ million} / 314 = \$127{,}388$$

A 2024 salary X with the same purchasing power as Ruth's 1931 salary is $80.000(314/15.2) = $1,652,631.

1.22 The real rate of return is approximately equal to the nominal rate of return minus the rate of inflation. Here, 2% = nominal – (–5%) implies nominal = –3%. A $100 investment would be worth $97 a year later, which is worse than just keeping cash in a checking account or safe deposit box.

1.23 Using either a future value or present value equation: $F = P(1 + R)^n$: $\$39{,}850{,}000 = \$30(1 + R)^{99}$ implies R = .153 (15.3%).

1.24 a. They got 730% by multiplying two times 365.

b. The effective annual return with daily compounding is $1 + R = 1.02^{365} = 1377.41$, so R = 137,641%.

1.25 The real value is equal to the nominal value divided by the price level.

a. Using the 12-cent payment in 1900 as a base, the real value of a tooth fairy payment was

$1/(114/8.4) = $.074 in 1987 and $5.84/(313/8.4) = .157 in 2024.

b. If tooth fairy payments had kept up with inflation, the payment should have been

$.12(114/8.4) = $1.63 in 1987, and $.12(313/8.4) = $4.47 in 2024.

1.26 Using the future value equation, $F = P(1 + R)^n$: $622{,}000 = 18(1 + R)^{59}$ implies R = .194 (19.4%).

1.27 Let X_0 be the initial investment, X_t the net inflows (contributions minus withdrawals) each year (expressed as positive numbers), and F the current value of the portfolio. The effective annual return R is given by the present value equation:

$$\frac{F}{(1+R)^n} + X_0 + \frac{X_1}{(1+R)^1} + \frac{X_2}{(1+R)^2} + \ldots + \frac{X_{n-1}}{(1+R)^{n-1}}$$

1.28 The implicit annual rate of return can be determined by this present-value equation:

$$\$5{,}000{,}000 = \$1{,}350{,}000 + \frac{\$1{,}350{,}000}{(1+R)^1} + \frac{\$1{,}350{,}000}{(1+R)^2} + \ldots + \frac{\$1{,}350{,}000}{(1+R)^{19}}$$

The answer works out to be 36.89%.

1.29 The present value of the \$443 million immediate prize is (1 − .25)\$443 million = \$332.25 million. The present value of the 30 payments is

$$P = (1-.25)\$10,536 + \frac{(1-.25)\$10,536(1.05)^1}{(1+R)^1} + \frac{(1-.25)\$10,536(1.05)^2}{(1+R)^2} + \ldots + \frac{(1-.25)\$10,536(1.05)^{29}}{(1+R)^{29}}$$

This works out to be \$372.38 million for a 2% required return, \$317.66 million for a 3% required return, and \$273.28 million for a 4% required return. So, for any after-tax required return greater than (roughly) 3%, the immediate \$443 million is more financially attractive. (The exact breakeven rate is 2.7%.)

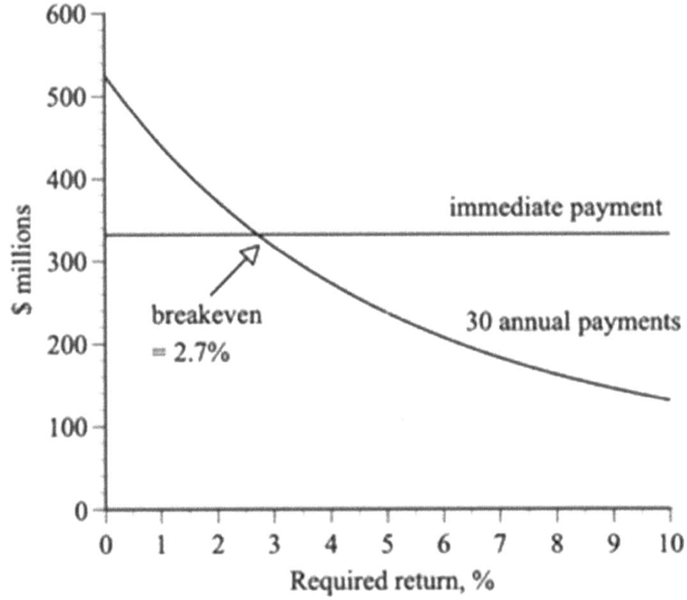

1.30 a. Solving the future-value equation, \$1,000(1+R)^{30} = \$17,000 implies $1 + R = (17,000/1,000)^{1/30} = 1.10$; the calculation assumed a 10% return.

b. I disagree. In current dollars, the cost is \$1,000. By the financial advisor's logic, why not invest for 100 years and call the true cost \$14 million?

1.31 Your wealth at the end of each year is

$$
\begin{aligned}
W_1 &= \$10,000 \\
W_2 &= \$10,000(1+R)+\$10,000(1+g) \\
W_3 &= \$10,000(1+R)^2+\$10,000(1+g)(1+R) \\
&\quad +\$10,000(1+g)^2 \\
&\vdots \\
W_{20} &= \$10,000(1+R)^{19}+\$10,000(1+g)(1+R)^{18} \\
&\quad +\ldots+\$10,000(1+g)^{19}
\end{aligned}
$$

For $g = .05$ and $R = .1$, $W_{20} = \$814{,}840$.

1.32 Using the future-value equation, $\$10{,}000(1.123)^{22} = \$128{,}338$, which is 74% more than $\$10{,}000(1.095)^{22} = \$73{,}639$.

1.33 You are not earning interest on $10,000 each year; you are earning 20% interest on your current wealth, which is growing every year. A 20% annual return is more accurate.

1.34 We can calculate the present value of each contract for a variety of required rates of return and determine a breakeven required return. Assuming that the payments are made annually, beginning in March 2023,

$$
P_O = \frac{\$46}{(1+R)^1} + \frac{\$46}{(1+R)^2} + \frac{\$46}{(1+R)^3}\ \frac{\$46}{(1+R)^4}
$$

$$
P_R = \frac{\$19.125}{(1+R)^1} + \frac{\$63.96}{(1+R)^2} + \frac{\$63.96}{(1+R)^3} + \frac{\$63.96}{(1+R)^4} + \frac{\$8.967}{(1+R)^5}
$$

The breakeven required rate of return turns out to be 50.6%, with the restructured contract having a higher present value for any required return less than 50.6%. The restructured contract was financially advantageous for Watson.

1.35 The appropriate present-value equation is

$$
\$100,000-\$14,350=\sum_{t=1}^{10}\frac{\$9,000}{(1+R)^t}
$$

The implicit rate of return is less than 1%: $R = .0091$ (.91%).

1.36 Daily compounding increases the effective yield by crediting interest daily so that the depositor can earn interest on interest each day.

Continuous compounding would give a (slightly) higher effective yield. The formulas are:

$$\text{daily: } 1+R=\left(1+\frac{.05}{365}\right)^{365}=1.051267$$

$$\text{continuous: } 1+R=e^{.05}=1.051271$$

1.37 The argument ignored the time value of money. The $1,129,000 figure is at age 64 but the $199,000 is spread over the ages 22 to 64. If the $199,000 is spread evenly over 43 years, the future value with as 7.5% interest rate is $1,321,530.

1.38 The present values for these two strategies are:

$$PV_A=\sum_{t=0}^{51}\frac{\$50{,}000(1.03)^t}{(1+R)^t}$$

$$PV_B=\sum_{t=0}^{3}\frac{-\$75{,}000(1.05)^t}{(1+R)^t}+\sum_{t=4}^{51}\frac{\$70{,}000(1.04)^{t-4}}{(1+R)^t}$$

1.39 The implicit annual rate of return R is the value that solves this future-value equation:

$$\$10{,}000=\$3\left(1+\frac{R}{52}\right)^{3120}+\$3\left(1+\frac{R}{52}\right)^{3119}+\ldots+\$3\left(1+\frac{R}{52}\right)^{1}$$

The answer works out to be R = .22% (about 1/5 of 1%).

1.40 The future-value equation $13,000,000 = $140,000$(1 + R)^{50}$ gives $1 + R = (13{,}000{,}000/140{,}000)^{(1/50)} = 1.095$, an annual return of 9.5%. We should also consider the rent savings and the mortgage payments, property taxes, maintenance, and other expenses.

1.41 a. The 39.5% figure was evidently arrived at by dividing the 257% return by 6.5 years: 257%/6.5 = 39.5%. This calculation ignores compound interest.

b. The appropriate future-value equation $357 = 100(1+ R)^{6.5}$ gives an annual return of R = .2163 (21.63%).

1.42 The future value is

$$\$3{,}000(1.10^{15})+\$3{,}000(1.10^{14})+\ldots+\$3{,}000(1.10^{1})=\$104{,}849$$

1.43 Using the future-value formula: $40,000$(1.1194^{40})$ = $3,643,108.

1.44 A total of 1,407,550 pennies divided by 34 years is \$413.98 per year. The future value is

$$F = \$413.98(1.10^{33}) + \$413.98(1.10^{32}) + \ldots + \$413.98 = \$101,622.44$$

1.45 The appropriate present value equation is

$$P = \frac{\$7,000}{(1+R)^1} + \frac{\$7,000}{(1+R)^2} + \frac{\$7,000}{(1+R)^3} + \frac{\$7,000}{(1+R)^{15}}$$

The solution is R = .62%. (If he lives to 85, R = 3.44%).

1.46 The rate of return calculations are very misleading. The ratio \$192,000/\$36,800 = 5.22, represents a 422% return, not a 500% return (just as \$1 that grows to \$1.10 is a 10% return, not 110%). In addition, the letter neglects the fact that the tuition is paid now, while the assumed additional tax revenue occurs in the future. If these additional tax dollars are spread evenly over 45 years, the annual amount is \$192,000/45 = \$4,266.67. Spreading the cost of college equally, too, the implicit return R is determined by this present-value equation:

$$0 = -\$9,200 - \frac{\$9,200}{(1+R)^1} - \frac{\$9,200}{(1+R)^2} - \frac{\$9,200}{(1+R)^3}$$
$$+ \frac{\$4,266.67}{(1+R)^5} + \frac{\$4,266.67}{(1+R)^6} + \ldots + \frac{\$4,266.67}{(1+R)^{48}}$$

The solution is R = .099 (9.9%). The value of R would be even lower if the \$192,000 in taxes were tilted more to the future because of the growth of income.

In addition, the fact that those who go to college make higher incomes on average does not prove that it is college attendance that is responsible for their high income. No doubt, many are motivated to pursue successful careers, with college one step on this path, and would earn higher-than-average incomes even if they didn't attend college. The correct comparison is not the income of those who attend college with the income of those who don't, but the income of those who attend college with what their incomes would have been if they hadn't attended.

The letter also assumes that without financial aid from the federal government, the average person attending college would not have attended. Most likely, many of those who attend college and pursue successful careers would attend college even without federal aid. The relevant comparison is the incomes with and without college enrollment of those who attend because of the additional federal aid.

1.47 Time is money. AMS receives almost all of the student's money in advance of when the payment is due to the college and is able to invest it in the meantime. Presumably, students could do this on their own. The only conceivable advantage of these early monthly payments is that they compel the student to put aside money that will later be needed for tuition.

1.48 Working with millions of dollars, the present value is

$$P - \frac{1+.03(10)}{(1+R)^{21}} + \frac{1+.03(9)}{(1+R)^{22}} + \ldots + \frac{1+.03(1)}{(1+R)^{30}}$$

The present value can be calculated for various assumed required rates of return; for example, P = \$4.34 million for R = .05 and P = \$1.09 million for R = .10.

1.49 Using the future-value formula, $(1 + .08 - .016)^{30} = 6.4306$ vs. $(1 + .08 - .002)^{30} = 9.5184$. Wealth is 50% higher with the low-expense fund; for example, with an initial \$10,000 investment, \$95,184 versus \$64,306.

1.50 The present-value equation is

$$\$1,000,000 = \frac{X(1.02)^1}{(1.023)^1} + \frac{X(1.02)^2}{(1.023)^2} + \ldots + \frac{X(1.02)^{25}}{(1.023)^{25}}$$

The solution works out to be \$41,547.

2

The Term Structure

2.1 What is your reaction to this dialogue from the *Sopranos* television show?

Financial adviser: T-bills, I was able to lock you in before the rates dropped.

Tony: What doesn't this kid know about money? You know, I trust him 1,000 percent. Thank you.

2.2 Here is some advice from *William E. Donoghue's Complete Money Market Guide* on how to get rich by predicting interest rates:

> The answer is simple, and to figure it out, all you have to do is to be able to read a figure that you can find in the financial section of many major newspapers.... This figure is called the average maturity index of money funds and it will give you the most accurate prediction available regarding what interest rates are going to do in the near future.

a. What is the logical basis for the argument that the average maturity of money-market fund portfolios is an interest rate predictor?

b. If the average maturity lengthens, is that a prediction that interest rates are headed up or down?

c. What is the flaw in the conclusion that you can use the maturity index to predict interest rates profitably?

2.3 Explain the error in this assertion from *Beyond Wall Street: The Art of Investing*: "If the yield curve were a crystal ball, all economists would be billionaires."

2.4 Explain why you agree or disagree with this advice: "In an inflationary era, when depreciation of the currency is the order of the day, a fixed, long-term obligation is not the thing to own."

2.5 Explain why this *Los Angeles Times* headline is puzzling: "T-Bill Investors Bet on Lower Interest Rates."

2.6 In 1992, it was reported that a "Ban the Bond" posse, which included some of Bill Clinton's closest financial advisors, wanted the U.S. government to stop issuing long-term bonds and thereby reduce the federal deficit: "the approximately $40 billion a year that the U.S. Treasury now raises through 30-year bonds should be borrowed at shorter terms—say, between one and 10 years, where rates are lower." Why might such a shift not, in fact, reduce the federal deficit in the long run?

DOI: 10.1201/9781003630166-2

2.7 On October 31, 2001, the U.S. Treasury surprised financial markets by announcing that it would no longer sell 30-year bonds to finance government debt. A bond strategist at Merrill Lynch argued that, "The Treasury is trying to shorten the maturity of their debt, which makes sense given the current climate of low yields." (At the time, interest rates on 2-year Treasury notes were about 2.4 percentage points less than interest rates on 30-year Treasury bonds.) Explain why a switch from 30-year to 2-year securities might not reduce the Treasury's interest expense in the long run.

2.8 Explain why you might hesitate to follow this financial advice that was given to a mid-size business: "Since short-term interest rates are currently less than long-term rates, it is better to borrow short-term."

2.9 In a *Wall Street Journal* article, a money manager argued that accelerating inflation usually means falling bond prices and that the path of inflation can be gauged by comparing the latest 12-month increase in the price index with the 12-month increase over a period ending 6 months ago.

a. Why does accelerating inflation usually mean falling bond prices?

b. How does the suggested comparison gauge whether inflation is accelerating?

c. Why, even if accelerating inflation causes bond prices to fall and the suggested comparison correctly gauges whether inflation has been accelerating, may this information be of little use to investors?

2.10 In June 1991, Prudential Securities advised clients that

> If a slowdown in the economy begins and a recession seems imminent, longer maturities can be used to lock in the current high rate of return. The traditional theory behind this latter scenario is that the economy needs to be stimulated to effect a turnaround. The most direct way to do this is by reducing interest rates.

Explain

a. why long-term bonds may do better than short-term bonds when interest rates fall.

b. which federal body will lower interest rates to bolster the economy, and how they will lower interest rates.

c. why lower interest rates bolster the economy.

d. why Prudential's advice is of little value even if the recession seems imminent to investors.

2.11 Evaluate this argument by a prominent economics professor:

> [W]e should curb the political influence that the banking community has achieved through its formal alliance with the Fed. It is not surprising, of course, that [banks] are more interested in relatively tight money and high interest rates than are debtors and consumers.

2.12 Merrill Lynch featured a graph like the figure below on the cover of the April 7, 1986, issue of the newsletter *Investment Strategy Focus*. The figure shows a striking correlation between the price of West Texas crude oil and the interest rate of 10-year Treasury bonds between January 1973 and March 1986, leading to the prediction that the two lines will converge because

> While it is not a perfect fit, there is enough correlation to provide an interesting reading. At the present time, the bond yield is about as far below the crude oil price as it was during the 1976/78 period.

What logical problem do you see with their analysis?

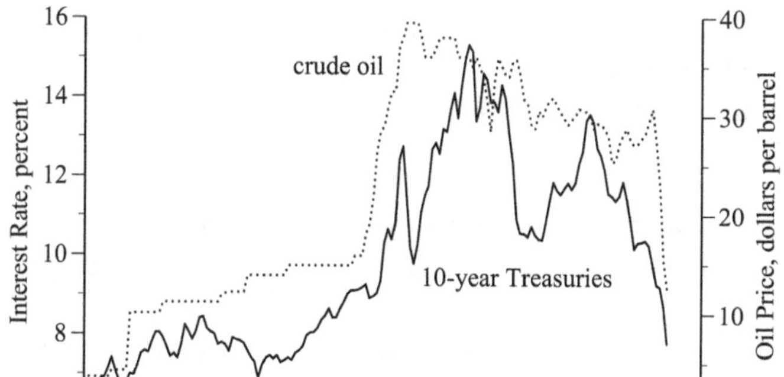

2.13 Prudential-Bache's Director of Economics & Fixed Income Research once proposed that the Fed target a flat term structure: if the interest rates on long-term bonds are 5%, the Fed should use monetary policy to set short-term interest rates at 5% too. If the liquidity preference hypothesis is correct, what interest rate expectations are consistent with a flat term structure?

2.14 In November 1988, 2-year Treasury zeros had 8 1/2% interest rates while 30-year Treasury zeros had 9% interest rates. An article in *The Wall Street Journal* began: "Why would anyone buy 30-year Treasury bonds right now when they can earn nearly the same returns on short-term issues that aren't as susceptible to price decline?"

a. Why are long-term zeros more susceptible to price declines?

b. Why would anyone buy 30-year zeros when the term structure is flat?

2.15 In 2023, the term structure was downward sloping. Is a downward sloping term structure more consistent with a financial market consensus that interest rates will rise or fall in the future? If you disagree with this consensus and believe that interest rates will not change much, should you buy bonds with short durations or long durations? Explain your reasoning.

2.16 In 1986, *The Wall Street Journal* reported that, "Falling interest rates prompt corporations to refinance short-term, high-cost debt with bonds with lower rates and longer maturities, reducing costs and making them less vulnerable to interest-rate moves.... Still, many corporations delay refinancing, expecting interest rates to drop further." Why might long-term debt have lower interest rates than short-term debt? In what way are those who borrow long-term still vulnerable to interest rate moves?

2.17 How would the expectations hypothesis explain the fact that when the Fed buys short-term Treasury bills, there is generally a much larger effect on short-term interest rates than on long-term interest rates?

2.18 In 1961 and 2011, the Federal Reserve announced that it would implement "Operation Twist," a policy intended to twist the term structure so that short-term interest rates would be higher than long-term interest rates. Should they have bought short-term bonds and sold long-term bonds, or vice-versa? What are the implications, if any, of the expectations hypothesis for Operation Twist?

2.19 Critically evaluate this advice from a financial advisor writing in *Money* magazine:

> The yield curve can help both large and small investors pick attractive maturities. Because investors' collective wisdom is often correct, yield curves can serve as a forecasting tool, though a limited one. Thus when a steeply rising yield curve is flashing an inflation warning, specialists urge investors to pick bonds with maturities of three to five years. Such securities capture reasonable returns but minimize the risk that your principal will shrink if rates continue to climb.

2.20 Give a rational explanation for a situation in which the yield to maturity on a 10-year Treasury bond with 2% coupons is higher than the yield to maturity on a 10-year Treasury bond with 5% coupons.

2.21 In 2001, Motorola sold more than $1 billion in new long-term bonds and used the proceeds to eliminate its short-term debt. With the term structure upward sloping, why might it want to do this?

2.22 Is the modified duration of a perpetuity that pays $100 a year forever infinite? Explain your reasoning.

2.23 It has been observed that long-term rates are more stable than short-term rates; for example, when the 1-year rate jumps from 10% to 13%, the 20-year rate might only rise from 10% to 12%. Do not use any numbers, but simply explain logically how the expectations hypothesis might explain the relative stability of long-term rates.

2.24 An economist recently argued that

> Short-term rates affect the demand for things normally financed on a short term basis, such as auto leases, computers, furniture,

and large appliances. Intermediate-term rates affect the demand for things normally financed on an intermediate-term basis, such as auto purchases and home improvements. Long-term rates affect the demand for things normally financed on a long term basis, such as housing and plant & equipment. In order to encourage long-term investment, the Fed should have these permanent target goals:

Short-term rates 5.50%
Intermediate-term rates 4.50%
Long-term rates 3.60%

How would you respond?

2.25 During the 10-year period 1982–1992, three-fourths of the professionally managed bond mutual funds did worse than the Salomon Brothers Broad Investment Grade Bond Index. A managing director of PIMCO, one of the few funds that beat the index, said that regulatory and accounting rules compel many investors to buy 1-year securities, making their interest rates artificially low. Investors who are not subject to such constraints can do better by buying a portfolio of 6-month and 2-year securities. Consider a 6-month Treasury zero with a 4% interest rate, a 1-year Treasury zero with a 3.5% interest rate, and a 2-year Treasury zero with a 4.0% interest rate. Instead of investing $1 million for 6 months in the 1-year zero, how should an investor divide $1 million between the 6-month and 2-year zeros so that her portfolio of 6-month and 2-year zeros has the same duration as a portfolio of 1-year zeros?

2.26 Use the expectations hypothesis to interpret this empirical observation from the book, *The Stock Market and Inflation*:

> A good measure of the stance of monetary policy is the yield curve....The yield curve is said to be inverted when short rates are above long rates... During recessions and the early stages of economic recovery the yield curve is positive (i.e., short rates are below long rates), implying easy, or at least cheap, money. During the late stages of the recovery cycle, when inflation is strong and monetary policy has been forced to tighten sharply, short rates rise and the yield curve usually becomes inverted.

2.27 The Fed raised short-term interest rates in the spring of 2000 to cool the economy and restrain inflation. Yet long-term interest rates were little affected and even fell, inverting the term structure. How would you explain this term-structure inversion?

2.28 Explain this analysis from Whitman and Shubik (*The Aggressive Conservative Investor*) of pension fund and life insurance companies that hold assets with an average duration of 8 years:

> A portfolio duration of eight years is about as long as one can obtain on conventional coupon-paying bonds, given double-digit

> interest rates, but investment horizons of 40 years are not uncommon for pension funds or life insurance companies....such portfolios will surely suffer when interest rates decline, even though the associated temporary increase in market value...may create the illusion of investment success.

2.29 Here are the interest rates on Treasury zeros on October 21, 2019:

Maturity	Interest Rate
1-year	1.67%
5-year	1.57%
10-year	1.84%

According to the expectations hypothesis, what was the implied anticipated 5-year rate on October 21, 2024?

2.30 Use these data to show how to calculate the real interest rate on 1-year zeros purchased on January 1, 2020. (Just set up the requisite calculations; do not do them.)

Maturity Date	Zero Rate (%)	CPI
January 1, 2018	1.80	247.87
January 1, 2019	2.58	251.71
January 1, 2020	1.53	257.97
January 1, 2021	.10	261.58

2.31 Critically explain and evaluate these excerpts from a *Wall Street Journal* article:

> With inflation abated and interest rates down sharply on money-market funds and bank accounts, consumers are turning to bond products for higher yields. Many investors have shifted dollars out of money funds paying around 7% and into [long- term] Treasury securities paying more than 10%....
>
> A California real estate attorney admits that he was "dumbfounded" to find that $192,000 in Treasury zeros he bought in January 1984 were valued at $156,000 when he went to sell them four months later...
>
> Nelson Chase, a West Bloomfield, Mich., attorney is representing a group [that invested in zeros and is now] suing New York-based Merrill Lynch & Co. "All the literature talks about how safe these investments are," he says. "Unless you can be absolutely sure you will hold to maturity, these aren't safe investments."

In particular, explain

a. what circumstances, if any, would dissuade you from shifting out of a bank paying 7% into Treasury zeros paying 10%.

b. how Treasury zeros could lose nearly 20% of their value in 4 months.

c. why zeros held to maturity may not be safe.

2.32 Critically evaluate this strategy from a bond-fund manager: "I was doing a barbell strategy, with half my money invested in 1-year zeros with a 1% interest rate and half in 29-year zeros with a 3% interest rate. Then I realized that I could get a higher return with the same duration by investing all my money in 15-year zeros with a 2.5% interest rate."

2.33 On October 13, 1992, the yield to maturity on 1-year Treasury zeros was 3.4% and the yield on 20-year Treasury zeros was 8.2%. If an investment bank wanted to bet that the term structure would flatten, would it buy 1-year zeros and sell 20-year zeros, or vice versa? Why would the investment bank buy one and sell the other, instead of just buying one or the other?

2.34 How would you respond to this investment strategy touted in March 2023?

> Corporate bonds are yielding more than T-bills right now. Why wouldn't I short corporate and go long T-Bills for the maximum possible amount I could get my hands on, and then some. Riskfree arbitrage, no? Greatest trade ever.

2.35 Suppose that the term structure for Treasury zeros is flat with 6% yields to maturity and will be flat with 5% yields to maturity 1 year from now. If so, what will be the 1-year rate of return on a 20-year zero purchased today? (Calculate the exact return, not an approximation.)

2.36 The annual interest rate on a 20-year zero is 5% and the annual interest rate on a 5-year zero is 4%.

a. What is the implicit annual interest rate on a 15-year zero 5 years from now that is embedded in this term structure? (Just set up.)

b. If you expect the annual interest rate on a 15-year zero 5 years from now to be 4%, what will your expected annual rate of return be if you buy the 20-year zero now and sell it after 5 years? (Just set up.)

c. Explain why you believe that the rate of return you calculate in Part (b) will be either higher than, lower than, or equal to 4%.

2.37 In his senior theses, an undergraduate economics major investigated the relationship between inflation and interest rates by estimating the following equation using monthly data for the 20-year period 1996–2015:

$$R = \underset{[25.26]}{15.98} - \underset{[21.29]}{.067P}, \qquad R^2 = .66$$

where R = interest rate on 1-year Treasury bonds, P = consumer price index (CPI), and the t-values are in brackets. What advice would you give this student?

2.38 The Fama bond strategy is based on the assumption that the implicit forward rates embedded in the term structure are worthless as predictors of future interest rates. Instead, the best predictor of future interest rates is current interest rates; for example, that the interest rate on 1-year Treasury zeros a year from now will be the same as it is today. Suppose that the interest rates on 1-, 2-, and 3-year Treasury zeros are 1.0%, 1.8%, and 2.0%, and you are going to buy one of these three zeros and hold it for 1 year. (If equations are needed, you must show these equations, but do not solve them.)

a. If the expectations hypothesis is correct, which of these three zeros has the highest expected return?

b. If Fama's theory is correct, which of these three zeros has the highest expected return?

2.39 Use the expectations hypothesis to explain how a term structure could pivot; for example, change from an upward-sloping term structure to a downward-sloping curve. Specifically, suppose that the interest rate on 5-year zeros is 3% and the interest rate on 10-year zeros is 4%. What would have to happen to the anticipated interest rate on 5-year zeros 5 years from now for the interest rate on 5-year zeros to rise to 4%, while the interest rate on 10-year zeros falls to 3%?

2.40 In 1988, a bank offered selected individuals a $35,000 line of credit, allowing them to borrow up to $35,000 whenever they wanted at a monthly interest rate of 2.5%, compounded daily. What is the effective annual interest rate? (Assume 12 months of 30 days each.)

Answers

2.1 Treasury bills mature in a year or less, so "locking in" means a guaranteed return for a year at most. When the T-bills mature, Tony will have to reinvest, and his advisor has already told him that rates have dropped—which means that he will earn a lower rate of return when he reinvests.

2.2 a. Money-market fund lengthen their portfolios, locking in today's rates if they expect interest rates to decline. They shorten their portfolios, rolling them over more frequently, if they expect interest rates to increase.

b. A lengthening of average maturity is consequently a prediction that interest rates are headed down.

c. However, there is no secret information in daily newspapers that gives readers an advantage over other bond traders. These expectations are no doubt already embedded in the term structure.

2.3 The term structure and yield curve reflect the interest rate expectations that investors use to price assets. If these expectations turn out to be correct, then asset prices were "correct," and no one makes abnormal profits. Investors become wealthy by purchasing assets that (after the fact) turn out to have been greatly undervalued by the market because of very inaccurate predictions.

2.4 Inflation reduces the real value of fixed, long-term obligations; however, if inflation is the order of the day, long-term bonds will have high interest rates that take this inflation into account.

2.5 Treasury bills are short-term bonds that mature in less than 1 year. Investors who buy Treasury bills are implicitly betting on an increase in interest rates so that they can roll over their investment at higher interest rates. (The article told how there had been aggressive buying the previous day at the U.S. Treasury's auction of 3- to-5-year Treasury notes, suggesting that, while the term structure was upward sloping at the time, with 1-year Treasury bonds paying 7.4%, 4-year Treasury bonds paying 7.8%, and 10-year Treasury bonds yielding 8.60%, these buyers expected interest rates to decline over the next 3 to 5 years. The headline writer mistakenly called these note buyers "T-bill investors.")

2.6 This strategy is intended to take advantage of the steep term structure of interest rates that then prevailed. Some banks tried to do the same thing by using short-term deposits to finance the purchase of long-term Treasury bonds. The expectations hypothesis explanation of an upward-sloping term structure is that interest rates are expected to increase. If interest rates do increase by more than the implicit forward rates embedded in the term structure, the U. S. Treasury will be forced to roll over its short-term debt at sharply higher interest rates, and its borrowing costs will be even higher than had it issued long-term bonds.

2.7 The upward-sloping term structure indicates that investors expect interest rates to increase over time. If so, rolling over short-term debt may be as expensive (or more so) than issuing long-term debt.

2.8 The expectations hypothesis implies that an upward-sloping term structure reflects expectations that short-term interest rates are expected to rise in the future. If they increase more than the forward rates embedded in the term structure, the business will end up paying more in the long run.

2.9 a. Increases in the rate of inflation tend to increase nominal interest rates, which reduce bond prices.

b. The comparison of a recent rate of inflation with the rate 6 months ago shows whether the rate of inflation is increasing or decreasing.

c. This information may be of little use to investors because it is widely known and already embedded in bond prices (as reflected in the term structure of interest rates).

2.10 a. A decline in interest rates increases the prices of fixed-income securities. The prices of long-term (actually long-duration) securities are most sensitive to interest rates.

b. The Federal Reserve Board can reduce the discount rate, reduce reserve requirements, or make open market purchases to lower market interest rates.

c. Lower interest rates reduce the cost of borrowing to buy cars, houses, and factories, and (for those who have cash to invest) make financial assets less attractive relative to real assets.

d. A well-anticipated recession and decline in interest rates should already be reflected in the term structure of interest rates.

2.11 Banks make money from the spread between what they pay depositors and what they charge borrowers, not from the level of interest rates. In fact, the high interest rates in 1979–1981 nearly bankrupted the banking industry.

2.12 Not only did Merrill Lynch not have a well-thought-out theory, there is a theory that makes sense: interest rates are affected by the rate of inflation (changes in prices), not the level of prices.

Imagine oil prices went up to $40 and stayed there permanently (and the overall CPI changed similarly). The initial rapid inflation might cause a spike in interest rates but once prices stabilized and stopped rising, interest rates should come back down—not stay at 16%, as implied by the graph.

In fact, the price of crude oil was $98 per barrel in 2013. If the Merrill Lynch figure had been a good predictor of interest rates, the 10-year rate would have been 30%. Instead, it was 3%. Even though the price level was high, the rate of inflation was low—and it is the rate of inflation, not the price level, that affects interest rates.

2.13 In the absence of liquidity preference, if investors expect no change in interest rates, the term structure will be flat. If the liquidity preference hypothesis is true, then long-term rates will be somewhat higher than implied by the expectations hypothesis. For a flat term structure, with long-term rates equal to short-term rates, investors would have to expect interest rates in the future to be lower than they are today.

2.14 Remember that the market will set prices so that someone is willing to hold these bonds.

a. Long-term bonds tend to have relatively long durations and more capital risk.

b. If the yield curve is flat, some investors may buy 30-year bonds if they are more concerned with income risk than capital risk, are unconcerned about risk, or think that interest rates are going to fall.

2.15 A downward sloping term structure is consistent with a financial market consensus that interest rates will fall. If you think that interest rates will increase (or, at least, not fall as much as implied by the term structure), then you should buy bonds with short durations, since rising interest rates will reduce bond prices and a bond's duration is a gauge of the sensitivity of its price to interest rate changes.

2.16 Long-term securities might have lower interest rates than short-term securities because the market expects interest rates to decline. If these expectations prove correct, the firm that borrows long-term will have locked itself in at what, in retrospect, turns out to be a high interest rate. Those who borrow long-term will be hurt financially if interest rates drop by more than the implicit interest-rate predictions embedded in the term structure.

2.17 For simplicity, consider a flat term structure. A Fed purchase of Treasury bills pushes T-bill prices up and T-bill rates down, say, by .5%. If investors believe that this signals a permanent .5% decline in T-bill rates, the expectations hypothesis implies that all interest rates will decline by .5%. If investors expect the decline to be temporary, so that future short-term rates will be higher than they are currently, then long-term rates will decline by less than .5%. (For a specific example, think about the interest rates on 1-year and 2-year zeros, where the current 1-year rate falls from 2% to 1.5% while the anticipated 1-year rate a year from now either falls from 2% to 1.5% or stays at 2%.)

2.18 The Fed should buy long-term bonds (pushing bond prices up and yields down) and sell short-term bonds (pushing prices down and yields up). The expectations hypothesis implies that long-term rates won't fall below short-term rates unless investors believe that interest rates are going to fall in the future. Thus, to maintain this twisted term structure, the Fed had to convince investors of an implausible scenario in which interest rates stay high while investors continue to believe that they will decline.

2.19 This advisor suggests using the expectations hypothesis to interpret the term structure, a hypothesis that assumes that bonds are priced so that all strategies are expected to do equally well. If so, there is no reason to pick any particular bond. It is circular (and useless) to choose a bond strategy based solely on the interest rate predictions embedded in the term structure.

2.20 The term structure is upward sloping, with interest rates expected to rise, which will generate more income from the reinvestment of the 5% coupons.

2.21 Perhaps Motorola believed that future short-term rates would be higher than the implicit rates embedded in the term structure and wanted to bet against the term structure. Or perhaps it was more concerned with income risk than with capital risk; i.e., it was concerned that a sharp increase in interest rates would push its interest obligations so high that it might be forced into bankruptcy.

2.22 The modified duration is approximately equal to the percentage change in the price resulting from a one-percentage-point increase in the required return. Since perpetuity prices do not change by infinite amounts, the modified duration is not infinite.

2.23 An expectations hypothesis explanation is that fluctuations in interest rates are thought to be temporary; for example, if the current 1-year rate increases by one percentage point, but future 1-year rates are revised upward by less than one percentage point (perhaps no change at all), short-term rates will have to increase by more than long-term rates for bonds to be priced so that all strategies to do equally well.

2.24 The term structure depends not only on Fed policy but also on investor preferences and expectations—specifically interest rate expectations and risk premiums. All the empirical evidence is that long-term bonds have risk premiums relative to short-term bonds. So, a downward-sloping term structure could only be a permanent market equilibrium if investors continually think interest rates are going to fall in the future.

2.25 She wants her investment in the 6-month and 2-year zeros to have the same duration as the 1-year zero, so that these two strategies will be affected equally by changes in interest rates. The 1-year zeros have a duration of 1 year. The duration of the portfolio is $\alpha(.5) + (1 - \alpha)2.0$. Equating the two durations, $1 = \alpha(.5) + (1 - \alpha)2.0$ implies $\alpha = 2/3$.

2.26 These empirical observations are consistent with the expectations hypothesis interpretation of the yield curve. When the term structure is upward sloping, interest rates are lower now than they are expected to be in the future, a situation consistent with the early stages of economic recovery, with inflation and interest rates expected to increase in the future. When the term structure is downward sloping, interest rates are higher now than they are expected to be in the future, a situation consistent with a tight monetary policy that will eventually reduce inflation and interest rates.

2.27 This inversion of the term structure suggests that investors expect the current rise in interest rates to be temporary, and that interest rates several years from now will be lower than they are today—which is consistent with a successful Fed policy that raises current interest rates, but reduces the future rate of inflation.

2.28 When interest rates fall, the market prices of their bonds will increase but their long-term-realized returns beyond the 8-year duration will be diminished by the rolling over of the coupons and maturation values of their bonds into new bonds with lower interest rates. Life insurance companies and pension funds have long horizons.

2.29 According to the expectation-hypothesis, the current return from a 10-year zero is equal to the current return from a 5-year zero times the return 5 years hence from a 5-year zero:

$$(1+R_{10})^{10} = (1+R_5)^5 (1+R_5^{t+5})^5$$

$$(1.0184)^{10} = (1.0157)^5 (1+R_5^{t+5})^5$$

$$R_5^{t+5} = \left(\frac{(1.0184)^{10}}{(1.0157)^5}\right)^{1/5} - 1 = 1.0211$$

The implied anticipated 5-year rate on October 21, 2024 was 2.11%. (The actual 5-year rate on October 21, 2024, turned out to be 3.88%.)

2.30 The real return r is given by this equation:

$$1+r = \frac{1+R}{1+\pi}$$

where R is the nominal return on a 1-year zero and π is the rate of inflation over the life of the bond.

Here, the real return is .1288%:

$$1+r = \frac{1.0153}{(261.58/257.97)} = \frac{1.0153}{1.0140} = 1.001288$$

2.31 a. You might believe that interest rates are going to rise substantially.

b. Zeros have considerable capital risk. A 20-year zero will lose about 20% of its value if interest rates rise by one percentage point.

c. There is still inflation risk. (They are also not safe in the sense that if interest rates increase, you could have made much more money rolling over short-term bonds.)

2.32 It would be surprising if the term structure did not take interest rate expectations into account. The upward-sloping term structure suggests that investors expect interest rates to rise, in which case rolling over the 1-year zeros will be at higher interest rates and make up for the initially low return.

2.33 If the term structure flattens, the yield spread will narrow so that the yield on 20-year zeros falls (and the price rises) relative to 1-year zeros. To profit from such a flattening of the term structure, the investment bank should buy 20-year zeros and sell (twenty times as many) 1-year zeros. By purchasing the 20-year zeros and selling the 1-year zeros, instead of just buying the 20-year zeros, the investment bank will profit from a flattening of the term structure even if the overall level of interest rates rises or falls.

Suppose, for example, that the 20-year rate goes up 1 percentage point while the 1-year rate goes up 2 percentage points. The bank will lose money if it had simply bought 20-year zeros, but make money if it bought 20-year zeros and sold 1-year zeros.

2.34 The corporates are long-term, and the T-bills are short-term, so you will have to roll over your money in the T-bills you buy now when they mature. The market is expecting T-bill rates to be lower in the future than they are now.

2.35 Letting the maturation value be F, the current price is $P_0 = F/1.06^{20}$; a year from now, the price will be is $P_1 = F/1.05^{19}$, giving a capital gain of $(P_1 - P_0)/P_0 = P_1/P_0 - 1 = (F/1.05^{19})/(F/1.06^{20}) - 1 = 1.06^{20}/1.05^{19} - 1 = .269$, or 26.9%.

2.36 a. According to the expectation-hypothesis, the current return from a 20-year zero is equal to the current return from a 5-year zero times the return 5 years hence from a 15-year zero:

$$(1+R_{20})^{20} = (1+R_5)^5 (1+R_{15}^{+5})^{15}$$

$$(1.05)^{20} = (1.04)^5 (1+R_{15}^{+5})^{15}$$

$$R_{15}^{+5} = \left(\frac{(1.05)^{20}}{(1.04)^5}\right)^{1/15} - 1 = 1.05335$$

The implied return 5 years hence from a 15-year zero is 5.335%

b. The current price of a 20-year zero paying X 20 years from now is

$$P_0 = \frac{X}{1.05^{20}}$$

You expect the price of the 20-year zero 5 years from now to be

$$P_5 = \frac{X}{1.04^{15}}$$

If you are right, your annual rate of return will be

$$(1+R)^5 = \frac{P_5}{P_0} = \frac{X/(1.04)^{15}}{X/(1.05)^{20}} = \frac{(1.05)^{20}}{(1.04)^{15}}$$

This works out to be an annual return of 8.058%.

c. For a 20-year zero with a 5% yield and a 5-year zero with a 4% yield to do equally well, future interest rates will have to rise above 5%. If you expect the 15-year rate 5 years from now to be only 4%, then you will do better buying the 20-year zero and selling it in 5 years than buying the 5-year zero. Thus, your return will be greater than 4%.

2.37 Theoretically, there is a positive relationship between the rate of inflation and interest rates, but this student incorrectly used the price level instead of the rate of inflation and got the wrong sign. The correct regression, using the rate of inflation, gives the correct sign (though the correlation is low):

$$R = \underset{[15.67]}{2.48} + \underset{[1.93]}{.7491\pi}, \qquad R^2 = .012$$

2.38 a. If the expectations hypothesis is correct, each zero has the same expected return—since the expectations hypothesis assumes that they are priced to give the same expected return.

b. Let the respective interest rates be R_1, R_2, and R_3. A \$1 investment in the 1-year zero will be worth $1 + R_1 = \$1.01$. A \$1 investment in the 2-year zero will be worth $(1 + R_2)^2$ after 2 years and

$$\frac{(1+R_2)^2}{1+R_1^{+1}}$$

after 1 year, where the denominator is the 1-year rate 1 year from now. If Fama's theory is correct, the 1-year rate 1 year from now will be 1.0%, the current 1-year rate. So, 1 year from now, a \$1 investment in the 2-year zero will be worth

$$\frac{(1+R_2)^2}{1+R_1^{+1}} = \frac{1.018^2}{1.010} = 1.026$$

Similarly, 1 year from now, a \$1 investment in the 3-year zero will be worth

$$\frac{(1+R_3)^3}{(1+R_2^{+1})^2} = \frac{1.020^3}{1.018^2} = 1.024$$

The 2-year zero has the highest expected return.

2.39 According to the expectations hypothesis, the interest rate on 10-year zeros is related to the current interest rate on 5-year zeros and the interest rate on 5-year zeros 5 years from now in this way

$$(1+R_{10})^{10} = (1+R_5)^5 (1+R_5^{+5})^5$$

$$(1+R_5^{+5})^5 = \frac{(1+R_{10})^{10}}{(1+R_5)^5}$$

In our example, the anticipated 5-year rate is initially:

$$\left(1+R_5^{+5}\right)^5 = \frac{(1.04)^{10}}{(1.03)^5} \Rightarrow R_5^{+5} = .0501$$

It then changes to

$$\left(1+R_5^{+5}\right)^5 = \frac{(1.03)^{10}}{(1.04)^5} \Rightarrow R_5^{+5} = .0201$$

So, if the anticipated 5-year rate 5 years hence falls from 5.01% to 2.01%, this will twist the term structure as described in the problem.

2.40 Using the compounding equation, $(1 + .025/30)^{360} = 1.3497$, an effective annual rate of 34.97%.

3

Amortized Loans

3.1 Before the 1969 Truth-in-Lending law, a finance company using the "add-on" method could loan you $1000; charge you $100 interest (with $1100/12 = $91.67 due each month for 12 months); and say that the interest rate was 10%.

a. What is the true annual interest rate on such a loan?

b. If the annual interest rate were really 10%, how big would the monthly payments be?

3.2 *Consumer Reports* gave the following advice about auto loans:

> The nice thing about auto loans is that you can locate the lemons before you sign on the dotted line. Just keep your eye on the APR—the Annual Percentage Rate.... Obviously, the lower the APR, the better. Another point to keep in mind: the shorter the loan the better ....a one-year loan is much cheaper than a four-year loan. Say you borrow $4000 at 11%. For a one-year loan, the total interest would be $242. The total interest for a four-year loan would be $963—about four times as much. Of course, the monthly payments for the longer loan would be smaller, but remember that you pay heavily for that convenience.

a. Why is the $242 total interest on a 1-year loan far less than 11% of $4000?

b. Why is the total interest on a 4-year loan more than on a 1-year loan?

c. What is the present value of the monthly payments for the 1-year loan and for the 4-year loan, each discounted by an 11% required return?

d. Assuming the same interest rate on each loan, are there any circumstances in which "the shorter the loan, the better" is not true?

3.3 For a 5-year, $100,000 loan at a 10.5% annual interest rate, most banks require 60 monthly payments of $2150, due at the end of each month, beginning a month from the signing of the loan papers. A Southern California lender requires 20 quarterly payments of $6450, due at the beginning of each quarter, starting on the day the loan is signed. What is the annual interest rate on this loan?

3.4 When a *Los Angeles Times* columnist interviewed Frank Sperling, a vice president at Security Pacific National Bank, about whether people

DOI: 10.1201/9781003630166-3

should pay cash for a car or get a car loan and invest the cash, Sperling said that,

> If you can earn an interest rate equivalent to half the interest rate on your loan, you'll come out ahead.

The *Times* columnist called this Sperling's Rule. For example, instead of paying $30,000 cash for a car, a buyer comes out ahead if the $30,000 is invested to earn 5% and the car is paid for with a 4-year amortized loan with a 9% loan rate: the 5% investment earns $6,465.19 in interest while the car loan has monthly payments of $746.55 and total interest of only $5,834.40. What is the flaw in Sterling's Rule? Do not do any calculations, but do explain your reasoning.

3.5 The owner of a Washington, D.C. real estate firm says this equation is basic to real estate:

Total Interest Paid = Principal × Interest Rate per Period × Interest Periods

a. Explain why the total interest paid on a $100,000 conventional 30-year mortgage at 10% is not $100,000 × 10%/year × 30 years = $300,000.

b. Is the correct total interest larger or smaller than $300,000? Explain your reasoning.

3.6 An elderly couple received a letter from their savings bank that began:

> We are very pleased to offer you the opportunity to save $1,370.91 in future interest on your mortgage loan. Yes, you can save $1,370.91 in future interest by increasing your monthly payment by only $25.00 per month beginning in August. This extra $25.00 per month will also pay off your mortgage 3 years and 7 months early.

An enclosed analysis showed that this couple had an unpaid balance of $8,479.53 on a 7.25% loan, with 11 years and 11 months of $89.00 monthly payments remaining, and that

> With your present monthly payment of $89.00, your future interest paid over the next 11 years 11 months will be $4,185.04
> By increasing your monthly payment
> by $25.00 per month, your future interest
> over the next 8 years 4 months will be $2,814.13
> Interest savings (will also pay off your
> mortgage 3 years 7 months early) $1,370.91

What would you advise the couple who received this letter? Why do you think the bank made this offer?

3.7 *Sylvia Porter's Personal Finance* book asked this teaser question:

> Want to build equity in your home fast, slash 60 percent off the total interest you pay on a mortgage held to maturity, retire the major debt of your lifetime—your home loan—before the kids' college bills come steamrolling in?

The "hot tip" is to get a 15-year mortgage:

> The 15-year-fixed- or adjustable-rate mortgage (ARM) can help you accomplish all that for a relatively low price. For $105 more per month, a 15-year, fixed-rate mortgage saves you $115,000 in interest charges (compared to a 30-year fixed rate mortgage) over the life of the mortgage.... If you can afford modestly higher monthly payments and meet stricter borrowing requirements, there's no denying the advantages of a 15-year versus a 30-year mortgage.

What is the flaw in these calculations? Assuming you can afford the higher monthly payments, is a 15-year loan always better than a 30-year loan?

3.8 In 2021, it was reported that, "Almost half (47%) of homeowners who refinanced over the past year of ultra-low rates are now saving at least $300 a month." However, financial advisor Suze Orman issued a warning to homeowners who were thinking of refinancing their high-interest mortgages at rates below 3%: "It makes me so crazy how most homeowners make a huge mistake when they refinance."

Consider a person who has been playing down a 30-year mortgage for 14 years at 6% and now refinances with a new 30-year mortgage at 2.75%. Orman writes: "This is so very wrong. Sure, the new mortgage is at a lower interest rate, but you just extended your mortgage payment on this home to 44 years! My rule of refinancing is that you are to never extend your total payback period past 30 years." The Yahoo Finance writer reporting this story noted that, "You'll pay tens of thousands less in interest over time," keeping the current mortgage with 16 years to go instead of replacing it with a new 30-year mortgage.

If you were a financial advisor, what would you advise?

3.9 In 1985, the *Los Angeles Times* described the "sudden, almost explosive, acceptance of the 15-year fixed rate mortgage," in place of the traditional 30-year mortgage, citing a Mortgage Bankers Association estimate that from "minimal acceptance" just a year ago, they now account for one-seventh of all new mortgages. In explanation, the *Times* cites "common sense economics":

> at the end of 30 years, that $100,000 mortgage [at 13%, with $1,106.20 monthly payments] has cost the home buyer a grand total of $398,232—a mind boggling $298,232 in interest... by cutting the same mortgage down to 15 from 30 years (and raising the monthly payments from $1,106.20 to $1,265.25), the total cost to the home buyer is $227,745 for a net saving in interest of $170,487.
>
> "While you certainly can't quarrel with the arithmetic of the 15-year mortgage—and the sudden popularity of it ... there are limits on how far the trend can go," according to Fred E. Case of UCLA's Graduate School of Management. "Not everyone who sees the sense of the 15-year mortgage is in a position to qualify for one."

The *Times* also quoted an anonymous "cynical Midwestern lender":

> I'd like to think that home buyers have suddenly gotten smart—that they've looked at those figures and realized how much interest they're paying over 30 years. God knows they've been dumb about it long enough.

Why, by their reckoning, is a 30-year mortgage so expensive? Is there any interest rate at which you would choose a 30-year rather than a 15-year mortgage at the same interest rate?

3.10 A consumer finance book advised, "A second method of reducing costs is to make the largest down payment possible and repay in the shortest period of time." How does this strategy reduce costs? Would you recommend that borrowers always follow this advice?

3.11 A *Los Angeles Times* financial writer recommended biweekly mortgages in which the monthly payments are calculated as if it were a conventional 30-year monthly mortgage, but then half this monthly amount is paid every other week:

> At 9.25% interest, a biweekly $100,000 mortgage pays off in slightly more than 21 years, instead of 30, and saves $63,819 in interest. On a $200,000 mortgage, the interest saved is $126,637.
>
> "And," as G. Randall Kinst, director of secondary marketing for Mortgage Loans America, a large wholesale mortgage banking firm located in Campbell, Calif., says, "a 30-year conventional loan would need an unheard of 6.7% interest rate to achieve the same savings realized on a biweekly."

How does a biweekly mortgage reduce the total interest paid? Would you choose a 9.25% biweekly or a 6.7% monthly?

3.12 A California mortgage banker set up a "simulated" biweekly plan:

> it simply sets itself up as a trust, collects biweekly mortgage payments from its clients and then turns around and pays their lender the regular monthly payment .... What it amounts to is simply one extra payment a year being made on the mortgage.

Why would a mortgage banker do this for its clients?

3.13 A "seven-and-seven loan" has an interest rate that is 7 percentage points over the prime rate and has initial fees that are equal to 7% of the size of the loan. If the prime rate is 10%, what is the effective interest rate on a seven-and-seven 10-year loan with amortized monthly payments? (Just set up.) Explain why the effective interest rate would be higher or lower if this were a 5-year loan.

3.14 The owner of Dial Auto Pawn in Long Beach, California, says, "We aren't lenders" and "we aren't pawnbrokers." However, the company will make a $10,000 "cash advance" to a customer who leaves a luxury car with Dial Auto Pawn; the customer can reclaim the car by paying back the $10,000 plus a storage fee of $39 a day. If the cash advance lasts

365 days (perhaps through a string of customers), what is the effective annual interest rate?

3.15 A finance professor began an article with this observation: "Adjustable rate mortgages (ARMs) have become an increasingly popular loan vehicle over the last four or five years ....the primary advantage to lenders is clear—elements of interest rate risk are shifted to borrowers." In what sense does an ARM shift interest rate risk to the borrower; specifically, what gamble were lenders taking before, that borrowers are now taking? Will lenders, in retrospect, ever regret avoiding this gamble?

3.16 A Letter to the *Los Angeles Times* financial advice column, "Money Talk," asked

> My husband and I are in the process of securing a $32,000 home equity loan through an out-of-state lender at an interest rate of 12.5% ....[T]he processing costs will be about $5,000. Does that sound reasonable?

Evaluate this loan, assuming that it is an amortized 30-year loan with monthly payments and that it is not repaid early. If it were repaid after 15 years, would the effective interest rate be higher or lower?

3.17 A finance textbook co-authored by a Nobel laureate asked:

> You have just decided to buy a house and need to borrow $100,000. One bank offers you a mortgage loan [at a 12% annual interest rate] to be repaid over 30 years in 360 monthly payments....Another bank offers you a 15-year mortgage loan [at a 10.4% annual interest rate] with a monthly payment of $1,100. Which is the better deal?

The authors note that the monthly payment of the 30-year mortgage is $1028.61, which is less than the $1,100 monthly payment on the 15-year mortgage but, because the annual interest rate is lower on the 15-year mortgage, they conclude that the 15-year mortgage is the better deal.

Is it always true that the loan with the lower interest rate is the better deal?

3.18 In the early 1980s, Pomona College loaned professors $85,000 at 7% and an additional $40,000 at 12% to help them buy homes near campus. Both of these loans were conventional 30-year mortgages with constant monthly payments. For simplicity, the Pomona College business office combined these two loans into one 30-year mortgage with a single interest rate:

$$R = \left(\frac{\$85{,}000}{\$125{,}000}\right)7 + \left(\frac{\$40{,}000}{\$125{,}000}\right)12 = 8.60$$

What single interest rate should they have used?

3.19 Explain why you either agree or disagree with this advice in the *Wall Street Journal*.

> Paying off the mortgage can also be safer than buying even super-safe Treasury bonds, says Steven Enright, a River Vale, N.J., financial planner. While the value of the bonds will drop if interest rates go up, as he expects in 1993, "you don't have that risk if you are paying down your mortgage."

3.20 In 2023, a Southern California banker said that he had a very low-interest variable-rate mortgage on his home, but he was concerned that interest rates may rise: "It will take at least a few years for this economy to return to a level where the Fed can raise rates significantly without killing the economy."

His strategy was to "reduce the principal as fast as I can while my rate is low so that if interest rates go up, at least the principal I am paying the higher rate on will be lower and hence the overall interest paid over the life of the loan will be pretty low—in fact lower than the rate I could get now if I refinanced at a fixed rate." Evaluate this strategy.

3.21 In 1986, a *Wall Street Journal* reporter said he was tempted to refinance his 25-year, 13.25% $55,000 mortgage with a new 9.5% loan but was dissuaded by the $3,500 to $4,000 he would have to pay in points and other closing costs. Critically evaluate his logic. How would you decide whether to refinance? (Use words, not equations.)

> With, say, a saving of $100 a month in principal and interest payments, I would pocket $36,000 over 30 years [net of closing costs], I thought at first. Not so. Since I have only 22 1/2 years left on my existing contract and if I convert it to 25 or 30 years to keep my payments low, I discovered that I could end up paying more total dollars in the long run.

3.22 A payday loan company charges $15 for a 14-day loan of $100; that is, they lend you $100 today and, 14 days later, you pay them $115. If they were to make 26 such loans consecutively over the course of a year, what would be their annual rate of return?

3.23 A homeowner recently obtained a 30-year $300,000 amortized mortgage at a 6% annual percentage rate (APR) with monthly payments of $1798.65.

Immediately after obtaining this loan, she called a lender she heard on the radio and was told that she could refinance at a 5.75% interest rate and have exactly the same monthly payments of $1798.65, and her mortgage would be fully paid off in 28 years. The savings of 2 years of monthly payments, 24($1798.65) = $43,167 would far exceed the $10,000 in fees it would cost her to obtain this loan. Are you persuaded? Would you advise her to refinance or not? Explain exactly how you would decide.

3.24 A *Wall Street Journal* article showed readers when it pays to refinance a mortgage. Readers were advised to calculate the one-time cost of refinancing C and their monthly savings S from the new mortgage. The ratio C/S gives the number of months that it will take for the refinancing to begin paying off. This number of months can be compared to the length of the mortgage and the length of time that the homeowner plans to stay in the current house. For instance, if it costs $5,000 to refinance a mortgage that will save $50/month in mortgage payments, the C/S is 100 months—making refinancing attractive for someone who plans to stay in the house for more than 100 months and has a mortgage with more than 100 monthly payments remaining.

Critically evaluate this advice.

3.25 A developer offered $100,000 30-year 12% mortgages with "no interest the first year." The loan has constant monthly payments for 30 years, but no interest is charged during the first year. What is the appropriate constant monthly payment? What is the effective interest rate consistent with these monthly payments? Just set up. Do you think that the effective interest rate is larger or smaller than 12%? Why?

3.26 On commercial loans, banks often require "compensating balances," with the borrower depositing perhaps 10% or 15% of the amount borrowed in a low-interest checking account. Suppose that a small business borrows $200,000 at a 10% annual interest rate (compounded monthly) in a 5-year balloon loan ($200,000 plus interest due after five years) and must keep $20,000 in a zero-interest checking account for 5 years. What is the effective annual interest rate on such a loan? (Just set up.)

3.27 A 1986 *Newsweek* article said of a 2.9% loan rate offered by General Motors and a 0% rate from American Motors,

> Don't think this is a never-again opportunity. The American auto market is going to be flooded with new cars in the years ahead ... there seems no way to avoid a market where there will be too many cars chasing too few passengers. So what will come next—a pitch featuring negative interest rates?

How would a negative interest rate work? In particular, what would be your monthly payment on a 4-year amortized monthly loan of $20,000 at –5%? Is the total of the monthly payments more or less than $20,000?

3.28 A 2024 homebuyer was offered two $800,000 interest-only mortgages:

a. 5.00% APR with 1.50 points.

b. 5.75% APR with .25 points.

Assuming these are 5-year loans, which do you recommend? You don't need to make a specific recommendation; you do need to show the calculations you would do in order to make your recommendation. (Ignore taxes.)

3.29 Explain the logic behind this conclusion by a *New York Times* columnist, and then explain why it is misleading:

> The essential difference between fixed- and adjustable-rate mortgages [ARM] is the party at risk. In fixed mortgages, the lender takes all the risk, profiting or suffering from changes in the interest rate.... With an ARM, the borrower, not the lender, is at the mercy of fluctuating interest rates.

3.30 In 2017, a Los Angeles mortgage broker said that he would not finance his own home with an adjustable-rate mortgage because, "I don't want to throw the dice and get burned." In what sense is a fixed-rate mortgage also a throw of the dice? What is a losing roll?

3.31 Here are some excerpts from a 1986 *New York Times* article:

> "In my view, making long-term fixed-rate mortgages is simply not a viable strategy any longer," said Dennis Jacobe, director of research at the United States League of Savings Associations.
>
> The widespread issuance of fixed-rate mortgages in the 1970's led to the collapse or merger of nearly a quarter of the nation's 4,000 savings associations then existing... Of those that survived, some remain in extremely poor shape....
>
> Adjustable-rate mortgages reached their height of popularity in late 1984, when 70 percent of the mortgages issued by savings and loan associations were adjustable-rate, according to the savings league.

a. What economic event caused trouble for S&Ls holding fixed-rate mortgages? How do adjustable-rate mortgages provide protection?

b. Some S&Ls moved to shorter-term mortgages and longer-term deposits. If the duration of their liabilities is greater than the duration of their assets, are they protected from interest rate fluctuations?

c. Why do you suppose many S&Ls wished they had issued fixed-rate mortgages during 1981–1984?

3.32 The federal government's budget is calculated on a cash flow basis. In 1987, several borrowers prepaid their loans from the federal Export-Import Bank, reducing the Bank's 1987 budget deficit by $1.5 billion.

a. Why do you think these borrowers voluntarily repaid their loans early?

b. Explain how a loan prepayment reduces the Export-Import Bank's budget deficit.

c. Do you think that these loan prepayments strengthened or weakened the financial condition of the Export-Import Bank?

3.33 A *Wall Street Journal* article warned of the dangers of interest-only mortgages. For example, a $350,000 30-year loan at an interest rate of 4% might be interest only for 10 years and then interest plus principal for the last 20 years. Show the formulas you would use to determine the monthly payments for

a. the first 10 years of this loan

b. the last 20 years of this loan

c. all 30 years if this were a conventional loan amortized over 30 years

Explain why (a) is either larger or smaller than (c), and why (b) is either larger or smaller than (c).

What would you advise a homebuyer?

3.34 Lew Sichelman, a syndicated real estate columnist, gave this advice on how to choose between these two $100,000 30-year, fixed-rate mortgages:

Option	Annual Interest Rate (%)	Points (%)	Monthly Payments ($)
1	7	0	665.30
2	6	5.75	599.55

> At 6%, you'd have to keep the house seven years and four months ... before the extra amount you pay every month adds up to more than the extra money [the 5.75 points] you'll pay at settlement. If you don't stay that long, you'll save money by making higher payments.

a. How did he come up with 7 years and 4 months?

b. Why is this calculation logically flawed?

c. Explain exactly how you would choose between these two options. (Set up the relevant equations, but don't solve them.)

3.35 A department store advertises that if a customer borrows money to buy a major appliance, the first 6 month's interest will be free and that no payments are due for 6 months. What is the effective interest rate if $1,000 is borrowed and, after the initial 6-month grace period, 18% annual interest is charged and the loan is paid off in 24 equal monthly installments? Just set up.

3.36 Ginnie Mae mutual funds buy a pool of residential mortgages that are guaranteed by the Government National Mortgage Association. Investors in these funds receive the monthly mortgage payments made by homeowners. While investors are protected against default, they can be hurt both by a rise in market interest rates and by a decline. Explain how this is possible.

3.37 Consider a $100,000 4-year loan with amortized monthly payments and a 5% APR. For each of the following *ceteris paribus* changes, state whether the duration goes up, goes down, or is unchanged.

a. The amount borrowed is increased to $250,000.

b. The length of the loan is changed to 8 years.

c. The amortized payments are made quarterly instead of monthly.

d. The APR is increased to 10%.

e. Instead of amortized payments, it is a balloon loan with the amount borrowed and all accrued interest paid at the end of 4 years.

3.38 Rank order the following assets (from 1 = highest to 4 = lowest) according to how sensitive the market values are to changes in the required return used to discount the cash flows:

a. 30-year amortized mortgage at a 10% interest rate

b. 30-year interest-only mortgage at a 10% interest rate

c. 30-year interest-only mortgage at a 5% interest rate

d. 30-year balloon mortgage

3.39 In 2023, a Michigan household received an offer that would allow it to borrow up to $150,000 at a 4.99% interest rate plus an initial "processing fee" equal to 4.99% of the amount borrowed.

a. If this is a conventional monthly amortized loan for n months, what equation would you use to determine the effective annual interest rate?

b. If this is a 5-year loan, is the effective annual interest rate larger or smaller than 4.99%?

c. If this is a 5-year loan, is the effective annual interest rate larger or smaller than 5.99%?

d. Would the effective interest rate be higher or lower if the loan were for 10 years instead of 5 years?

3.40 In 2024, a homebuyer compared 15-year and 30-year fixed-rate amortized mortgages at 6%. Without doing any calculations.

a. Which loan has the higher monthly payments?

b. Which loan has the higher unpaid balance after 5 years?

c. Which loan has the higher total payments over the length of the loan?

d. If the mortgage is paid off after 5 years, which loan's stream of payments (including the unpaid balance after 5 years) has the higher present value at a 6% required return?

e. If the mortgage is paid off after 5 years, which loan's stream of payments (including the unpaid balance after 5 years) has the higher present value at a 10% required return?

Answers

3.1 a. The appropriate amortized-loan present value equation is

$$\$1,000 = \frac{\$91.67}{(1+R/12)^1} + \frac{\$91.67}{(1+R/12)^2} + \ldots + \frac{\$91.67}{(1+R/12)^{12}}$$

The solution is an annual rate of R = .1798 (17.98%).

b. If the annual percentage rate was really 10%, the monthly payments X would be given by this equation:

$$\$1,000 = \frac{X}{(1+.10/12)^1} + \frac{X}{(1+.10/12)^2} + \ldots + \frac{X}{(1+.10/12)^{12}}$$

The solution is X = $87.92.

3.2 a. With an amortized loan, the average amount borrowed is much less than the initial loan amount, here about half the amount.

b. The total interest on a 4-year loan is more than on a 1-year loan because the money is borrowed for a longer period of time.

c. $4,000, because the present value of the payments discounted by the loan rate is the amount borrowed.

d. "The shorter the loan, the better" is not true if it is a favorable loan rate (lower than your required return, based on what you can earn on your investments).

3.3 The usual amortized-loan equation confirms that the $2,150 payments are correct for a 10.5% annual interest rate:

$$\$100,000 = \frac{\$2,150}{(1+.105/12)^1} + \frac{\$2,150}{(1+.105/12)^2} + \ldots + \frac{\$2,150}{(1+.105/12)^{60}}$$

The implicit annual interest rate R on the second loan is higher because the quarterly payments start immediately and accelerate the repayment:

$$\$100,000 = \$6,450 + \frac{\$6,450}{(1+R/4)^1} + \frac{\$6,450}{(1+R/4)^2} + \ldots + \frac{\$6,450}{(1+R/4)^{19}}$$

The annual interest rate works out to be R = .1144 (11.44%), nearly a full percentage point higher than the rate on the first loan.

3.4 The car loan is amortized. Each monthly payment covers the interest due and also reduces the unpaid balance until it hits zero at the end. Instead of borrowing $30,000 for 4 years, the car buyer borrows $30,000 at the beginning and almost nothing at the end, so that the average amount borrowed is about half the initial loan. Sterling's Rule is based on a flawed comparison of the return on $30,000 with the interest on roughly half of $30,000.

3.5 a. This equation incorrectly assumes that payments are made annually with no payment of principal until the very end.

b. The actual total interest is much less than the reported $300,000 in interest because payments are, in fact, monthly with a continual repayment of principal. You pay less than the reported $300,000 interest because you don't borrow $100,000 for all 30 years. The monthly payments are $877.57. The total payments are 360($877.57) = $315,925.20, implying that the total interest is $315,925.20 – $100,000 = $215,925.20.

3.6 Paying off a mortgage early does reduce the interest and the total payments over the life of the loan, but this doesn't necessarily mean that it is a good idea. It depends on the loan rate. The bank offered this opportunity because, at the time, 7.25% was a below-market rate that had been locked in 20 years earlier. Interest rates had risen, and the bank wanted these low-interest loans paid off as soon as possible, so that it could loan the money out at higher rates.

3.7 The author is not taking into account the time value of money. A more relevant question is whether the mortgage rate is high or low.

3.8 The relevant question is whether you want to borrow more at (a possibly tax-deductible) 2.75%, perhaps because you can make a better return invested in stocks.

3.9 If the loan rate is lower than what I can earn on safe investments, I would like to borrow a lot for a long time.

3.10 You borrow less money if you make a large down payment and if you repay the loan as soon as possible. If the loan rate is advantageous (for example, a low-interest loan from an employer, a housing contractor, or automobile dealership), then, contrary to this consumer finance book's advice, you are better off borrowing as much as possible for as long as possible.

3.11 There are two parts to the biweekly "secret." First, paying half of each monthly payment 2 weeks early reduces the interest charges. Second, there are 52 weeks in a year, so there are 26 biweekly payments, which are two extra biweekly payments compared to 12 monthly payments.

Biweekly payments accelerate the mortgage payoff, which reduces the total interest and the total payments. This financial writer did not take into account the time value of money, and it seems unlikely that a present value analysis would favor a 9.25% biweekly over a 6.7% monthly.

3.12 The bank gets to invest your money for 2 weeks every month, without paying you any interest, in essence, an annual 6-month interest-free loan.

3.13 For a 10-year \$100,000 monthly amortized loan at 10% + 7% = 17%, the monthly payments are X = \$1,737.98:

$$\$100{,}000 = \frac{X}{(1+.17/12)^1} + \frac{X}{(1+.17/12)^2} + \ldots + \frac{X}{(1+.17/12)^{120}}$$

The borrower receives \$100,000 – 7%(\$100,000) = \$93,000 and \$1,737.98 monthly payments on a \$93,000 loan implies an effective annual interest rate of R = .1903 (19.03%):

$$\$93{,}000 = \frac{\$1{,}737.98}{(1+R/12)^1} + \frac{\$1{,}737.98}{(1+R/12)^2} + \ldots + \frac{\$1{,}737.98}{(1+R/12)^{120}}$$

With a 5-year loan, the initial 7% fees become more burdensome, raising the effective interest rate (to 20.41%).

3.14 There is no compounding so the customers pay back 365(\$39) after one year:

$$R = 365(\$39)\$10{,}000 = 1.4235\ (142.35\%).$$

3.15 With fixed-rate mortgages, the lender wins if interest rates decline; with adjustable-rate mortgages, the borrower wins if interest rates decline (and the lender wins if interest rates increase). In retrospect, lenders will regret not issuing fixed-rate mortgages if interest rates do, in fact, decline.

3.16 The monthly payments are X such that

$$\$32{,}000 = \frac{X}{(1+.125/12)^1} + \frac{X}{(1+.125/12)^2} + \ldots + \frac{X}{(1+.125/12)^{360}}$$

The monthly payments are X = \$341.52. Since the borrower only gets \$32,000 – \$5,000 = \$27,000, the effective annual interest rate R is such that

$$\$27{,}000 = \frac{\$341.52}{(1+R/12)^1} + \frac{\$341.52}{(1+R/12)^2} + \ldots + \frac{\$341.52}{(1+R/12)^{360}}$$

The solution is R = .1501 (15.01%).

If the loan is repaid after 5 years, the \$5000 processing costs will be more important, and the effective interest rate will be higher (17.21%).

3.17 The loan with the lower interest rate is generally the better deal; however, there are some situations in which borrowing for longer at a somewhat higher loan rate is better. For example, a 30-year loan at 1.1% is generally better than a 1-day loan at 1%.

3.18 The appropriate monthly payments can be calculated for each loan

$$\$85{,}000 = \frac{X_1}{(1+.07/12)^1} + \frac{X_1}{(1+.07/12)^2} + \ldots + \frac{X_1}{(1+.07/12)^{360}}$$

$$\$40{,}000 = \frac{X_2}{(1+.12/12)^1} + \frac{X_2}{(1+.12/12)^2} + \ldots + \frac{X_2}{(1+.12/12)^{360}}$$

X_1 = \$565.51 and X_2 = \$411.45. The total monthly loan payment is \$565.51 + \$411.45 = \$976.96, so the implied annual loan rate R is given by this amortized loan equation:

$$\$125{,}000 = \frac{\$976.96}{(1+R/12)^1} + \frac{\$976.96}{(1+R/12)^2} + \ldots + \frac{\$976.96}{(1+R/12)^{360}}$$

The solution is R = .0868 (8.68%)

3.19 As with long-term Treasury bonds, there is no cash-flow risk from paying down a fixed-rate mortgage: you can be absolutely certain about how much you save each month by not having to make the monthly payments. The monthly savings are analytically equivalent to receiving fixed monthly income from Treasury securities. And, as with the purchase of long-term Treasury securities, the repayment of a fixed-rate mortgage will turn out to be a financial mistake if interest rates rise. (The repayment of variable-rate mortgage is equivalent to rolling over Treasury bills, and involves the very same reinvestment risk; you will regret paying off the mortgage if interest rates decline.)

3.20 In general, borrowing money at low interest rates is profitable, and borrowing money at high interest rates is unprofitable. It is not profitable to pay down a low-interest loan. It would make more sense to invest the money now and pay down the loan *after* interest rates have risen. The only advantage of paying the loan down now is if he does not have the discipline to save for a future pay down.

3.21 All his calculations ignore the time value of money. He might consider refinancing for 22 1/2 years at 9.5%, choosing the size of this new loan to give him the same monthly payments he has now, and see if this new loan covers his unpaid balance plus the closing costs. It would cover these costs.

(His current monthly payments are \$630.69, and the unpaid balance is \$54,173.34. He could borrow \$70,190.12 at 9.5% for 22 1/2 years, with monthly payments of \$630.69. The \$70,190.12 cash from the new loan is \$16,016.78 more than the unpaid balance on his current loan, which would allow him to pay \$3,500 to \$4,000 in closing costs and pocket more than \$12,000.)

3.22 Compounding for 26 2-week periods, the annual rate of return is 3,685.68%:

$$(1+R) = (1.15^{26}) = 37.8568$$
$$R = 36.8568$$

3.23 A comparison of the current $10,000 in fees with a saving of $43,167 in monthly payments 28–30 years from now ignores the time value of money.

To compare apples with apples, she should compare two 30-year loans, each with $1798.65 monthly payments. If the new loan is for more than $310,000, she can repay the initial loan, pay the $10,000 fees, and make a profit.

As it turns out, she could borrow $308,213.44—not enough to pay the $10,000 fees.

3.24 There are two major problems with a payback criterion:

a. Dollars in equals dollars out does not ensure a positive net present value. For example, a $5,000 refinancing cost with $50/month saving has a payback period of 100 months; but the present value of $50/month for 100 months at 10% is only $3,383. The present value does not exceed the $5,000 cost until 216 months have passed.

b. A payback-period criterion ignores the value of the cash flow beyond the payback period. For example, a $1,000 refinancing cost with $50 monthly savings has a payback period of 20 months, but the size of the saving depends on whether there are 2 years or 28 years left on the mortgage.

To further illustrate this point, which of these three financial arrangements is the most attractive?

	Payback Period
a. pay $1000 and save $50/month for n months	20
b. pay $2000 and save $100/month for n months	20
c. pay $6000 and save $250/month for n months	24

Present value calculations give a very different answer than does the pay-back period:

	Present Value (net of financing cost)		
n	Option a	Option b	Option c
20	– $82	– $165	– $412
30	322	645	612
60	1,353	27,07	5,766
120	2,783	5,567	12,918
240	4,181	8,362	19,906
360	4,698	9,395	22,488

3.25 If the monthly payments are X, then, after 1 year with no interest being charged, the unpaid balance has declined to \$100,000 – 12X. At this point, the present value of the remaining 29 years of payments at a 12% annual interest rate is equal to this unpaid balance:

$$\$100,000 - 12X = \sum_{t=1}^{29(12)} \frac{X}{(1+.12/12)^t}$$

The effective annual rate R equates the present value of the 360 monthly payments to the size of the loan:

$$\$100,000 = \sum_{t=1}^{30(12)} \frac{X}{(1+R/12)^t}$$

The monthly payments work out to be X = \$918.56; the effective annual interest rate is R = 10.55%, which is less than 12%, because of the interest-free year.

3.26 The business has the use of \$180,000 and, after 5 years, must pay interest on \$200,000. The effective interest rate R can be determined by calculating the total amount due after 5 years and subtracting the \$20,000 held as a compensating balance:

$$\$180,000(1+R)^5 = \$200,000(1+.10/12)^{60} - \$20,000$$

The effective interest rate works out to be 11.42%.
Equivalently, the net present value (NPV) equation is:

$$0 = \$200,000 - \$20,000 - \frac{\$200,000(1+.10/12)^{60}}{(1+R)^5} + \frac{\$20,000}{(1+R)^5}$$

3.27 Using the present-value equation with a monthly rate of R = –.05/12 = –.004167,

$$\$20,000 = \frac{X}{(1-.004167)^1} + \frac{X}{(1-.004167)^2} + \ldots + \frac{X}{(1-.004167)^{48}}$$

The requisite monthly payments are X = \$375.52. With a negative interest rate, the total payments are less than \$20,000: 48(\$375.52) = \$18024.96.

3.28 With interest-only mortgages, the monthly payments are (.05/12)\$800,000 = \$3,333.33 or (.0575/12)\$800,000 = \$3,833.33. After points, the homebuyer receives (1 – .015)\$800,000 = \$788,000 or (1 – .0025)\$800,000 = \$798,000. In each case, the borrower pays back

$800,000 after 5 years. If the borrower's annual required return is R, the NPVs are

$$NPV_a = \$788,000 - \sum_{t=1}^{60} \frac{\$3,333.33}{(1+R/12)^t} - \frac{\$800,000}{(1+R/12)^{60}}$$

$$NPV_b = \$798,000 - \sum_{t=1}^{60} \frac{\$3,833.33}{(1+R/12)^t} - \frac{\$800,000}{(1+R/12)^{60}}$$

The difference in NPVs is

$$NPV_a - NPV_b = -\$10,000 + \sum_{t=1}^{60} \frac{\$500.00}{(1+R/12)^t}$$

Choose (a) if the difference in NPVs is positive; choose (b) if the difference is negative. Option (a) wins for any required return that is less than 56.14%:

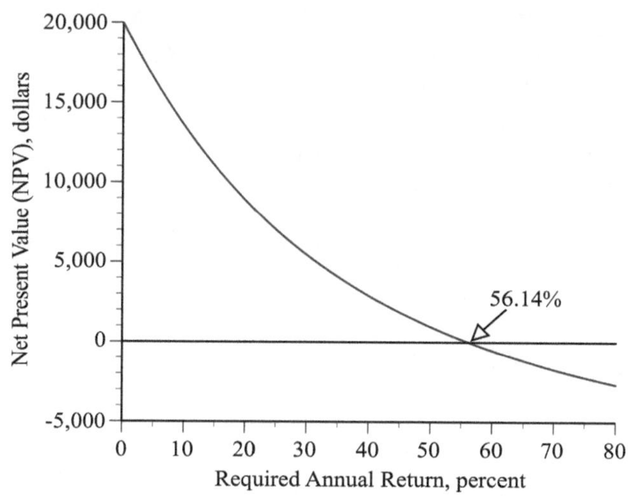

3.29 There is interest-rate risk for both the bank and the borrower. With a fixed-rate mortgage, a decline in interest rates benefits the bank and hurts the borrower, while the reverse is true of an increase in interest rates. With an adjustable-rate mortgage, an increase in interest rates benefits the lender and hurts the borrower, while the reverse is true of a decline in interest rates.

A fixed-rate mortgage is implicitly a wager on rising interest rates by the borrower and a bet on falling interest rates by the lender. An adjustable-rate mortgage is a bet on declining interest rates by the borrower, a bet on rising interest rates by the lender.

3.30 A fixed-rate mortgage is a wager that interest rates will not decline (a losing roll), leaving the homeowner with a relatively high-interest mortgage.

3.31 a. An unanticipated increase in interest rates hurt S&Ls who had borrowed short and lent long, thereby holding assets with longer durations than their liabilities. Adjustable-rate mortgages alleviate this imbalance by reducing the duration of their assets.

b. If the duration of their liabilities exceeds the duration of their assets, their net worth will be reduced by an unanticipated decline in interest rates: the market value of their liabilities will increase by more than the market value of their assets.

c. Interest rates declined significantly, increasing the market value of long-term, fixed-rate mortgages considerably.

3.32 The analysis is very similar to home mortgages issued by a savings and loan association.

a. They prepaid early because they could borrow elsewhere at lower interest rates.

b. These prepayments reduced the Export-Import Bank's cash-flow deficit because it brought in more cash, ignoring the fact that it also diminished future cash flow.

c. Since these were presumably high-interest loans, the Export-Import Bank was made worse off by their prepayment.

3.33 The present-value equations are:

$$\text{a. } X = \left(\frac{.04}{12}\right)\$350,000$$

$$\text{b. } \$350,000 = \sum_{t=1}^{20(12)} \frac{X}{(1+.04/12)^t}$$

$$\text{c. } \$350,000 = \sum_{t=1}^{30(12)} \frac{X}{(1+.04/12)^t}$$

The monthly payments for (a) are smaller than (c) because (a) is interest only and (c) includes principal repayments. The monthly payments for (b) are larger than (c) because the loan is amortized over 20 rather than 30 years.

The relevant question is whether one wants to pay off a 4% loan or use money borrowed at 4% to make investments. If the borrower can make more than 4% and expects their income to be high enough 10 years from now to make the higher mortgage payments, I would advise taking the interest-only loan.

3.34 a. The monthly saving is \$665.30 – \$599.55= \$65.75, and (5.75%)(\$100,000)/\$65.75/month = 87.45 months.

b. It should be a present value calculation, and it should take into account the difference in the unpaid balance if you don't stay 30 years.

c. For different repayment dates n, calculate the unpaid balances and compare the present values of the cash flows at the borrower's required return:

$$P_1 = \sum_{t=1}^{n} \frac{\$665}{(1+R/12)^t} + \frac{B_1}{(1+R/12)^n}$$

$$P_2 = \$5{,}750 + \sum_{t=1}^{n} \frac{\$600}{(1+R/12)^t} + \frac{B_2}{(1+R/12)^n}$$

The difference in present values is

$$P_1 - P_2 = -\$5{,}750 + \sum_{t=1}^{n} \frac{\$65}{(1+R/12)^t} + \frac{B_1 - B_2}{(1+R/12)^n}$$

It turns out that the breakeven repayment date n is equal to 120 months if R = .06 and is equal to 128 months if R = .07.

3.35 The monthly payments X are determined by equating the unpaid balance to the present value of the payments:

$$\$1{,}000 = \frac{X}{(1+.18/12)^1} + \frac{X}{(1+.18/12)^2} + \ldots + \frac{X}{(1+.18/12)^{24}}$$

The effective annual interest rate R equates the present value of the payments to the initial loan:

$$\$1{,}000 = \frac{X}{(1+R/12)^7} + \frac{X}{(1+R/12)^2} + \ldots + \frac{X}{(1+R/12)^{30}}$$

The solution is X = \$49.92 and R = .1193 (11.93%).

3.36 If interest rates increase, the market value of the mortgages (and the mutual fund shares) will drop. If interest rates decrease, many homeowners will refinance their mortgages, reducing the portfolio's average interest rate.

3.37 Think of the duration as the present-value weighted average wait until the funds are received.

a. Unchanged. The average weight does not depend on the size of the loan.

b. Up. The lengthened loan increases the average wait.

c. Up. The deferral of payments to a quarterly lengthens the loan.

d. Down. A higher discount rate reduces the weights given to distant payments.

e. Up. A balloon loan lengthens the average wait.

3.38 We can answer this question by thinking of the durations—the present-value weighted average wait until the cash flow is received. An interest-only mortgage has more of the payments at the end than does an amortized mortgage. A 5% interest-only mortgage has lower monthly payments than does a 10% interest-only mortgage, with the same payment at the end. A balloon mortgage is a zero and has an even longer duration. The assets are in order, from highest sensitivity to lowest: d, c, b, and a. (The 4 durations, from a to d, are 8.49 years, 9.58 years, 15.59 years, and 30 years.)

3.39 a. The monthly payments X for a loan lasting n months are determined by this equation:

$$P = \sum_{t=1}^{n} \frac{X}{(1+.0499/12)^t}$$

The effective annual interest rate R is then determined by this equation:

$$P(1-.0499) = \sum_{t=1}^{n} \frac{X}{(1+R/12)^t}$$

For a 5-year $150,000 loan, the monthly payments are $2,830.00 and the effective interest rate is 7.12%.

For a 10-year $150,000 loan, the payments are $1,590.25 and the effective interest rate is 6.11%.

b. The effective annual interest rate is larger than 4.99% because of the processing fee.

c. The 5% processing fee is paid up front so it is more expensive than paying an extra 1-percentage-point loan rate.

d. The effective interest rate is lower if the loan is for 10 years because the processing fee is spread out over a longer horizon.

3.40 a. The monthly payments are lower on the 30-year mortgage, so that the loan is not paid off as quickly.

b. The 30-year mortgage has the higher unpaid balance after 5 years, because the monthly payments are lower.

c. The 30-year mortgage has the higher total payments because the funds are borrowed for a longer period of time and, consequently, more interest must be paid.

d. For either loan, no matter when the mortgage is paid off, the present value of the payments at a 6% required return (the interest rate on the loan) is equal to the amount borrowed.

e. In comparison with the 15-year mortgage, the 30-year mortgage has lower monthly payments and a higher unpaid balance after 5 years; it therefore has the longer duration. An increase in the required return will reduce the present value of the loan with the longer duration, here the 30-year mortgage. Thus, the 15-year mortgage has the higher present value at a 10% required return.

4

Bonds

4.1 The *Encyclopedia of Investments* stated that, "The effective rate of return [on a Treasury bond] .... is normally referred to as the security's yield to maturity." Explain why an investor's realized rate of return is not necessarily equal to the bond's yield to maturity, even if the bond is held until maturity.

4.2 A *Wall Street Journal* article began,

> At first glance, "premium bonds" may sound like a mad investment scheme straight out of a Marx Brothers movie: The investor pays even more for a bond than its face value.

Imagine that you are employed by an investment bank that makes a market in municipal bonds, and that a client who read this article asks you why someone would buy a premium bond. What is your answer?

4.3 A *New York Times* article recommended bond-swapping—selling a bond that had gone down in price and buying a similar bond:

> Some 30-year A-rated bonds of Municipal Electric Utilities, for example, were marketed four or five years ago with a 7% coupon. Currently, many of these bonds are worth only sixty cents on the dollar.... The process of turning lemons into lemonade, so to speak, involves bond-swapping.

Why do you suppose these bonds were only worth 60% of their face value? What is the flaw in this advice?

4.4 Explain why you agree or disagree with this advice from a *Los Angeles Times* financial columnist:

> Investors flee from bonds when interest rates rise—or when they think they're going to rise—because bond prices move in the opposite direction from interest rates. Thus bonds—which are interest-bearing debt securities issued by governments and corporations to raise money—are a good investment during periods of low interest rates.

4.5 Explain why this financial writer's explanation of a bond's yield to maturity is incorrect: "[A] $1,000 bond might carry a stated annual yield, known as the coupon, of 8 percent, meaning that it pays $80 a year to the bondholder. If that bond was bought at 87, the actual yield would be 9.2 percent ($80 annual interest on $870 of principal)."

4.6 John Kenneth Galbraith wrote that "anyone who buys a junk bond known as a junk bond deserves on the whole to lose." Why would any rational investor buy a junk bond when it is clearly labeled a junk bond?

 DOI: 10.1201/9781003630166-4

4.7 In 1948, a distinguished economist proclaimed that, "Never in the lifetime of anyone in this room will government two-and-a-halves [2.5% coupon bonds] sell below par." Was he right?

4.8 Vanguard founder John Bogle wrote:

> It is reasonable, for example, to assume that a U.S. government bond with an 8% coupon will achieve an annual total return of +8% if held to its 20-year maturity.

a. Why did the Bogle specify a U.S. government bond?

b. Explain why the "reasonable" conclusion is either correct or incorrect.

4.9 A *Wall Street Journal* article argued that people buying 30-year Treasury bonds with 6.7% yields were imprudent: "room for further slippage is limited. Interest rates have never been less than zero yet," and while bond prices might decline "a bit more," "the premium for making this bet is all of four-fifths of a percentage point, since one can get 5.84% without the risk on a two-year note."

a. Explain why interest rates are unlikely to be negative.

b. Explain why investors in 30-year Treasuries may make much more than four-fifths of a percentage point if interest rates decline.

4.10 Bonds can be bought on margin—30% for corporate bonds and as little as 5% for Treasury bonds. Why would anyone want to buy Treasury bonds on margin, since the loan rate charged by the broker is presumably higher than the interest rate on Treasury bonds?

4.11 Explain the error(s) in this September 1991 *Los Angeles Times* newspaper column:

> Thomas M. Poor, manager of the Scudder Short-term Bond Fund in Boston, suggests that you focus on a volatility index known as "duration." This is a calculation in which you determine the present value of a bond's future interest payments and principal repayment. Sound complicated? It is. Suffice it that bond funds with lower duration numbers are less volatile.
>
> According to Poor, money market funds have a duration of zero, while a portfolio filled with 30-year Treasury bonds would have a duration of 10.

4.12 In May 1992, a Japanese newspaper, *The Nikkei Weekly*, reported that Japanese life insurance companies traditionally "had concentrated on high-coupon bonds, disregarding those with coupon rates of less than 6%." Tadao Nishioka, section chief at Nippon Life Insurance Co., says, "We used to buy bonds with coupon rates of 6% or more even if their prices were ¥10 above face value of ¥100."

a. Why might a bond with a 4% coupon be more attractive than an equally risky bond with an 8% coupon?

b. Show how to calculate the yield to maturity on a 10-year bond with a coupon rate of 6% and a price 10% above its face value. (Assume that the coupons are semi-annual.)

4.13 A *Los Angeles Times* financial columnist wrote that,

> Demand for the bonds of states, cities and public authorities, which offer tax-exempt interest payments, has been tremendous. So many have rushed to buy what bond houses advertise as the last tax shelter of the middle class that customary price differentials between tax-exempt and taxable bonds have narrowed. Crowd psychology rather than economics is at work.

Consider tax-exempt and taxable bonds with the same coupons, maturity, and default risk. Explain clearly why a huge surge in the demand for tax-exempt should not cause the price differential between tax-exempt and taxable bonds to narrow.

4.14 In January 1990, the Mexican government bought 30-year zero-coupon U.S. Treasury bonds paying $33 billion in 2020. To price these 30-year zeros, the U.S. Treasury used the prevailing 7.925% interest rate on 30-year Treasury coupon bonds rather than the prevailing 7.625% interest rate on Treasury 30-year zeros.

a. Who did this benefit?

b. How much difference did it make?

c. Was the term structure upward sloping, downward sloping, or flat at the time?

4.15 An investment textbook states that "bond investors will prefer to buy short-term bonds [rather than long-term bonds] whenever they expect interest rates to rise." What is the logic behind this assertion? Why is it incorrect?

4.16 In a *New York Times* interview, John T. Haggerty, National Director of Personal Financial Planning for Prudential-Bache Securities, advised

> I wouldn't buy any bond, except maybe a Treasury, that was 30 years in maturity. I don't know if the world is going to be around 30 years from now.... If I had to buy, or if I wanted to buy, I'd probably be looking at discount bonds. There you have the maturities working in your favor. You know the bond's going to be going up in price, because it's getting closer to maturity with the passage of time.

a. Why is the existence of the world 30 years from now of little relevance to an investor's choice between short-term and long-term bonds?

b. Evaluate Haggerty's apparent claim that the returns from bonds selling at a discount are inherently more certain than the returns from bonds selling at par or for a premium.

c. Interest rates subsequently dropped substantially. Why, in retrospect, were 30-year bonds an especially profitable investment?

4.17 Prudential Securities advised clients that "during periods of escalating inflation, shorter [bond] maturities are preferred, since they are less volatile and offer greater flexibility to shift into higher yielding instruments while providing little risk to principal." Explain why

a. short-term bonds may do better than long-term bonds during an escalating inflation.

b. Prudential specified an escalating inflation, rather than a steady inflation.

c. short-term bonds have risks, other than risk to principal.

d. there may be no advantage from shifting into higher-yielding instruments if investors are well aware of the escalating inflation.

4.18 In February 1985, Edward Yardeni of Prudential-Bache wrote that, "The Fed must lower interest rates to offset the erosion of the financial system's net worth.... Otherwise the financial system will collapse." How can lower interest rates bail out financial intermediaries?

4.19 In April 2023, JPMorgan Chase CEO Jamie Dimon said that stress tests administered by the Fed before the failure of Silicon Valley Bank "never incorporated interest rates at higher levels." Why might higher interest rates contribute to the failure of an otherwise well-managed bank?

4.20 Explain why the following observation in a Fidelity Investments newsletter is right, but not for the reason given:

> All bonds do not react the same way to changing market conditions....bonds with longer maturities are more likely to fluctuate in price. This is because the longer an investor's money is tied up at a certain rate, the greater the likelihood that interest rates—and therefore bond yields—will change before the bond matures.

4.21 Answer the questions following this quotation from a *Wall Street Journal* columnist:

> With most economists now expecting interest rates to rise later this year, buying any kind of long-term bond carries a growing risk of principal loss for those who can't hold the issue until maturity. Zeros are especially risky because they react more extremely than conventional bonds to changes in interest rates.

a. Do zero-coupon bonds have to sell at a discount?

b. How can there be a principal loss if the bond issuer doesn't default?

c. Why are zeros especially risky?

d. Is there no risk for those who hold until maturity?

e. Why would anyone buy a long-term zero if it is clear that interest rates will rise? Give an example.

4.22 Explain why you either agree or disagree with this reasoning by a prolific financial writer:

> Another way of achieving security is to put up as little money as possible to purchase financial instruments that will almost certainly appreciate in future years. Inevitably, many bond issues are at a discount because they were originally offered with lower coupon rates than are presently obtainable. Deep discount bonds may also be the result of interest rate fluctuations or a business's running into difficulties and not paying its bondholders. While the company struggles to revamp itself or undergoes reorganization under the court's protection, the bonds will fall sharply. Buyers of such deeply discounted bonds stand to make substantial capital gains and accrued interest if or when the company emerges from its troubles.

4.23 Vanguard founder John Bogle warned investors that a long-term bond fund's current yield (income divided by current market value) may be a misleadingly high measure of the investor's rate of return, particularly for funds that hold lots of bonds issued at par when interest rates were higher than they are today. Ignoring taxes, transaction costs, and default risk, and assuming that the current level of interest rates is expected to persist indefinitely, explain why a bond fund's current yield may be misleadingly high

a. if the bonds are callable after some future date.

b. even if the bonds are not callable.

4.24 Other things being equal, which would you expect to have the higher yield to maturity,

a. corporate or Treasury bonds?

b. corporate or municipal bonds?

c. AA or A corporate bonds?

4.25 What do you predict would happen to the yield spread between equally risky corporate and municipal bonds

a. if the current progressive tax system were replaced with a flat 25% tax? (Municipals would still be tax-exempt.)

b. if municipal bonds lost their tax-exempt status?

4.26 In 2005, Columbia/HCA Healthcare, the nation's largest for-profit hospital company, issued \$200 million in 100-year debt, rated A3 by Moody's and BBB+ by Standard & Poor's. A *Wall Street Journal* article said that "most investors avoid 100-year bonds like the plague," forcing the company to offer a 7.5% yield, compared to the 6.25% yields then prevailing on 30-year Treasury bonds. The *Journal* asked, (a) "Why would investors buy the IOU of a company when chances are they won't live to see their principal returned?," and also pointed out that (b) "even though investors get interest every year, by the time they get their principal back, inflation, even at its current low levels, would have eroded the principal's value to virtually nothing." Explain why these two concerns are of little importance and identify two much more important risks.

4.27 In 1993, Walt Disney Co. issued 100-year bonds with 7.5% coupons and 7.5% yields to maturity. Morgan Stanley (the investment bank handling this issue) estimated that "if long-term yields ... were to rise one percentage point, investors in the Disney bond would have a total return of negative 4.19% over the [first] year. If long-term rates were to fall one percentage point, however, the total return would be nearly 23%."

a. Did this bond initially sell at a premium or discount from par value?

b. Estimate the duration of this bond, without using a complicated mathematical formula for the duration.

4.28 An investment management firm said that its "fixed-income manager will maintain a portfolio duration between 80% and 120% of the duration of the Lehman Brothers Aggregate Index."

a. What is a "fixed-income manager"?

b. When would a fixed-income manager want a portfolio duration equal to 80% of the duration of the Lehman index?

c. When would a fixed-income manager want a portfolio duration equal to 120% of the duration of the Lehman index?

d. Why do you suppose they don't allow their fixed-income manager to go outside the 80%–120% range?

4.29 An article in the *American Association of Individual Investors Journal* explained duration with a graph showing that (a) bond price risk is highest when the bond is held only a short while and declines to a minimum when the holding period is equal to the bond's duration; and (b) reinvestment rate risk is highest when the bond is held until maturity and declines to a minimum when the holding period is equal to the bond's duration. Thus, "When a bond is held to its duration, the price risk and the reinvestment risk are at a minimum." Explain why you disagree.

4.30 Identify the economic event that is most likely to explain this *Wall Street Journal* headline: "Zero-Coupon Returns Lead Bond Funds With Average 7.05% Gain in 1st Quarter." Explain your reasoning.

4.31 A lawsuit alleged that there had been fraud and misrepresentation in a land sale. The defendant had allegedly misrepresented part of the land as suitable for the development of condominiums that would generate an estimated net cash flow of $120,000 a month. This land turned out to be unbuildable. One side of the lawsuit argued that the present value of this anticipated $120,000 monthly cash flow should be calculated using a Treasury bond rate; the other side argued that the corporate Baa bond rate is more appropriate.

a. Which of these interest-rate arguments do you suppose was made by the defendant and which was made by the plaintiff (the person suing for damages)?
b. If you were the judge, what interest rate would you use to calculate the present value?

4.32 Between 1989 and 1992, Treasury-bill interest rates fell from 9% to below 4%, provoking a half-joking commentary from economic analyst Ed Yardeni that "there could be interest riots in Florida. The American Association of Retired Persons (AARP) might start a campaign to force the Fed to raise interest rates." Explain Yardeni's reasoning. Don't investors make capital gains when interest rates decline and suffer capital losses when interest rates increase?

4.33 Explain this observation in an article in the *Financial Analysts Journal* regarding life insurance companies and pension funds:

> Contemporary accounting practice tends to promote the view that increases in bond prices are a positive outcome even when the long-run impact of the associated decline in interest rates is negative.

4.34 The British government first consolidated its debts in 1751 by issuing (*consol*) bonds that pay a constant coupon and never mature. However, these and subsequent British consols could be redeemed by the government and either retired or exchanged for new consols with different coupons. Calculate the yields to maturity on the British consol bonds that were purchased for £100 in 1927 and paid £4 annual coupons at the end of each year.

a. forever.
b. until they were redeemed for £100 in 2015.

4.35 Series EE U.S. savings bonds are sold for half of their face value; for example, it costs $25 for a bond that will be worth $50 when it matures. The number of years until maturity is set to give a specified rate of return. The maturities on Series EE bonds issued between November 1982 and October 1986 were set to give a 7.5% return. In November 1986, the maturities of new EE bonds were set to give a 6% return. Were the maturities shortened or lengthened in November of 1986? Explain your reasoning. Why do you suppose savings bond interest rates were reduced in November of 1986?

4.36 Explain this quotation from *The Wall Street Journal*:

> Suppose you buy a 10-year Treasury note today at a yield to maturity of 6% and interest rates shoot up to 8%. What happens to your investment?
>
> A. You lose money.
>
> B. You make money.

C. Nothing happens.

D. All of the above.

The answer: D. All of the above. How is that possible? The trick is how long you hold the investment.

4.37 In his keynote address to the American Association of Individual Investors' National Meeting for Investment Education, Vanguard founder John C. Bogle said that investors should, "Consider the impact of income yield and principal change on total return in light of the length of time that you expect to own the investment." To illustrate this point, he presented a graph showing the terminal value (the market value of the bond plus the value of the reinvested coupons) for a 25-year Treasury bond with 8% coupons over horizons of 1–25 years under three scenarios: interest rates rise to 10%, interest rates stay at 8%, and interest rates fall to 6%.

a. For a horizon of 25 years, which of these three scenarios gives the highest terminal value?

b. For a horizon of 1 year, which of these three scenarios gives the highest terminal value?

c. For what horizon is the terminal value the same for all three scenarios?

4.38 In 2012 Alan Sloan, a senior editor at Fortune, warned that, "Municipal bonds are a train wreck waiting to happen."

> Let's look at a security that I own: a New Jersey transit trust fund bond bought at about face value when it was issued four years ago. This bond, which pays 5.25% annual interest and is due in June 2023, currently trades for 120.505% of face value, according to the most recent Bloomberg quote. On the surface, its yield looks pretty good in these ultra-low-rate days: 4.36%. You get that by dividing the 5.25 of interest by the bond's market value of 120.505....
>
> New Jersey has the right to redeem the bond at face value in June 2018, less than six years from now. If rates remain anywhere near their current levels in 2018, this bond will be redeemed fast enough to break the sound barrier. That produces some sorry math: Pay the aforementioned $12,051 for your bond, get redeemed out for $10,000 in 2018, and your "yield to worst," as it's known, is 1.66%. Yechhhh!

a. Why is the yield to maturity if the bond is held for 11 years not 4.36%?

b. What is the correct value of the yield to maturity? (Assume that coupons are paid every 6 months, beginning 6 months hence.)

c. Show how to calculate the yield to call if the bond is called at par in 6 years.

4.39 Ten years ago, a company issued 30-year 12% bonds with a maturation value of $1,000. Now it can exercise the bond's call provisions and retire these bonds by paying 110% of par—$1,100 apiece. It can issue new 20-year bonds at 9%, but will have to pay its investment banker a fee equal to 5% of the par value of the new issue. Should it call these bonds and issue new ones? (For simplicity, assume that the coupons are paid annually, with the next coupon due 1 year from today.)

4.40 For each of the following pairs, identify the asset with the longer duration:

a. a conventional 30-year amortized mortgage at 8% or a 15-year zero with an 8% yield to maturity.

b. a conventional 30-year amortized $400,000 mortgage at 6% or a conventional 30-year amortized $800,000 mortgage at 6%.

c. a 5-year zero with a 10% yield to maturity or a 10-year zero with a 5% yield to maturity.

d. a 10-year 7%-coupon bond with a 5% yield to maturity or a 10-year zero with a 6% yield to maturity.

Answers

4.1 If it is a coupon bond, the effective return will be higher or lower than the yield to maturity, depending on whether the rate of return earned on the reinvested coupons is higher or lower than the yield to maturity. It will equal the yield to maturity if the return on the reinvested coupons is equal to the yield to maturity.

4.2 If a bond's coupons are larger than its yield to maturity, then the bond sells for a premium over its face (or maturation) value. The generous coupons make up for the high price.

4.3 Bond prices go down if interest rates go up or if the chances of default rise. The problem with this advice is that, if bonds are fairly priced, selling one bond to buy a different bond doesn't gain anything. It's like, when apple prices decline, you sell one apple in order to buy another apple.

4.4 Yes, bond prices and interest rates move in opposite directions. No, bonds are not necessarily good investments when interest rates are low. Is the columnist hoping that interest rates will fall (and bond prices rise) and thinking this is more likely when interest rates are already low? There is no momentum in interest rates and, in addition, there is less room for interest rates to fall when interest rates are already low.

4.5 The author calculates the yield by dividing the annual interest by the market price: $80/$870 = .092 (9.2%). This 9.2% figure is the not-very-informative "current yield," which is not the same as the yield to maturity unless the bond is selling for its maturation value. In the example here, the investor will get a capital gain at maturity in addition to the annual coupons. The yield to maturity y is given by the present value equation (assuming annual coupons),

$$\$870 = \frac{\$80}{(1+y)^1} + \frac{\$80}{(1+y)^2} + \ldots + \frac{\$80}{(1+y)^m} + \frac{\$1,000}{(1+y)^m}$$

For example, with m = 5 years until maturity, the yield to maturity is y = 11.57%.

4.6 At some (low) price, a junk bond will attract buyers who believe that it is a gamble worth taking. In fact, (almost) every investor has a sufficiently low price at which they would buy a junk bond.

4.7 He was wrong. Bonds sell below par when interest rates increase, and interest rates have subsequently been higher than 2.5%.

4.8 a. Bogle specified a government bond so that there would be no default risk.

b. As Bogle goes on to explain: "Only if the semiannual interest coupon is reinvested at the same interest rate of 8% will the cumulative return equate to +8% annually."

4.9 a. Interest rates are unlikely be negative because investors can get a 0% return simply by holding cash.

b. A 30-year bond has a long duration and its price will increase substantially if interest rates decline.

4.10 The return on Treasury bonds includes capital gains or losses as interest rates fluctuate. Investors might buy Treasury bonds on margin if they expect interest rates to decline significantly and give a total return (coupons plus capital gains) that is larger than the loan rate.

4.11 The present value of a bond's future interest payments and principal repayment is its price, not its duration. The duration is the present-value-weighted average length of time until the coupons and maturation value are received. Money market funds do have a duration of essentially zero. The duration of a portfolio filled with 30-year Treasury bonds depends on their coupons (and interest rates); for example, a portfolio of 30-year Treasury zeros has a duration of 30 years.

4.12 a. The price of the bond with the 4% coupon could be sufficiently low to make it more attractive.

b. The yield to maturity y is given by

$$110 = \frac{3}{(1+y/2)^1} + \frac{3}{(1+y/2)^2} + \ldots + \frac{3}{(1+y/2)^{20}} + \frac{100}{(1+y/2)^{20}}$$

The solution works out to be y = .0473 (4.73%).

4.13 The taxable bond has the lower price and higher before-tax rate of return. If the demand for tax-exempts surges, the prices of tax-exempts will rise, widening the price and interest-rate differentials.

4.14 a. It benefitted Mexico.

b. ($\$33$ billion$/1.07625^{30}$) – ($\$40$ billion$/1.07925^{30}$) = \$3.640 billion – \$3.349 billion = \$291 million.

c. The term structure was downward sloping, because this is when coupon-bond yields are higher than zero yields.

4.15 When interest rates are expected to rise, they can anticipate rolling over their short-term bonds into bonds with higher interest rates. The problem is that the term structure will take into account anticipated increases in interest rates—so that long-term bonds will be priced to offer higher returns that short-term bonds. The statement would be okay if it referred to investors who expect future interest rates to be higher than those already embedded in the term structure.

4.16 a. Investors can sell their bonds before they mature.

b. Bond returns consist of coupons and capital gains (or losses). There is no reason to think that coupons are less certain than maturation value. In fact, for bonds with default risk, early coupons are safer than later maturation values.

c. The decline in interest rates increased the market value of long-duration bonds.

4.17 a. To the extent that escalating inflation raises nominal interest rates, it reduces the prices of fixed-income securities. The prices of long-term (actually long-duration) securities are most sensitive to interest rates.

b. Other things being equal, an escalating inflation will raise nominal interest rates, while a steady inflation is consistent with constant nominal interest rates.

c. Short-term bods have income (or reinvestment) risk.

d. A well-anticipated inflation should already be reflected in the term structure.

4.18 Financial intermediaries, such as savings and loan associations, that have borrowed short-term and lent long-term, will benefit from a decline in interest rates since the market value of their assets will increase by more than the market value of their liabilities.

4.19 If a bank has mainly long-term assets (like Treasury bonds, mortgages, and stock) and mainly short-term liabilities (like deposits) so that the duration of its assets is longer than the duration of its liabilities, its net worth will fall when interest rates increase. Most banks have tremendous leverage, so it doesn't take much of an increase in interest rates to bankrupt them.

4.20 The prices of long-term (actually long-duration) bonds are more sensitive to interest rates, but not because interest rates are more likely to change in the distant future. It is just a mathematical fact that a given interest rate change has a larger percentage effect on the present value of a distant cash payment. (It is unclear why the quotation distinguishes between interest rates and bond yields.)

4.21 a. Yes; otherwise, the rate of return would not be positive.

b. The market values fluctuate with interest rates.

c. With no cash flow before maturity, a zero has a duration equal to its maturity; coupon-paying bonds have shorter durations than their maturity—and duration gauges the sensitivity of market value to interest rate changes.

d. There is inflation risk and also opportunity-loss risk, in that, if interest rates increase, one could have done better rolling over short-term bonds than holding on to a zero.

e. The term structure may reflect this anticipated increase in interest rates. In fact, if others expect interest rates to increase by a larger amount than you do, the upward sloping term structure will be so steep that you might anticipate making more money buying a long-term zero than rolling over short-term bonds. For example, if 1-year Treasury bills pay 8% and 30-year zeros pay 12%, and you expect Treasury bill rates to increase to 10% over the next 30 years, the 30-year zero is a much better investment.

4.22 Bonds with low coupons will have low prices that take into account the coupons and maturation values and give investors anticipated returns comparable to those on high-coupon, high-priced bonds. Bonds issued by distressed companies are cheap because it is uncertain whether the companies will meet their bond obligations.

4.23 a. When interest rates have declined, bond issuers are likely to exercise their call provisions, and investors will consequently not receive the generous coupons until maturity.

b. Because high-coupon bonds sell at a premium to maturation value, their yields to maturity will be less than their coupon rate.

4.24 The differences involve default risk and taxes.

a. Corporates because the coupons and maturation value are riskier than for Treasury bonds.

b. Corporate bonds because the income is more highly taxed than is the income from municipal bonds.

c. A-rated bonds because the coupons and maturation value are riskier than for AA bonds.

4.25 a. The municipal-bond interest rate, at least for states with no income tax, would probably be about 75% of the corporate-bond interest rate; for example, if AAA corporate bonds yielded 4%, then AAA municipal bonds would be priced to yield about (1 − .25)4% = 3%. Municipals issued within states with income taxes would yield somewhat less.

b. They would probably be priced to yield approximately the same rate of return.

4.26 Some of the buyers are institutions, not individuals, and may well be around 100 years from now. No matter what, investors can sell their bonds before maturity. The maturation value may be worth little 100 years from now, but that is only a small part of the value of the bond. Two more important concerns are the default risk for a BBB+ bond and the interest-rate risk for a bond with such a long duration.

4.27 a. Because the yield to maturity is equal to the coupon rate, it sold for par.

b. The total return is the 7.5% coupon plus the capital gain (or loss) x:

$$7.5\% + x\% = -4.19\% \text{ implies } x = -11.69\%$$

$$7.5\% + x\% = 23\% \text{ implies } x = +15.5\%$$

The duration is evidently between 11.69 and 15.5 years. (Because of the nonlinearity, the actual percentage changes are not exactly equal to each other or to the duration.) Halfway between is (11.69 + 15.5)/2 = 13.6. (The actual duration is 13.8 years.)

4.28 a. A fixed-income manager is in charge of the bond portfolio.

b. A portfolio duration equal to 80% of the duration of the Lehman index would beat the index if future interest rates turn out to be higher than the values embedded in the term structure.

c. A portfolio duration equal to 120% of the duration of the Lehman index would beat the index if future interest rates turn out to be lower than the values embedded in the term structure.

d. They don't want their fixed-income manager to make large bets that might cause them to underperform other fixed-income managers drastically—and cause their customers to flee.

4.29 A bond's price risk is highest when the bond is held only a short while and declines to a minimum when the holding period is equal to the bond's maturity. Reinvestment rate risk is highest when the bond is held until maturity and declines to a minimum when the holding period is brief. The total risk, price risk plus the reinvestment risk, is highest when the bond is either held for a short while or held until maturity and is at a minimum when the holding period is equal to the bond's duration.

4.30 Long-term interest rates must have fallen and zero-coupon bonds did relatively well because they have longer durations than coupon bonds with the same maturity.

4.31 a. The plaintiff wanted to use a low interest rate, the Treasury bond rate; the defendant wanted to use a high interest rate, the Baa rate.

b. Since condominium developments are riskier than Treasury bonds, the projected cash flow should be discounted by a higher interest rate, perhaps even higher than Baa corporate bonds.

4.32 If retirees invest mainly in bank accounts and short-term securities, a halving of interest rates cuts their interest income in half. When these investors roll over their short-term securities, the decline in income resulting from lower interest rates outweighs any temporary capital gains.

4.33 For horizons longer than the duration of the assets, a decline in interest rates reduces the future value of a portfolio, because the long-run decline in reinvestment income more than offsets the short-run increase in market value.

4.34 In either case, the yields to maturity are 4%. The yield on a zero is equal to the annual income divided by the initial price. The yield on a coupon bond selling for its maturation value is equal to its coupon rate.

4.35 If you pay $25 for a bond that will be worth $50 at maturity, the sooner you get your $50, the higher is your annual rate of return. In order to reduce the interest rate on a bond that sells for a fixed price and pays a fixed dollar amount, the maturity must be lengthened. The interest rates were reduced because market interest rates had declined. The federal government no longer had to pay a 7.5% interest rate to find buyers.

4.36 In the short run, the increase in interest rates gives the investor capital losses (answer A). As time passes, the extra income on the reinvested coupons boosts the return (answer B). For a horizon equal to the duration of the bond (here, about 7 1/2 years), the total return—reinvested income plus capital gain or loss—is (approximately) unaffected by changes in interest rates (answer C).

4.37 This analysis relates to capital risk, income risk, and immunization

a. For a horizon of 25 years, the reinvestment risk is most important (the value of the bond is simply equal to its maturation value), and the terminal value is largest if interest rates rise to 10%.

b. For a horizon of 1 year, there has been almost no reinvestment of coupons, and the capital risk is most important. The terminal value is largest if interest rates fall to 6%.

c. The terminal value is (approximately) the same, regardless of whether interest rates go up or down (by small amounts) for a horizon that is equal to the duration of the bond. (The duration of a 25-year 8% bond is 11.2 years and, as expected, Bogle's graph shows the three terminal values to be equal at this point.)

4.38 a. The 4.36% number is the coupon divided by the market price. The yield to maturity is less than this because the market price will fall to the maturation value when the bond matures.

b. The yield to maturity is the value of R that solves this equation:

$$\$12,050.50 = \frac{\$525/2}{(1+R/2)^1} + \frac{\$525/2}{(1+R/2)^2} + \ldots + \frac{\$525/2}{(1+R/2)^{22}} + \frac{\$10,000}{(1+R/2)^{22}}$$

The solution is 3.05%.

c. The yield to call is the value of R that solves this equation. The value is 1.66%.

$$\$12,050.50 = \frac{\$525/2}{(1+R/2)^1} + \frac{\$525/2}{(1+R/2)^2} + \ldots + \frac{\$525/2}{(1+R/2)^{12}} + \frac{\$10,000}{(1+R/2)^{12}}$$

4.39 One way to answer this question is to set the size of the new bond so that the annual coupons are \$120, the same as the existing bonds. Since they both mature in 20 years, the only question is whether the proceeds P from issuing the new bonds more than cover the cost of retiring the old bonds:

$$P = \frac{\$120}{(1+.09)^1} + \frac{\$120}{(1+.09)^2} + \ldots + \frac{\$120}{(1+R)^{20}} + \frac{\$1000}{(1+.09)^{12}}$$

P works out to be \$1,273.86, which more than covers the \$1100 redemption price and the \$50 investment banker fee.

4.40 The duration is the present-value weighted average wait until receiving the cash flow; here, the asset with the longer duration is:

a. the 15-year zero.

b. equal.

c. the 10-year zero.

d. the 10-year zero.

5

Stock Exchanges

5.1 Peter Lynch, a legendary mutual fund manager, wrote that, "When you buy a share of stock, even a very risky stock, you are contributing something to the growth of the country. That's what stocks are for." When you buy 100 shares of Microsoft stock, is the money you spend on this stock used to pay the company's expenses or expand its operations?

5.2 In Las Vegas, in the long run, the average gambler loses money. In the stock market in the long run, the average gambler/investor has made approximately 12% annually. How can this be? If investors are making profits of 12% a year, are firms suffering losses of 12% a year?

5.3 Critically evaluate this October 2017 claim by Donald Trump that the stock market boom during his presidency reduced the national debt accumulated by his predecessor:

> The last eight years, they borrowed more than it did in the whole history of our country. So they borrowed more than $10 trillion, right? And yet, we picked up $5.2 trillion just in the stock market. Possibly picked up the whole thing in terms of the first nine months, in terms of value. So you could say, in one sense, we're really increasing values. And maybe in a sense we're reducing debt.

5.4 The great economist Irving Fisher compared the 1929 stock market crash to a run on a bank that had issued paper bank notes whose value exceeded the gold in its vaults. In his analogy, the bank was U.S. industry, the bank's paper money was stock, and the bank's real assets were the country's factories and machines. Explain why this is not an apt analogy.

5.5 After the October 19, 1987, stock market crash, a veteran *Los Angeles Times* financial columnist wrote an article titled, "Wall Street's Disaster was All Too Real." He argued that

> More than $500 billion was wiped off stock prices on Oct. 19 … Yet there is hope, even a growing belief, that somehow that $500-billion loss doesn't touch the real American economy.
>
> Unfortunately, the hope is false—as you'll see if you think about it. The $500 billion was real enough when it increased corporate cash flow; real enough when investors paid it out for stocks at high prices. Stocks do not rise on air, but on somebody paying real money to buy them.

DOI: 10.1201/9781003630166-5

> Where is that real money now? It is gone. It is as if that $500 billion had built 10,000 factories and office buildings and homes and shopping centers and they had all burned down in a single day.

a. Do investors increase a corporation's cash flow when they buy its stock?

b. If the market value of a company's stock rises by $1 million, must investors have purchased $1 million worth of stock?

c. Where does the money that investors spend on stock go?

d. If you were the President of the United States, would you rather have the stock market fall by $500 billion or have $500 billion worth of factories destroyed by fire?

5.6 The *Wall Street Journal* awarded its tongue-in-cheek 1986 "Charity Begins at Home Award":

> To Merrill Lynch Capital Markets, for its underwriting of Home Shopping Network. Merrill priced the stock at $18 a share. The day it began trading, the stock more than doubled to $42.625 ... By June the stock had more than doubled again to $100.

The creators of Home Shopping Network sold 2 million shares to the public and kept 10 million shares for themselves. What was the total market value of the company at a price of $18? At $42.625? At $100? At $5, the price 1 year later? Did it really make any difference to anyone whether the 2 million shares were initially sold at $18 or $42?

5.7 The Morgan Stanley investment banking firm went public on March 21, 1986, by selling 4,500,000 shares at $56.50. The stock closed at $71.25 that day on the NYSE. Who gained and lost from this mispricing?

5.8 During the 1920s, the president of Chase National Bank made a $4 million profit selling Chase stock short. What are short sales? Did these short sales give him an incentive to manage the bank efficiently or inefficiently? Why might bank presidents today be hesitant to short-sell their bank's stock?

5.9 Fred Schwed, Jr., author of *Where are the Customers' Yachts?*, wrote,

> One [bear-raid strategy] is the effort to depress a certain stock a few points in the hope of 'touching off' some stop-loss orders.... A more extensive operation, looking for a larger profit, is to help depress stocks to the point where margin calls will be sent out.

Explain the apparent purpose of a bear-raid, who would benefit from it, and Schwed's description of its techniques to someone who doesn't understand stop-loss orders or margin calls.

5.10 In the spring of 1920, there was a struggle between investors who sold shares of Stutz Motor Company stock short and Allan Ryan, the president of Stutz, who personally bought up virtually all of the company's stock. The stock's price surged from 100 in early 1920 to 391 on March 31, at which point Ryan announced that he was willing to sell stock to the short sellers at $750 a share. The New York Stock Exchange responded by announcing an indefinite suspension of trading in Stutz stock and declaring the short sellers' contracts void. It claimed that "there is not a word of truth in the statement that the action ... was dictated by a desire to benefit the short interests." Why would short sellers buy stock from Ryan at $750 a share? Why would short sellers benefit from a voiding of their contracts?

5.11 Explain the following recommendation in the PaineWebber brokerage firm's analysis of the 1986 Tax Reform Act:

> Investors who have short-term [capital] gains should try to defer them, whenever possible, into 1987 when they will be taxed at a maximum of 38.5%, much lower than the current 50%. One possible strategy is to "short against the box."

5.12 A 25% margin requirement requires an investor to put up 25% of the cost of buying a stock. Thus, $750 is the most that can be borrowed for the purchase of $1,000 worth of stock. What is the degree of leverage if an investor borrows $750 to purchase $1,000 worth of stock?

5.13 In 1929, many speculators bought stocks with a 10% margin. Assuming a very short period of time, so that dividends and interest costs are negligible, how much do stock prices have to increase to double the speculator's equity? How much do stock prices have to fall to wipe out the speculator's equity?

5.14 In the first 8 months of 1986, Japanese stock prices rose 44%, putting prices at 50 times earnings. Comparing this runup with the 1929 surge in stock prices in the United States, two *Financial Times* correspondents wrote that "a major difference is that most of it is now being done with real money, not on margin, so that there is no monetary reason why it cannot go on." Can speculative booms happen with "real money"?

5.15 Andrew Tobias, an astute market observer, wrote that, "Margin is how brokerage firms make it easy for you to overextend yourself with leverage." Louis Rukeyser, who was the long-time host of the popular public television show, *Wall Street Week*, said, "If you and your broker are nonetheless determined to give margin a try, be prepared for an intense and perilous relationship that may well last till debt do you part." Explain how margin gives you leverage and why it might be a perilous strategy.

5.16 Explain how stop-loss orders could do the damage described by Louis Rukeyser, who was the long-time host of the popular public television show, *Wall Street Week*:

> A friend of mine who was out in the Far East in 1963 had stop-loss orders on all his stocks. When President Kennedy was assassinated. . the market took a fierce immediate plunge ... The market then recovered its nerves, turned around almost immediately and

> went right up past its previous level. But by the time the news reached my unfortunate friend, all he could do was get back in with 80 shares where he had formerly had 100.

5.17 a. In a *Wall Street Journal* story, a Merrill Lynch vice president said that when a customer calls and asks, "How's the market?" a standard reply is something like, "The Dow is up three dollars." What is misleading about that answer?

b. Explain why this *Cape Cod Times* headline is confusing: "Dow drops 8.92 to 2,575.49 despite gains by blue chips."

5.18 A financial writer said that the Dow Jones Average

> is taken as gospel. The state of the economy, the fate of politicians, often are read in the twists and turns of Wall Street's most recognizable indicator, the Dow Jones Industrial Average.

In 1979, Chrysler and Esmark, which had fallen by 44% and risen by 42%, respectively, during the preceding 20 years, were replaced by IBM and Merck, which had both increased by nearly 400%. If the substitution had been made 20 years earlier, would the Dow have told a happier or sadder tale during the 1960s and 1970s?

5.19 In October 2024, Berkshire Hathaway stock sold for nearly $700,000 a share. What would have happened to the divisor for the Dow Industrial Index if Berkshire had been added? How important would Berkshire have been to movements in the Dow?

5.20 Explain the 1.71 number used in the following quotation from a *Businessweek* article and explain whether you agree or disagree with the conclusion that movements in the Dow overstate the volatility of the 30 stocks in the Dow:

> Investors who hate stock market volatility, take heart: It ain't as bad as it seems. That is, it's not as bad as the Dow Jones industrial average might have you believe.
>
> Those pulse-pounding swings in the Dow overstate the rise or fall of prices of its 30 blue chips by more than 70%. Put another way, every time a Dow stock loses or gains a dollar, the average currently moves by 1.71 points.

5.21 A *Wall Street Journal* article written by two portfolio strategists argued that wealthy investors often don't pay capital gains taxes because they only realize gains when they can realize capital losses to offset the gains. In fact, investors who realize more losses than gains get a break on their income taxes. They also argued that this strategy is facilitated by purchasing volatile stocks. Respond to this argument from a reader: "This article is patently asinine. Do wealthy investors really seek out volatile securities so they will generate losses to offset capital gains on others? … Anyone dull enough to believe this rubbish won't benefit from the general excellence of the rest of the *Journal*."

5.22 The Nikkei 225 average of Japanese stock prices fell from a peak of 38,915 on December 29, 1989 to 17,948 on April 15, 1992. What was the annual compound decrease in prices during this 2 1/4-year period?

5.23 Answer this question posed by *The Wall Street Journal*: "Which is less damaging [to your portfolio], inflation of 50% or a 50% drop in your portfolio's value?"

5.24 Nobel laureate William F. Sharpe offered this advice for investors:

> The first thing is to get some feel for the lessons history might teach us about what may happen in the future....I like to make sure that people take a hard look at 1973–1974. It's terribly important to get people focused on real returns—that is, not only how much you won or lost but how much more it cost you to eat. And '73'–74 was really a shocking time—you lost a lot of money on stocks, and it cost you a whole lot more to eat. That was a disastrous time.

The nominal return on the S&P500 (dividends plus capital gains) was −14.7% in 1973 and −26.4% in 1974. Consumer prices increased by 8.7% in 1973 and by 12.9% in 1974. What was the annual real rate of return for S&P500 investors over this 2-year period? (Show how to calculate the exact value, not an approximation.)

5.25 Below are the closing prices on Friday, October 16, 1987 and on Monday, October 19, 1987. Do these data indicate that stock prices fell more on this Black Monday for large established companies or for smaller, more speculative firms?

	Friday	**Monday**
Dow Industrials	2246.74	1738.74
NYSE Composite	159.13	128.62
Nasdaq	406.33	360.21

5.26 The S&P 500 index was introduced on March 4, 1957, with an initial value of 43.73. Sixty-seven years later, on March 4, 2024, its value was 5,130.95. Over the same time period, the Dow-Jones Industrial Average increased from 471.48 to 39,989.83. Which index increased more in percentage terms? What conclusion do you draw from these numbers?

5.27 Critically evaluate this analysis of a new corporation by a prolific financial writer:

> The founder of the Widget Works decides to sell 100,000 shares at $10 out of a total issued capitalization of 250,000, thus leaving him with three-fifths, or 60%, of the company. He retains majority control while the corporation receives the proceeds of the sale—$1,000,000 less expenses .... the investors' shares are immediately devalued, since the $1 million reflects the worth, not of the 100,000 shares that were purchased, but of the total issued capitalization of 250,000. And these 250,000 shares are now worth $4 apiece.

5.28 In April 1987, the bid and ask prices for a seat on the NYSE were $750,000 and $1.5 million. Which price was the bid, and which the ask? Do you think this market was very liquid? In what sense?

5.29 A full-page 1988 newspaper advertisement boasted that D.H. Blair & Co. had managed "the top performing initial public offering and 4 of the top 5 performers." A table showed that the price of Management Technologies' stock had increased by 370.83% between its initial sale and December 31, 1987, more than any other new stock. Three other Blair-managed offerings increased by 135.42%, 130%, and 127.50% between the initial sale and December 31, 1987. Investors who "believe in investing in exciting super growth stocks early" were urged to contact D.H. Blair. Why are such comparisons potentially misleading? Which readers of this ad were not happy to see that the price of Management Technologies' stock quadrupled?

5.30 In 1983, the SEC enforcement chief said that, "Anyone who engages in insider trading is clearly a thief." Explain what the following insiders are stealing and from whom they are stealing:

a. A chemist discovers a cure for baldness and buys stock in the company he works for before revealing his discovery.

b. A company's chief executive officer sells half of his stock in the company before releasing a disappointing earnings report.

c. A merger and acquisitions lawyer working for a corporate raider buys stock in the target company before the offer is announced.

Answers

5.1 Unless it is a new issue, the money you spend to purchase shares of stock is not used to pay the company's expenses or expand its operations. Instead, the money goes to the shareholders you buy the stock from.

5.2 Unlike Las Vegas, which is a zero-sum game, firms produce things and make profits, thereby generating earnings that are either distributed to shareholders or reinvested in the firm. Profitable firms can pay dividends without shrinking. As they expand and their earnings and dividends increase, their shares are also worth more, thereby providing capital gains to shareholders.

5.3 Changes in stock prices do not affect the national debt, except for the minor effects that realized capital gains have on tax revenue.

5.4 The stock exchanges are a secondary market. Unlike depositors withdrawing money from a bank, stockholders who sell their shares do not constitute a run on industries, because businesses are not obligated to redeem these shares.

5.5 a. Unless it is an IPO or the company is issuing new stock, no money goes to the company.

b. A stock's price and market value can rise or fall greatly even if only a few shares are purchased and sold.

c. The money that investors spend on stock goes to the shareholders who sold the stock.

d. I would rather have the stock market fall by $500 billion, which is a paper loss and can easily be reversed (as it was after the crash on October 1, 1987).

5.6 The total market value is the total number of shares multiplied by the price per share, here $216 million, $511.5 million, $1,200 million, and $90 million. If the 2 million shares had been sold at $42 instead of $18, the company could have raised an additional $48 million.

5.7 Investors who bought shares at 56.50 benefited from being able to buy at a bargain price. The firm (and its pre-offering owners) lost because, if the 4,500,000 shares had been sold at $71.25 instead of $56.50, the firm would have received an additional 4,500,000($71.25 – $56.50) = $66,375,000.

5.8 A short seller sells borrowed stock, hoping to buy it back at a lower price. Managers who sell their company's stock short have an incentive to manage their company poorly. A more likely explanation for this bank president's short sales is that he had nonpublic knowledge of bad news about the bank. Nowadays, bank presidents risk insider-trading fines and/or imprisonment for such behavior.

5.9 A bear raid is intended to drive down a stock's price, presumably benefiting investors who have sold the stock short. If the price drops a bit, it might trigger stop-loss orders, which automatically sell a stock when the price goes below the preset stop-loss price. Stockholders who bought the stock on margin might have to sell their stock when the price falls and their brokerage firms demand additional margin.

5.10 Short-sellers have to replace the stock they borrowed. They would not be happy about paying $750/share, but they have little alternative if Ryan owns all the stock. Short-sellers welcomed the voiding of their contracts because it freed them of the requirement that the borrowed stock be returned (since Ryan owned almost all of the stock, they owed Ryan stock).

5.11 Investors short-sell against the box when they own a stock and then borrow shares to sell short. Because they already own the stock, they can use the shares they own to replace the shares they borrowed, and they neither gain or lose if the stock's price goes up or down. Thus, they have locked in the profit they had before the short sale, and can realize it after the capital gains tax is reduced.

5.12 An investor who puts up $250 to purchase $1,000 worth of stock has 4/1 leverage:

$$\text{leverage} = \frac{\text{total assets}}{\text{net worth}} = \frac{\$1,000}{\$250} = 4$$

5.13 The investor has 10/1 leverage, so that a 10% increase in stock prices will double the speculator's equity, and a 10% decrease will wipe the speculator out.

5.14 Being able to borrow money and buy on margin can help fuel a speculative bubble, but bubbles can happen even when there is no margin buying.

5.15 With, say, a 50% margin requirement, an investor can buy $1,000 of stock with $500 cash and a $500 loan, thereby creating 2/1 leverage. If the investment goes up 10% to $1,100, the $100 gain is a 20% profit on the investor's $500 (neglecting dividends on the borrowed stock and interest on the borrowed money).

Leverage is a two-edged sword in that if the value of the investment drops 50%, to $500, the 2/1 leverage gives the investor a 100% loss—if the investment is sold to repay the borrowed money, the investor has nothing left.

5.16 Stop-loss orders automatically become orders to sell at the market price when the price drops below the stop-loss price. Thus, the friend was forced to sell after the temporary dip.

5.17 a. The Dow is a stock price index and is not measured in dollars. When the index rises three points, this does not mean that the price or the average price of anything increased by three dollars.

b. The Dow is an average of the prices of 30 blue chips. (The accompanying story reported that the percentage drop in the S&P 500 that day was twice as large as the drop in the Dow. Thus, the Dow dropped, even though the blue chips in the Dow did somewhat better (that is, fell less) than the broader market averages, and the headline writer misstated this event.)

5.18 If the substitution had been made 20 years earlier, the Dow would have been higher in 1979 because IBM and Merck did better than Chrysler and Esmark.

5.19 The Dow is a simple average of the prices of the 30 stocks in the Dow. When a high-priced stock like Berkshire Hathaway replaces a lower-priced stock, the divisor must be *increased* to keep the Dow at its level at the time of the substitution. Because the price of Berkshire is orders of magnitude higher than the prices of the other 29 stocks, movements in the Dow would be essentially movements in Berkshire.

5.20 There are problems with the Dow, but this isn't one of them. The 1.71 figure reflects the fact that the Dow divisor was less than 1, more precisely 1/1.71 = .585 when this article was written. A dollar change in the price of a Dow stock does indeed change the value of the Dow Index by 1.71, but the index was never intended to measure the dollar value of the component stocks. When the divisor was greater than 1, did the Dow misleadingly underestimate the volatility of stocks? If the average price of the 30 Dow stocks changes by 10%, the Dow Industrial Average will also change by 10%, no more, no less—no matter what the value of the divisor.

5.21 The advantage of a portfolio of volatile securities is that it generates capital gains, which do not have to be realized and taxed, and capital losses, which can be realized to obtain a tax break. A strategy of postponing gains and harvesting losses is profitable.

5.22 Using the future-value formula: $38{,}915(1 + R)^{2.25} = 17{,}948$, the solution is $R = -.2910$ (–29.10%).

5.23 The effects are approximately equal for small changes, but not for large changes. For example, a 100% drop in the value of your portfolio is clearly more damaging than a 100% rise in prices. Here's the example given by the *Journal*: "If you have $100 to spend on cappuccino and your favorite cappuccino costs $1, you can buy 100 cups. What if your $100 then drops in value to $50? You can only buy 50 cups. And if the cappuccino's price instead rises to $1.50? If you divide $100 by $1.50, you'll find that you can still buy 66 cups, and even leave a tip."

5.24 The nominal value of an invested dollar went from 1 to (1 – .147)(1 – .264), and the price level went from 1 to (1 + .087)(1 + .129). Therefore, real wealth fell by 49%:

$$\frac{W_2 / P_2}{W_0 / P_0} = \frac{W_2 / W_0}{P_2 / P_0} = \frac{(1-.147)(1-.264)}{(1+.087)(1+.129)} = .5116$$

The annual real rate of return was –28.5%:

$$(1+R)^2 = .5116$$
$$R = -.285$$

An approximation would calculate each real return as the nominal return minus the rate of inflation: –14.7 – 8.7 = –23.4 in 1973 and –26.4 – 12.9 = –39.3 in 1974, so that $1 goes to $1(1 – .234)(1 – .393) = .4650, and the approximate annual real rate of return is –31.8%:

$$(1+R)^2 = .4650$$
$$R = -.318$$

5.25 The Dow fell by 22.61%, the NYSE Composite by 19.17%, and the NASDAQ by 11.35%, indicating that stock prices fell more for large established companies than for smaller, more speculative firms.

5.26 The S&P increased by a factor of 117.33, a 7.37% annual rate of increase. The Dow increased by a factor of 84.82, a 6.85% annual rate of increase. The blue chips in the Dow did not do as well as the broader market. (These calculations ignore dividends.)

5.27 This conclusion assumes that the only value of the company is the $1 million in cash it raised. It must have other assets, such as patents or a business idea, if investors are willing to pay $1 million to own 40% of the company. The company is evidently worth $1,000,000/.40 = $2,500,000. Since there are 250,000 shares outstanding, each is worth $10.

5.28 The bid is what someone is willing to pay to buy it; the ask is what someone is willing to accept to sell it. Here, the bid is $750,000 and the ask is $1.5 million. The market is not very liquid in that it is very expensive to buy a seat and then sell it soon after.

5.29 These four stocks were not randomly selected and might be potentially misleading. It would be better to see all of the public offerings that D.H. Blair managed. Management Technologies' managers and pre-offering owners were not happy to see that the company had sold stock for far less than investors were willing to pay and consequently raised much less money than could have been raised.

5.30 a. The chemist is stealing information about the company's products and is able to buy stock cheaply from the company's shareholders.

b. The CEO is stealing information about the company's profitability and is able to sell stock at high prices to investors who don't yet know about the disappointing profits.

c. The lawyer is stealing information from the corporate raider and is able to buy stock at low prices from the target company's shareholders.

6

Dividend-Discount Models

6.1 A famous stock adviser once argued that a conspiracy between stock specialists and bankers is demonstrated by the fact that "When you're having a decline in stock prices you can always anticipate an increase in interest rates." What he apparently meant is that when market makers lower stock prices so that insiders can accumulate stocks cheaply, banks simultaneously raise interest rates so that the public cannot borrow money to purchase stocks at these bargain prices. Provide a reasonable non-conspiratorial explanation for the observation that a drop in stock prices is often accompanied by an increase in interest rates.

6.2 Explain the error in this assertion in a book on the "Art of Investing":

> [John Burr] Williams had declared that the price of a security rests on the expected stream of future dividends, adjusted by the effect of inflation that makes one dollar received tomorrow worth less than a dollar already in an investor's pocket—the so-called 'dividend discount' model.'

6.3 A financial columnist wrote that, "Whenever the Fed decides that inflation is too high or the dollar needs strengthening, it takes actions that make everybody's borrowing expensive and more difficult. That hurts profits, which pushes stock prices down." Why, even if profits were unaffected, might this Fed tightening reduce stock prices?

6.4 A Goldman Sachs portfolio strategist once argued that if the rate of inflation was used in place of interest rates in the dividend-discount model, the S&P 500 would appear to be fairly valued rather than 15% overvalued. Which discount rate would you use? Why?

6.5 Critically evaluate: "We gauge whether the overall stock market is cheap or expensive by using the constant-growth dividend-discount model $P = D/(R - g)$. Since our average holding period is 3 months, we use the 3-month Treasury bill rate plus a 3% risk premium as our required return."

6.6 There is an old Wall Street saying, "A bargain that stays a bargain isn't a bargain," suggesting that buying a stock for a price less than its intrinsic value (a "bargain") is not a good investment if the price doesn't increase afterwards ("stays a bargain"). How would a value investor respond?

DOI: 10.1201/9781003630166-6

6.7 Explain why you either agree or disagree with this statement by two senior Morgan Stanley analysts:

> Companies that can invest a lot today at high returns on capital will not only grow faster than the average company, their stocks will have valuations that are more sensitive to changes in the discount rate.

6.8 In an October 2017 interview with CNBC, Warren Buffett said that, "Valuations make sense with interest rates where they are." A *Business Insider* columnist wrote:

> Wrong, says John Hussman, the president of the Hussman Investment Trust and a former economics professor. In his mind, Buffett only gets half of the equation right. While Hussman acknowledges that low lending rates do, by nature, improve future cash flows, he argues that they must also be accompanied by strong growth—something that he notes the US is not currently enjoying....
>
> "It's an incomplete sentence," Hussman wrote in a recent blog post. "Unfortunately, the convenience of investing-by-slogan, rather than carefully thinking about finance and examining evidence, is currently leading investors into what is likely to be one of the worst disasters in the history of the U.S. stock market." Hussman calculates that stock valuations are stretched 175% above their historic norms, and predicts the S&P 500 will see negative total returns over the next 10 to 12 years. Along the way, the benchmark index will experience an interim loss of more than 60%.

Do you agree with Hussman's reasoning? (Not his conclusion, his reasoning.)

6.9 Warren Buffett once said that the ratio of total U.S. stock market valuation to GDP is "the best single measure of where valuations stand at any given moment." He has since walked back that assertion, but this ratio is nonetheless called the Buffett Indicator and used by many to gauge whether stocks are cheap or expensive. Why might value investors hesitate to rely on this indicator?

6.10 At a Thanksgiving dinner, a relative said, "I bought [XYZ] stock because it is one of the largest companies in the world and its stock is selling for only $5 a share." Give two distinct and very different reasons why the intrinsic value of the shares of the largest company in the world might be only $5 a share, when the shares of much smaller firms sell for more than $100 a share.

6.11 In valuing a company's stock, a handbook published by McKinsey & Company recommends adding a company-specific risk premium to a risk-free rate of return. For the risk-free return, they suggest the interest rate on government securities that have a duration comparable to that of stocks.

a. What kind of risk are government securities free of?

b. Why would the value of corporate stock depend on the interest rate on a government bond?

c. Why would you want to use a bond with a duration comparable to that of stocks?

d. Does the duration of T-bills or 10-year T-bonds more nearly match the duration of the S&P 500?

6.12 Suppose that the price of ABC stock is always equal to its intrinsic value. ABC pays annual dividends, with the next dividend equal to $2 and paid 1 year from today. The dividend is expected to grow by 4% a year and the shareholders' required return is 12%.

a. What is the current price of ABC stock?

b. What will the price be 1 year from now?

c. What is the shareholder percent return (dividend plus capital gains) for this first year?

6.13 The dividend yield (dividend/price) is usually less than the interest rate on Treasury bonds. Why?

6.14 Explain the logic behind this observation by Louis Rukeyser, who was the long-time host of the popular public television show, *Wall Street Week*: "Almost invariably, the higher the yield [the ratio of a stock's dividend to its price] the lower the growth."

6.15 Suppose that a company called Movie Treasures owns the rights to thousands of old movies and pays out all of the royalties it receives as dividends. Its annual dividend is currently $4/share. Shareholders project the dividend to decline steadily by 5% a year, and they require a 10% return on their stock.

a. What is the stock's intrinsic value?

b. What will happen to the intrinsic value as time passes? (Be specific.)

c. Why would anyone invest in a negative-growth stock?

6.16 Explain this observation by a *Forbes* columnist:

> It's natural to assume that interest rates drive stock prices, and sometimes they seem to.... But somehow it doesn't always work out.

6.17 Ian MacKinnon, Senior Vice President of the Vanguard Fixed Income Group, wrote that,

> With ... a [dividend] yield of just over 2% on the Standard & Poor's 500 Index and nearly 7% on ten-year Treasury bonds—that's a gap of 400 to 500 basis points a year that the stockholder has to hope to make up by price appreciation and dividend increases."

If we let x be the annual price appreciation and y be the annual dividend increase, does the phrase "price appreciation and dividend increases" mean (a) $x = y = 400$ to 500 basis points, or (b) $x + y = 400$ to 500 basis points? Explain your reasoning.

6.18 A 2023 article in the *Wall Street Journal* said that it had been "a disastrous 2022" for investors who had followed a classic 60-40 investment strategy (60% stocks, 40% bonds): "Last year's tandem declines in stocks and bonds blindsided many of the strategy's followers who were counting on bonds to help cushion their portfolios when equities had a bad year." What economic event is likely to have caused both bond and stock prices to fall?

6.19 A Harvard Business School professor wrote that "High growth may look good on paper—but it could destroy your stock market value." How is this theoretically possible? Shouldn't an increase in a company's growth rate always increase the market value of its stock? Be as specific as possible, using a hypothetical example to illustrate your reasoning.

6.20 Critically evaluate the following prediction by a panelist on the popular public television show, *Wall Street Week*:

> It's true that interest rates are rising, but that shouldn't affect growth stocks since they don't yield much [dividends] anyway.

6.21 A *BusinessWeek* article on recent dividend increases argued that "the outlook is good for continued increases. The average [dividend] yield is just 2.9%, low by historical standards. With interest rates rising, dividend yields may have to rise, too, to stay competitive." Explain how dividend yields can rise, even if dividends do not.

6.22 The managing director of the Bond Portfolio Analysis Group at Salomon Brothers once argued that the duration of a portfolio of bonds and stocks may be much greater than the duration of the bonds alone. How is this possible?

6.23 An article in *The Wall Street Journal* noted that, over the preceding 5 years, stock prices increased by 200% while the economy grew by only 40%, suggesting that stock prices had lost touch with fundamentals. This provoked an irate letter to the editor claiming that,

> The market is telling us the future of profits from the nation's capital stock looks that much better than it did five years ago. Either there will be more sustained growth or there will be fewer recessions affecting that income stream, or both.

What other rational explanation might there be?

6.24 In 2018, a former JP Morgan managing partner wrote that,

> Historically, stock prices have gone up about 10% a year. Bitcoin prices have gone up even more, though there is a lot less return history. Any argument for buying stocks now could also be used as an argument for buying Bitcoin.

How would a value investor respond?

6.25 A finance professor wrote a *MarketWatch* column in 2023 arguing that, from a value investor's standpoint, stocks are attractively priced relative to bonds. A prominent economics professor immediately sent this e-mail:

> Good column from an overall aggregate perspective and the low-interest rate scenario, but remember that a black swan event (contagion from a financial disaster like Lehman Brothers; pandemic that shuts down the economy short-term; etc.) can result in stocks falling 30-50% in short order, even if stocks are a better deal than bonds, or are "fairly priced."

Write a brief, logical response that the MarketWatch author might have written.

6.26 In 2007, the *New York Times* reported that parking spaces in midtown Manhattan could be rented for an average cost of $6,888/year ($574/month) or purchased for an average price of $165,019. Using the annual rent and a 10% required rate of return, what annual rate of growth of rents would justify this price?

6.27 Many econometric attempts to estimate asset demand equations assume that realized returns are equal to shareholder anticipated returns. For instance, if a stock sells for $20 at the beginning of the year, pays a $1 dividend, and sells for $22 at the end of the year, they assume that people buying the security at the beginning of the year anticipated a return of $R = D/P + \%P = \$1/\$20 + (\$22 - 20)/\$20 = .05 + .10 = .15$ (15%). Unfortunately, the returns calculated this way are sometimes negative, and it is difficult to explain why people willingly buy something with a negative return. How would you advise them to estimate shareholder anticipated returns?

6.28 You have decided to endow a finance chair at your college named, coincidentally, in your honor. Assuming that salaries are paid once a year, at the end of each year, and that the college can earn 10% a year on your gift, how much must you donate in order to provide $250,000 a year forever? A trustee points out that salaries increase each year. If so, how large an endowment is needed to provide $250,000 at the end of the first year and 5% more each succeeding year, forever? 15% more each succeeding year, forever?

6.29 A 2016 *Los Angeles Times* article reported that California's largest public pension fund CalPERS had a disappointing year, in that the CalPERS "bond portfolio saw a particularly dramatic uptick of 9.3%, ... but the same factors that drove up the value of bonds cost CalPERS in other areas, specifically its stock investments, which make up more than half of the pension fund's portfolio and lost 3.4% for the year." Explain why this story does or does not make sense.

6.30 What does John Burr Williams' yield to perpetuity π measure? (R_n is the rate of return on an n-year Treasury zero.)

$$\frac{1}{\pi} = \frac{1}{(1+R_1)} + \frac{1}{(1+R_2)^2} + \frac{1}{(1+R_3)^3} + \cdots$$

6.31 Explain why you either agree or disagree with economist David Rosenberg that "a stock by definition has an infinite duration."

6.32 In 2013, Marc Basto, InvestorPlace Assistant Editor, wrote that,

> If you plan to buy and hold Walt Disney (NYSE:DIS) stock in perpetuity, why not glom on to Disney's 7.55% Coupon 2093 Maturity long-term note? The price of this offer is now well above par (the $100 mark), but its 3.56% yield to maturity is a nice return, fully 2 percentage points better than Disney's current dividend yield.

Why might a value investor buy Disney stock instead of Disney bonds?

6.33 On July 19, 1984, Chrysler sold all of the stocks in its pension fund and bought bonds with the proceeds. In January 1987, the *Wall Street Journal* reported that rumors that Chrysler was going back into stocks

> prompted some guffaws on Wall Street because, on the surface, it might appear that Chrysler has missed an enormous stock rally and now wants to get back in at the top. But it isn't quite that simple, because the bond market did nearly as well as the stock market in the 2 1/2 years between July 1984 and December 1986. In that period … the S&P 500-stock index returned 25% annually, …. [while] the Shearson Lehman aggregate bond index returned 22.4% annually…. In fact, the bonds held by Chrysler equaled the stock market's performance because they were slightly longer in maturity than the Shearson index.

What economic event could explain simultaneous bond and stock market rallies? What does maturity have to do with performance?

6.34 The *Wall Street Journal* reported that some investors were beginning to think that the Fed might reduce interest rates soon, and that "Lower interest rates are considered good for stocks because they reduce the cost of corporate debt, thus helping profits, and encourage consumer spending." Explain why you agree or disagree that a company's stock price should not be affected by interest rates if it has no debt and is little affected by changes in consumer spending.

6.35 Answer this e-mail: "How can economists say that stock prices are inversely related to interest rates when the attached figure, using monthly data for the past 5 years, clearly show a positive relationship between the S&P 500 and the federal funds rate (the interest banks charge each other on overnight loans)?"

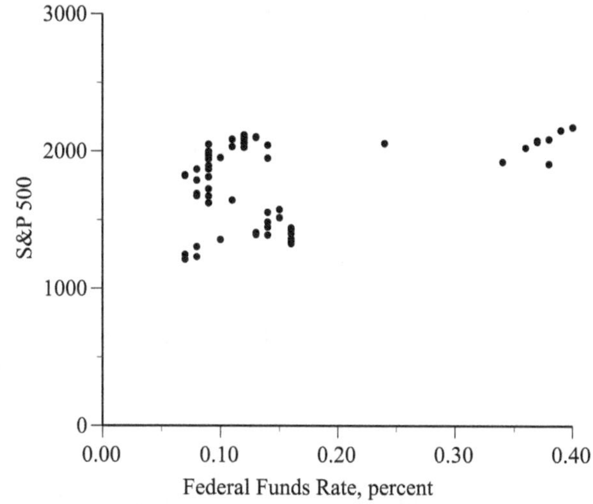

6.36 Identify two fundamental errors in this analyst's estimate of the fundamental value of General Electric (GE) stock:

> The quarterly dividend has increased from 18¢ a share to 25¢ a share over the past five years, an annual growth rate of 6.7%. The current market price of $35.28 is equal to the present value of dividends only if the required return is a relatively low 7.409%:
>
> $$P = \frac{D}{R - g}$$
>
> $$\$35.28 = \frac{\$.25}{.07409 - .067}$$
>
> However, the current price represents not only the present value of dividends, but also the present value of future capital gains. Therefore, we need to add together the present value of future dividends and the present value of future capital gains.

6.37 Merrill Lynch routinely tracks the characteristics of the stocks in the S&P 500 and has found that stocks with relatively high dividend yields consistently have low projected earnings growth. How do you explain this empirical relationship?

6.38 In 1989, a former Marquette University finance professor advised that

> Baseball cards, on average, have been the decade's best investment, appreciating [more than] 25 percent yearly over the last 10 years.... Knowledge of baseball isn't a prerequisite. You can buy cards and make money without it. But if you do know the game, you can do much, much better.... A portfolio consisting of cards of players chosen rookie of the year by Sporting News produced about a 45% annualized return.

Would a value investor consider baseball cards an investment or speculation? Explain your reasoning. What is the intrinsic value of the 1952 Mickey Mantle baseball card in near perfect condition that sold for \$12,600,000 in 2022?

6.39 Respond to this analysis of the stock market by a first-year MBA student:

> The dividend discount model is P = D/(R − g). I estimated the required return from the 10-year Treasury rate of 2.33% plus a 5% risk premium: R = .0233 + .05 = .0733. The dividend growth rate was 11.89% last year and I assume that this growth rate will continue in the short-run because the economy is improving. Therefore, for a short-run investor, the intrinsic value of the S&P 500 is infinite and investors should buy the S&P 500 regardless of the price.

6.40 Answer this question from a financial planner's client:

> The dividend yield on the S&P is around 1.7% and the rate on 10-year Treasury bonds is a little over 1.82%. Do you still think stocks look relatively cheap?

6.41 Explain why you agree or disagree with this assertion from the Hume MoneyLetter: "low interest rates are far more friendly to stocks than to cash or bonds."

6.42 A car buyer estimated how much money she would save on gas by buying a fuel-efficient car. Car A is predicted to average 20 miles per gallon, and Car B, 40 miles per gallon. Gasoline currently costs \$4.00 a gallon. The buyer estimated that whichever car is purchased will be driven 10,000 miles a year for 10 years, then sold. Using a 10% discount rate, the estimated present value of the gas savings was

$$\frac{\$4.00\left(\dfrac{100{,}000 \text{ miles}}{20 \text{ mpg}} - \dfrac{100{,}000 \text{ miles}}{40 \text{ mpg}}\right)}{1.10^{10}} = \$3{,}855.43$$

What errors do you see? How would you estimate the savings?

6.43 Suppose that a company currently pays no dividend and is priced to give shareholders a 10% return. The earnings are expected to grow by 15% a year for 10 years, after which the company begins paying half of its earnings out as dividends and its growth rate slows to 5% a year forever. If this stock's price is always equal to its intrinsic value and these expectations are correct, what will be the annual percentage increase in the price of the stock

a. each year for the next 10 years?
b. each year thereafter?

6.44 Consider a stock with a current price of $22.73 that pays annual dividends. Its next dividend will be $1 1 year from now. Its annual dividend will increase by 20% for 1 year and then increase by 5% annually forever. The shareholders' required return is 12%. According to the dividend-discount model, what will be the percentage increase in its price in the first year? Give a numerical answer.

6.45 In 1986 Michael Sherman, the head of Shearson Lehman's investment policy committee, recommended a portfolio of 70% stocks, 30% long-term bonds, and no short-term bonds: "If you have cash [short-term bonds] in your account, it means you don't trust what you're doing.... More stocks than bonds generally indicates a positive outlook both in Treasury rates and the economy." (The opposite occurred in early 1982, when more bonds than stocks in portfolios said that investors liked interest rates but not the economy.)

Explain why forecasts of interest rates and the economy should influence the portfolio allocation between stocks and bonds. Are there any circumstances in which you would recommend holding a substantial amount of cash?

6.46 Suppose a stock's price is equal to the present value of the after-tax dividends using a required rate of return R that is 2% higher than the after-tax interest rate on Treasury bonds: $R = (1 - t)S + .02$, where S is the before-tax interest rate on Treasury bonds and t is the tax rate on Treasury bonds. Use the constant-dividend-growth model to determine the percentage increase or decrease in the stock's price if the tax rate on dividends is increased from .15 to .40. (Assume that t, S, and the dividend cash flow do not change.)

6.47 Explain why you either agree or disagree with this argument by Edward Kerschner, chief strategist at PaineWebber, that a decline in interest rates affects stock prices more than zero-coupon bond prices:

> If interest rates go down, a zero-coupon security goes up more in price than a 30-year bond, which goes up more than a 10-year bond, which goes up more than a five-year bond. A zero coupon has the biggest gain because it pays you nothing until the end. The S&P 500 is out there somewhere past the zero coupon because it's never going to pay back principal. So in a period of falling interest rates, stocks ... will see their prices rise more than a terminal asset like bonds.

6.48 Explain why you agree or disagree with this conclusion by a Smith Barney analyst of the effects of the Fed lowering interest rates: "Declining interest rates would benefit the faster growing companies more, in terms of changing valuation, than they would help yield-oriented stocks."

6.49 Is a conservative investor with a high required return more interested in high-dividend or high-growth stocks? Consider Stock A paying a $2 dividend that is expected to grow by 2% a year, and Stock B paying a $2 dividend that is expected to grow by 6% a year. If both market prices are equal to intrinsic values using a 10% required return, which will appear more overpriced to an investor who has a 12% required return? Explain your results.

6.50 For each of the following pairs, identify the asset with the longer duration. (Assume that each is priced to give a 10% required return.)

a. a stock with a dividend that will always equal $1 or a stock with a dividend that is currently $1 and will grow by 5% a year.

b. a stock with a dividend that is currently $2 and will grow by 3% a year or a stock with a dividend that is currently $1 and will grow by 5% a year.

c. a consol bond with a $10 quarterly coupon or a no-growth stock that will pay a $5 quarterly dividend forever.

Answers

6.1 Fundamental analysis tells us that an increase in interest rates raises shareholder required returns, reducing the present value of a given cash flow. Rather than a drop in stock prices causing interest rates to increase, it is more plausible that increases in interest rates cause stock prices to decline.

6.2 According to Williams (and others who attempt to assess intrinsic value), the value of a security (not necessarily the price) is the expected future dividends, discounted by the investor's required rate of return—which is not necessarily equal to the rate of inflation. Dollars tomorrow are worth less than dollars today because dollars can be invested.

6.3 Higher interest rates increase shareholders' required returns, which reduce the present value of any given cash flow, including that from stocks.

6.4 The Goldman Sachs strategist's model works if we are more concerned with the conclusion than the assumptions. We should discount by the return available on alternative investments, such as Treasury bonds, adjusted for risk.

6.5 This is like saying that 30-year bonds should be valued by discounting the coupons by a 3-month interest rate if you plan on holding the bonds for only a few months. This is clearly wrong for bonds and is wrong for stocks as well.

6.6 Value investors don't buy a stock because they expect the price to go up but because they think that the anticipated cash flow (dividends) is a bargain at the current stock price. If the price goes down and the income projections haven't changed, they will buy more. In market panics, value investors say, "Wall Street is having a sale." They back up a truck and fill it with bargains.

6.7 They are correct. Ceteris paribus, high returns on capital allow companies to grow faster, and growth stocks have a relatively long duration—so they are very sensitive to changes in interest rates (and required returns).

6.8 Buffett's argument does not assume that low interest rates will increase future cash flows. For a given cash flow, low interest rates—by themselves—increase the present value of the anticipated cash flow—and justify high stock prices. (As of October 2024, stock prices have more than doubled since Hussman's apocalyptic prediction.)

6.9 GDP is not necessarily closely correlated to corporate profits and dividends, which are what matter for fundamental values. In addition, this measure ignores interest rates completely. When interest rates are low, stock prices should be higher relative to cash flow.

6.10 The large company might not be very profitable or it might have a very large number of shares outstanding.

6.11 a. Government securities are free of default risk.

b. The value of corporate stock depends on the interest rate on a government bond because bonds are an alternative asset for investors.

c. You might use a bond with a duration comparable to that of stocks because they then have comparable sensitivity to fluctuations in interest rates.

d. Treasury bills have a year or less until maturity and consequently have a duration of less than a year. The cash flow from corporate stocks is much more distant, and they consequently have a duration closer to that of 10-year Treasury bonds.

6.12 a. Using the constant-growth dividend-discount model, the current price of ABC stock is

$$P = \frac{D}{R-g} = \frac{\$2}{.12-.04} = \$25$$

b. Again, using the constant-dividend-growth model with the dividend 4% higher, the price will be 4% higher:

$$P = \frac{D}{R-g} = \frac{\$2(1.04)}{.12-.04} = \$26$$

c. Total shareholder return (dividend plus capital gains) is

$$\frac{D}{P}+\frac{\Delta P}{P}=\frac{\$2}{\$25}+\frac{\$1}{\$25}=.08+.04=.12$$

The stock is priced to give shareholders their 12% required return.

6.13 The dividends from stocks are expected to increase over time; the coupons from a bond won't.

6.14 Consider the constant-dividend-growth model's equation, R = D/P + g. For two stocks to have comparable returns when one has a higher anticipated dividend growth rate, the other stock must be priced to have a higher dividend yield. It is true that firms that pay high dividends have less money to retain for financing growth; but the dividend yield D/P reflects not just the level of dividends D, but the price P determined in the stock market. A firm with a high D need not have a high D/P. It will be priced to have a high D/P if its growth rate is meager.

6.15 a. Using the constant-dividend-growth model,

$$V=\frac{D}{R-g}=\frac{\$4}{.10-(-.05)}=\$26.67$$

b. The intrinsic value will decline by 5% a year, as dividends fall by 5% a year.

c. A negative-growth stock is attractive if the market price is lower than the intrinsic value.

6.16 Stock prices depend not only on interest rates but also on the economy. Sometimes the economy is expanding while interest rates are increasing, or the economy is contracting while interest rates are falling—in each case, the effects of the economy on stock prices offset (and may be even stronger than) the effects of interest rates.

6.17 MacKinnon is using the constant-dividend-growth model, where R = D/P + g, with g the growth rate of dividends and prices. Here, R = 7% (ignoring a risk premium) and D/P = 2%+, so that g = 4% to 5%. Because g is the growth rate of both dividends and prices, the answer is x = y.

6.18 A sharp increase in interest rates (caused by the Fed trying to cool inflation) was bad for both bond and stock markets.

6.19 Consider the constant-dividend-growth model with earnings per share E = \$1, required return R = .10, return on assets ρ = .05, and the stock's price always equal to its intrinsic value. The growth rate is $(1 - d)\rho$, where d is the payout ratio, the fraction of earnings paid out as dividends, and 1 – d is the retention ratio. The market price P is

$$P=\frac{D}{R-g}=\frac{dE}{R-(1-d)\rho}=\frac{d}{.10-(1-d).05}$$

Here are the growth rates and prices for different retention ratios:

1 − d	g = (1 − d)ρ	P
.00	.00(.05) = .00	\$10.00
.25	.25(.05) = .0125	\$8.57
.50	.50(.05) = .025	\$6.67
.75	.75(.05) = .0375	\$4.00

A higher retention rate increases the growth rate but lowers the market price because the firm's return on assets is less than the shareholders' required return.

6.20 According to the intrinsic value model, growth stocks have long durations and are actually very sensitive to changes in required yields.

6.21 A stock's dividend yield is its dividend divided by its price: D/P. The dividend yield can increase even if dividends do not, if the price falls.

6.22 It will be true if the duration of the stocks is greater than the duration of the bonds, which is often true (depending on the specific bonds and stocks).

6.23 Stock prices should increase faster than the cash flow from stocks if there is an unanticipated decline in interest rates. Another possibility is that the cash flow from stocks increased faster than the overall economy.

6.24 Here is one response:

> I don't think so!
>
> If corporate profits quadruple in 30 years, stock prices will be much higher than they are today. Not necessarily quadrupled, but much higher. Even if the average P/E falls 50%, prices will still be double what they are today. Plus, there is a 2% dividend yield from stocks.
>
> Bitcoin pays no dividends and has no logical relationship to the economy since it generates no cash flow.

6.25 He wrote, "Yep, but we value investors have our eye on 2031 and beyond."

6.26 Using the constant-dividend-growth model, a 5.83% annual growth rate of rents would justify the \$165,019 price.

$$P = \frac{D}{R - g}$$

$$\$165{,}019 = \frac{\$6{,}888}{.10 - g}$$

$$g = .10 - \frac{\$6{,}888}{\$165{,}019} = .0583$$

6.27 One possibility is $R = D/P + g$, where the anticipated dividend growth rate g can be estimated either from $g = (1 - d)\rho$, where $1 - d$ is the retention rate and ρ is the firm's return on assets, or from past rates of growth of dividends.

6.28 We can use the constant-dividend-growth model:

$$P = \frac{D}{R-g} = \frac{\$250,000}{.10-g}$$

For $g = 0$, $P = \$2,500,000$; for $g = .05$, $P = \$5,000,000$; for $g = .15$, an infinite amount is needed; i.e., no donation could be large enough to endow such a chair. (The above formula only applies if $R > g$.)

6.29 This explanation is puzzling because bond prices generally can only go up if interest rates go down, but lower interest rates are good for stock prices. So, "the same factors" must be wrong. Stock prices must have been negatively affected by the economy or investor sentiment. (Low-rated bonds are affected by default risk (and, hence, the economy), but it is unlikely that CalPERS owns many low-rated bonds.)

6.30 The left-hand side of this equation is the perpetuity formula, the value of $1 discounted by a constant rate π forever. So, π is the constant required return that gives the same present value as $1 discounted by a term structure of required returns.

6.31 It may have an infinite life, but the duration is finite. If the duration were infinite, then a one percentage-point change in the required return would have an infinite effect on the value of the stock, which is clearly untrue. We can estimate the duration by taking the derivative of the value of the stock with respect to the discount rate or directly from the duration formula. Taking derivatives,

$$P = \frac{D}{R-g}$$

$$\frac{dP}{dR} = -\frac{D}{(R-g)^2}$$

$$-\frac{1}{P}\frac{dP}{dR} = \frac{1}{R-g}$$

The duration is not infinite unless $g = R$, in which case the value is also infinite.

6.32 We can expect Disney stock to have a higher long-run return than Disney bonds if dividends increase by more than 2% a year.

6.33 A drop in interest rates (and required returns) raises the present value of a given cash flow. Bonds with long durations (which are roughly related to maturity) are especially sensitive to interest rates. Because stocks have relatively long durations, their prices are also very sensitive to interest rates. In addition, low interest rates may stimulate the economy, increasing the cash flow from stocks, but not from bonds.

6.34 The fundamental values of all securities are sensitive to interest rates because the present value of the cash flow depends on required rates of return, which are influenced by interest rates.

6.35 In theory, stock prices depend on longer-term rates (or a complete term structure). Also, there was very little variation in the federal funds rate in these data.

6.36 First, we should use the *annual* dividend with the annual required return and growth rate (or else use the quarterly dividend, required return, and growth rate). Second, the dividend growth model takes into account capital gains, and it would be double-counting to add together both present values. Using annual values, the implied required return is 9.534%:

$$\$35.28 = \frac{\$1.00}{.09534 - .067}$$

6.37 Consider the constant-dividend-growth model,

$$P = \frac{D}{R - g}$$

$$R = \frac{D}{P} + g$$

If the firm has a low g, then it must have a low P and high D/P to provide shareholders their required return. (Less satisfactory is the alternative explanation that firms that pay large dividends retain less and therefore grow slower. D may affect g, but it is P that determines D/P.)

6.38 The intrinsic value of a 1952 Mickey Mantle card is the present value of what you would pay each year to rent the card, for the enjoyment of looking at it and remembering past baseball games. This is surely much less than $12,600,000—making baseball cards speculation rather than a value investment. This conclusion is reinforced by the fact that a player's signature dramatically reduces the market price of a baseball card, but not its intrinsic value.

6.39 The constant-dividend-growth model P = D/(R − g) assumes that stocks will be held forever. The dividend growth rate should be the long-run growth rate, which is surely not 11.89%.

6.40 Stocks are disguised bonds: Treasury bonds pay 1.8% with fixed coupons while stocks pay 1.7% dividends that are very likely to grow by several percent a year. Stocks are likely to do better over the next 10 years.

6.41 This is true for stocks that have longer durations than bonds but not if they don't (for example, a no-growth stock and a 30-year zero).

6.42 The miles driven each year may stay at 10,000, but the cost of gasoline may not stay at \$4.00/gallon. The annual savings should be discounted each year, not the total savings over 10 years. There is an issue of whether the gasoline is bought at the start of the year or the end. It would probably be better to use monthly discounting with the gasoline bought at the beginning of each month.

$$\sum_{t=1}^{120} \frac{\$4.00(1+g/12)\left(\dfrac{100,000/12\text{ miles}}{20\text{ mpg}} - \dfrac{100,000/12\text{ miles}}{40\text{ mpg}}\right)}{(1+R/12)t}$$

which can be calculated for various assumed values of g and R.

6.43 This can be answered with a detailed dividend-discount model analysis. A clever shortcut is as follows: the fundamental-value model implies that the shareholders' actual return, dividend yield plus capital gain, will equal their required return, here 10%.

a. Since the dividend yield is 0% for the first 10 years, the annual price increase will be 10%.

b. Thereafter, the stock price will be determined by D/(R – g) and will increase at the rate g, 5% a year.

6.44 This can be answered with a detailed dividend-discount model analysis. A clever shortcut is as follows: the stock will be priced so that the dividend yield (1/22.73) plus capital gain will equal the shareholders' required return (.12). Therefore, the anticipated percentage increase in the stock's price is .12 – 1/22.73 = .076 (7.6%).

6.45 If you are worried (relative to the expectations already embedded in bond and stock prices) that interest rates will increase and the economy will slump, then short-term bonds (cash) are appealing.

6.46 Using the constant-dividend-growth model, we have

$$P = \frac{(1-\omega)D}{R-g}$$

where P is the stock price, D is the next dividend, w is the tax rate on dividends, and g is the growth rate of dividends. A change in w from .40 to .15 will change P from

$$P = \frac{.85D}{R-g} \text{ to } P = \frac{.60D}{R-g}$$

which is a 29.41% decrease:(.60 – .85)/.85 = .2941.

6.47 An asset's duration is the present-value weighted average time until receiving its cash flow—which is not infinite and may be less than 30 years. In the constant-growth dividend-discount model, for example, the percent change in price from a one-percentage-point change in the required return is

$$P = \frac{D}{R-g}$$

$$-\frac{\delta P}{\delta R}\frac{1}{P} = \frac{1}{R-g}$$

$$-100\frac{\delta P}{\delta 100R}\frac{1}{P} = \frac{1}{R-g}$$

This is less than 30 for many values of R and g. For example, with $R = .10$ and $g = 0$, it is 10.

6.48 Low interest rates increase the present value of any cash flow, but especially distant cash flows, which is beneficial to growth stocks since much of their present value consists of distant cash flows.

6.49 The higher discount rate reduces the value more for a stock whose cash flow is further in the future. Comparing the market price P using $R = .10$ with this investor's present value V using $R = .12$, the fast-growth stock is 50% overpriced, the slow-growth stock is only 25% overpriced:

$$\frac{P_A}{V_A} = \frac{\left(\dfrac{\$2}{.10-.02}\right)}{\left(\dfrac{\$2}{.12-.02}\right)} = \frac{\$25}{\$20} = 1.25$$

$$\frac{P_B}{V_B} = \frac{\left(\dfrac{\$2}{.10-.06}\right)}{\left(\dfrac{\$2}{.12-.06}\right)} = \frac{\$50}{\$33.33} = 1.50$$

6.50 a. The second stock, because a growth stock has a longer duration than a no-growth stock.

b. The second stock, because the higher the growth rate, the longer the duration.

c. Equal, because both are no-growth.

7

Earnings and Assets

7.1 A senior Morgan Stanley manager argued that, because shareholders own the firm, the value of their stock should equal the present value of the firm's future profits:

> To find the present value of the future earnings of a company in perpetuity, financial theorists use the model,
>
> $$P = E / (r - g)$$
>
> where P = Price, E = Earnings, r = the discount rate of the asset, and g = the growth rate of the earnings.

a. Explain his mistake.

b. He said that he uses r = .10 because "as an investor, I always have the choice of simply investing in an index fund" and these have returned 10% "throughout the modern period." Explain why you agree or disagree with this logic.

7.2 A seasoned *Los Angeles Times* financial columnist wrote:

> The underlying U.S. economy today is not strong enough to support the market's enthusiasm, and it is not gaining. The force driving stock prices up is declining interest rates (and oil prices). Well, interest rates decline when lenders have lots of money but borrowers don't have lots of need for it; that is, when business is slow. Like now.
>
> Every new statistic—retail sales off a bit, unemployment up a bit—indicates that the economy is only so-so. Which wouldn't be so bad if the outlook for the economy were better. But it's not. Despite lower interest rates, business doesn't seem in a hurry to invest in new plant and equipment....
>
> What does it all mean? Only that the economy will putter along—no disaster but no great glory either—and the stock market will probably take a sharp decline.

Is there any rational explanation for why the stock market might be strong, even while the economy is not?

7.3 A *Wall Street Journal* article quoted international money managers saying that Toyota and Honda "make beautiful cars" and that Toyota "is the premier car company in the world;" but the article argued that purchasing Toyota or Honda stock "would be a classic mistake—confusing

DOI: 10.1201/9781003630166-7

a great company with a great stock." How could a great company have an unattractive stock?

7.4 Explain why you either agree or disagree with this investment advisor's reasoning:

> A stock with a high P/E is inherently riskier than one with a low P/E. Suppose that Stock A has a P/E of 5 and Stock B has a P/E of 10. This means that if each company has a 1% increase in earnings, the price of Stock A will increase by 5% and the price of Stock B will increase by 10%.

7.5 Here is a graph of CAPE going back to 1880.

a. What is CAPE?

b. Why might the 2020 value of CAPE suggest that stock prices were above fundamental values?

c. What is the most important reason why that conclusion might be wrong?

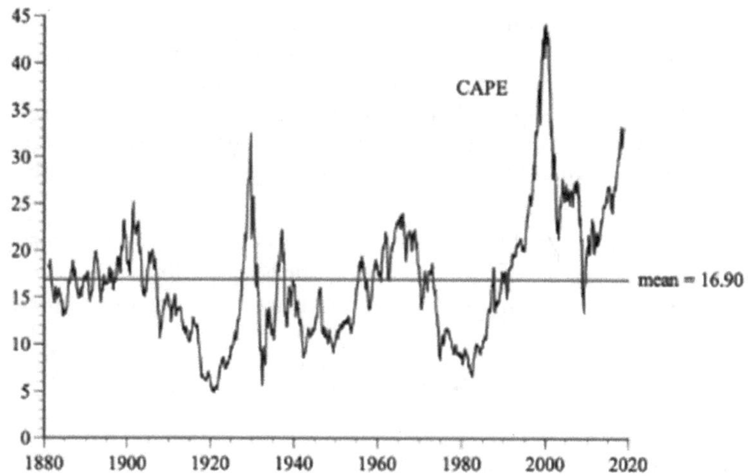

7.6 Robert Shiller's cyclically adjusted price-to-earnings ratio (CAPE) is equal to which of the following?

a. current S&P 500 price divided by average real S&P 500 earnings over the past 10 years

b. average S&P 500 real price over the past 10 years divided by average real S&P 500 earnings over the past 10 years

c. average S&P 500 real price over the past 10 years divided by current S&P 500 earnings

d. average value over the past 10 years of the ratio of the S&P 500 real price divided by the S&P 500 real earnings.

Explain Shiller's choice.

7.7 Carefully explain the inadequacies of this stock-selection advice from Peter Lynch, the legendary manager of Fidelity's Magellan Fund:

> The p/e ratio can be thought of as the number of years it will take the company to earn back the amount of your initial investment—assuming of course that the company's earnings stay constant.... If you buy shares in a company selling at two times earnings (a p/e of 2), you will earn back your initial investment in two years, but in a company selling at 40 times earnings (a p/e of 40) it would take forty years to accomplish the same thing.

7.8 Peter Bernstein, a prolific financial writer, said that stock and bond returns were negatively correlated during most of the 1960s but positively correlated for much of the 1970s. Is this theoretically possible if bond and stock prices are equal to their fundamental values?

7.9 Explain why you either agree or disagree with this interpretation of Tobin's q from investopedia.com:

> A ratio devised by James Tobin of Yale University, Nobel Laureate in Economics, who hypothesized that the combined market value of all the companies on the stock market should be about equal to their replacement costs .... A low Q (between 0 and 1) means that the cost to replace a firm's assets is greater than the value of its stock, which implies that the stock is undervalued. Conversely, a high Q (greater than 1) implies that a firm's stock is relatively more expensive than the replacement cost of its assets, which implies that the stock is overvalued.

7.10 In 2024, a finance professor proposed a new valuation model stating that a stock's future price is equal to its current price multiplied by the ratio of the current price/earnings ratio to the future price/earnings ratio:

$$P^{future} = P^{current}\left(\frac{PE^{current}}{PE^{future}}\right)$$

The professor gave this example:

> The current price of NVDA as of 6/6/2023 is \$400 and the current $PE^{Current} = 200$ while the forward 1 year and the future $PE^{Future} = 150$; then the future price is 400*(200/150)=\$533.3. Based on these figures, NVDA is expected to further rise and grow; and the upside is great for the future 1 year target. Hypothetically, if the $PE^{Future} = 250$, then the future price will be 400*(200/250) = \$320. That means the current price for NVDA is way overbought and expensive.

Explain why this model is either sensible or not.

7.11 In 2010, a portfolio manager wrote that

> If you're buying a company that historically looks cheap and it's at 11 or 12 times earnings, that sounds great right now with interest rates where they are. But if the 10-year is at 7%, that might not look so great.

a. What does "11 or 12 times earnings" mean?

b. What is the "10-year"?

c. Why might an increase in the 10-year make 11 or 12 times earnings not look so great?

7.12 A professor of business history wrote that,

> A century ago, when buying stock was a lot like placing a bet at the tracks, science had little to do with what we now know as market analysis. If there was anything close to a market theory, it was that a company was worth the net value of its visible assets. Any amount that its stock price rose above that level was somehow illegitimate. The difference between a stock's market price and the value of its underlying assets was known as 'water,' a term used with derision.

Use fundamental analysis to explain why a stock's market price may be larger than what it would cost to replace the firm's visible assets.

7.13 An investment textbook states that, "Book and market values will probably be equal when the stock is issued, but after that, it appears that only coincidence will keep them equal at any given moment." If a firm's book value is approximately equal to the replacement cost of its assets, can you think of any logical, not-coincidental reason why market value should be above, below, or equal to book value?

7.14 Warren Buffett has described a "wonderful business" as one that grows without borrowing or retaining a substantial amount of earnings, and the "worst business" as one that grows a lot, but does so by reinvesting virtually all of its earnings. Consider two companies that do not acquire other companies, issue new debt or equity, or engage in financial chicanery. How can a company that retains 20% of its earnings grow faster than one that retains all of its earnings?

7.15 Explain why you disagree with this logic: "I invested in this stock because its earnings of $5.70/share far exceeds the industry median of $2.48/share."

7.16 In March 2000, Wharton professor Jeremy Siegel wrote a *Wall Street Journal* article arguing that the price-earnings ratios for large tech stocks were probably not justified. For example, JDS Uniphase had a 1999 P/E of 668.3, paid no dividends, and had a total market value of $99 billion. Analysts' seemingly optimistic prediction was that its earnings would grow at 44% a year for the next 5 years. Siegel calculated that if its earnings grew at 44% a year for 10 years and "investors expect to receive an average 15% annual return," its P/E ratio in 10 years would be 68.3. Henry Goldstein, professor emeritus of economics at the University of Oregon, responded by arguing that

> the latest Barron's gives a consensus earnings forecast of $1.09 a share for JDSU for 2001. If such earnings were to rise by 44%

> annually over the following 9 years, the company's earnings in 2010 would be $29.02 per share. With the stock's price constant at its recent … level of $266 per share, its P/E in 2010 would then be a mere 9.2. So: Is this stock 'a buy' or 'a steal'?

Do not check their calculations. Instead, identify the logical error that explains their quite different conclusions. In your opinion, which economist's approach makes more sense?

7.17 IBI stock is selling for $70 a share. The company has $35 in assets per share and consistently earns a 20% return on its assets. This coming year, it is expected to earn an after-tax profit of $7 a share and to pay a dividend of $3.50 per share. Analyst 1 calculates the stockholders' return as $3.50/$70 = .05 (5%). Analyst 2 says the stockholders' return as $7/$70 = .10 (10%). Analyst 3 argues that the stockholders' return must equal the firm's profit rate, 20%.

a. Explain and evaluate the logic behind each analyst's calculation.
b. If you had to come up with a rough estimate of the shareholders' return using these data, what would your estimate be?
c. What is the value of q for this firm?
d. If IBI were to reduce its dividend by 10 cents a share and use these additional retained earnings to expand its operations, would you predict that this action will raise or lower the price of its stock? Explain your reasoning.

7.18 Use a numerical example to explain this reasoning by a prominent portfolio manager:

> One of the reasons why people get burned in growth stocks—well, one of them is that growth is hard to predict—but the other is that not all growth is created equal. If you are growing without a really good return on invested capital, you're not giving your shareholder any real benefit.

7.19 Why do the stocks of financially shaky companies tend to sell at relatively low P/Es? Shouldn't these stocks command a risk premium?

7.20 In an August 2017 MarketWatch column, Mark Hulbert argued that "the stock market is overvalued according to almost any standard valuation measure." For example, looking at the S&P 500, the P/E ratio was 24.6, compared to an average of 15.7 going back to 1871, and the dividend yield was 1.9%, compared to a historical average of 4.4%.

a. How much higher (or lower), in percentage terms, would the S&P 500 have had to have been in August 2017, for the P/E to equal its historical average?
b. Identify two logical reasons why P/E ratios might be higher than average and dividend yields might be lower than average.

7.21 In July 2022, a very successful investor tweeted that:

> This is what worries me about valuation. S&P PE multiples are still above long run average.

and included a link to a figure showing the P/E ratio for the S&P 500 since 1950:

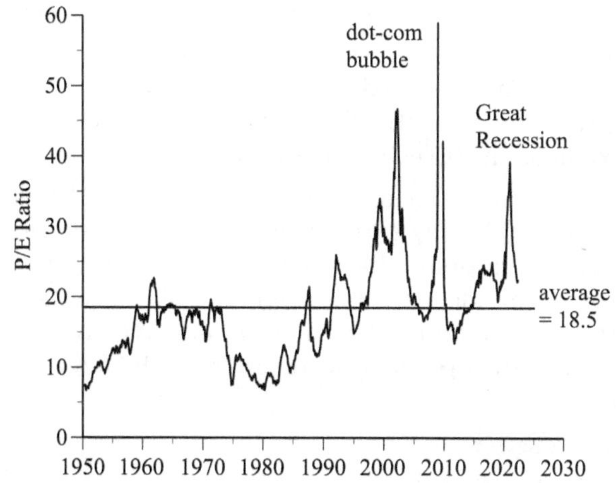

(Nine months in 2009 were omitted because the Great Recession caused a collapse of earnings and the P/E went above 70.) Give a rational reason why the S&P 500 could have a historically high P/E even if earnings have not collapsed.

7.22 A 1995 article in the *Wall Street Journal* included a graph of the S&P500 earnings yield E/P and the interest rate R on 30-year Treasury bonds, from 1985 to 1995:

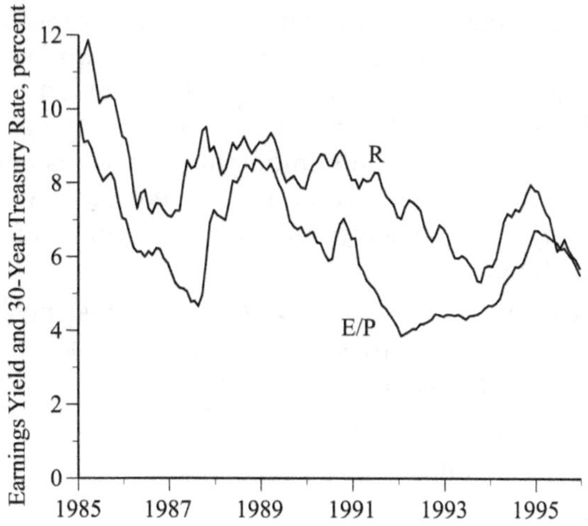

a. Why is there a connection between these two series?

b. How do you explain the fact that the Treasury rate was almost always above the earnings yield?

7.23 Explain the logic behind this advice from Burton Malkiel:

> For two companies whose expected growth rates are the same, you are better off with the one whose dividend payout is higher.

7.24 L and M are two mature companies that routinely earn a 20% return on their assets. Each has no debt outstanding. Yet L consistently has the smaller price-earnings ratio, currently 8.6 versus M's 11.3. Is there any logical explanation? (Use logic, not numbers.)

7.25 The economic value added (EVA) model says that firms create value for their stockholders by earning profits that exceed the stockholders' required return. Suppose that a firm has no debt and that all earnings are paid out as dividends. It has assets K that earn an annual return ρ, and shareholders' required rate of return is R. Which of these equations for the value of the firm is most consistent with EVA analysis? Explain your reasoning.

a. $V = (\rho K - RK)/R$

b. $V = K + (\rho K - RK)/R$

c. $V = K$

d. $V = \text{sum of } (\rho K - RK)$

7.26 The Financial Accounting Standards Board (FASB) and the SEC both require companies with proven oil and gas reserves to estimate the future cash flows from these reserves using current year-end prices and costs (unless other prices are established by existing contractual arrangements) and to take into account the timing of these flows by applying a 10% discount rate. The FASB noted that 70% of 102 petroleum evaluation engineers surveyed believed that the "present value" of proven reserves should be reported and that 58% supported a standard 10% discount rate. Yet, the FASB cautioned that, "The Board is concerned, at the same time, that users of financial statements understand that it is neither fair market value nor the present value of future cash flows. It is a rough surrogate for such measures." Why is a constant 10% discount rate problematic?

7.27 Explain why you expect a stock's P/E to be either positively or negatively related to each of these three factors, in each case holding the other two factors constant:

a. The firm's growth rate of dividends and earnings

b. Treasury bond rates

c. The firm's plowback ratio

7.28 Yahoo Finance calculates the "fair value" of a stock ("the appropriate price for shares of a company") as the price that sets the P/E ratio equal to the percentage earnings growth rate. For example, on June 12, 2020, Apple's annual earnings per share were $12.73, and the projected 5-year growth rate of earnings was 11.47%, giving a fair value of 12.73(11.47) = $146.01, compared to the current market price of $336. Thus, Yahoo concluded that Apple was dangerously overvalued.

What basis is there for Yahoo's calculation? Why is it logically flawed? Give a specific example of a hypothetical stock that has a P/E far above g but is nonetheless fairly valued.

7.29 A 2022 *Advisors Perspectives* article about Tobin's q said, "It might seem logical that fair value would be a 1:1 ratio. But that has not historically been the case." Theoretically, when will the value of Tobin's q be above 1? Below 1?

7.30 Between March 1985 and March 1986, bond rates dropped by about three percentage points, while the economy "muddled along," with essentially unchanged profit expectations.

a. Do you think Tobin's q went up or down during this period?

b. Does this change in q foretell an increase or decrease in business investment spending?

c. Why might businesses change their investment plans even if profit expectations are unchanged?

7.31 Suppose that a firm with no debt and 1 million shares outstanding has annual earnings of $5 million, on which $2 million is paid out as dividends and $3 million is invested in new capital that earns a rate of return ρ. For what values of ρ do this firm's earnings per share increase? Why might the firm's shareholders be worse off even though the firm's earnings per share increase?

7.32 A long-time investor said, "I was looking for companies with growing earnings. Calpine had just acquired a geothermal facility in northern California and had just arranged to expand operations elsewhere in the United States. Together, these actions should increase its earnings growth rate." If these actions do, in fact, increase Calpine's earnings growth rate, must they also increase the fundamental value of its stock?

7.33 Here are some balance-sheet data (millions of dollars) for a hypothetical company:

Assets		Liabilities	
Plant and equipment	100	Debt	0
		Book value of equity	100
Total	100	Total	100

and some annual end-of-year data:

total revenue	25
operating expenses	10
taxes	5
net after-tax income	10
dividends	4
retained earnings	6
rate of return on assets	10%
shareholders' required return	8%

Assume that dividends are paid annually and that the firm's dividends, earnings, and assets are all growing at the same constant rate. Use the constant-growth dividend-discount model to estimate the value of Tobin's q.

7.34 In 2008, *Fortune* magazine reported that, in the aggregate, the nation's five largest investment banks (Bear Stearns, Goldman Sachs, Lehman Brothers, Merrill Lynch, and Morgan Stanley) had a leverage ratio of 40:1. What rate of return on assets would cause their rate of return on equity to be –100%?

7.35 Consider a company that has 1 million shares outstanding, assets A = \$100 million, and a profit rate $\rho = 15\%$, so that it will earn \$15 million in profits during the coming year, E = \$15 million. The company always retains one-third of its earnings for investment in new assets and uses the remainder to pay dividends at the end of each year. It has no debt and its assets increase each year by the amount of retained earnings. Its market price is always equal to its fundamental value. The shareholders' required rate of return is 10%. Use the constant-growth dividend-discount model to determine the value of Tobin's q. Use the economic value added model to estimate the value of this firm.

7.36 A company has no debt and \$100 million in assets. It will earn a 30% return on its assets for the next 2 years and a 10% return on its assets every year thereafter. All its profits for the first year will be reinvested in the firm at the end of the first year; similarly, all its profits for the second year will be reinvested in the firm at the end of the second year. Starting in the third year, all its profits for each year will be paid out as dividends at the end of the year.

a. Fill in this table:

year	assets at the beginning of year (\$)	profits during year (\$)	dividends paid at end of year (\$)
1	100		
2			
3			
4			

b. If the firm's stockholders require a 10% return, use the dividend-discount model to determine the current value of the firm.

c. Use the Economic Value Added (EVA) model to value the firm.

7.37 An interview with John Neff, a highly respected managing partner of Wellington Management Company, gave this example of market irrationality:

> Two companies, one expected to grow at 8 percent and the other expected to grow at 15 percent. Both have the same total return—because an 8 percent grower typically pays a [dividend] yield of 7 percent while the 15 percent grower pays little or no yield. Yet the fast grower usually sells at a much higher [price-earnings] multiple. "Now does that make sense?" asks Neff with exasperation. "The market gives away yield. It's just damn stupid."

To investigate the rationality of such data, consider these three hypothetical companies (all data are annual per share):

Firm	Earnings/ Share E, $	Dividends/ Share D, $	Return on Equity ρ, %
1	10	6	20
2	10	3	20
3	10	6	35

For each firm, assume a 15% required return and use the constant-growth model to determine the plowback rate, growth rate, price, dividend yield, and price/earnings ratio. Why are the price-earnings ratios higher for the low-yield, high-growth stocks than for the high-yield, low-growth stocks? What are the shareholder rates of return on these three companies?

firm	plowback rate	growth rate	price	dividend yield	P/E	shareholder return
1						
2						
3						

7.38 A company has a 20% return on equity ρ, a 50% plowback rate $(1 - d)$, and earns \$4 a share. Use the present value equation, $P = D/(R - g)$, where $g = \rho\,(1 - d)$, to calculate the dividend-price ratio, the earnings-price ratio, and the price-earnings ratio when the shareholders' required return is (a) 20%; (b) 14%. Now redo (a) and (b), assuming that the company increases its plowback rate to 60%. Explain why this increase in the plowback rate does or does not affect the price-earnings ratios.

7.39 Legendary fund manager Peter Lynch popularized the PEG ratio (the ratio of a stock's P/E to its percentage growth rate) as a way of gauging whether a stock is cheap or expensive. Lynch argues that a fairly priced stock has a PEG of 1, while a stock with a PEG greater than 1 is overpriced and a stock with a PEG less than 1 is underpriced. For example, a company with a 20% growth rate that is selling for 10 times earnings would have a PEG of .5, which is "a very attractive ratio that would make the company an immediate buy." Explain the general logic of comparing the price-earnings ratio to the growth rate. Then use the constant-growth model to show that a company with a value ratio of .5 is not necessarily an "immediate buy."

7.40 The PEG is the ratio of a stock's price-earnings ratio to its growth rate g, where g is expressed as a percent,

$$\text{PEG} = \frac{P/E}{g}$$

Thus, a company with a P/E of 10 and a growth rate of 10% would have a PEG of 10/10 = 1. Legendary fund manager Peter Lynch popularized the PEG ratio as a way of gauging whether a stock is cheap or expensive. Lynch argues that "The p/e of any company that's fairly priced will equal its growth rate of earnings" (a PEG of 1), while a stock with a PEG greater than 1 is overpriced and a stock with a PEG less than 1 is underpriced.

A research analyst at a major investment firm used the constant-dividend-growth model to derive this equation:

$$\text{PEG} = \frac{P/E}{g} = \frac{\left(\frac{D}{R-g}\right)\frac{1}{E}}{g} = \frac{D/E}{(R-g)g} = \frac{d}{(R-g)g}$$

The analyst gave this example of a typical stock with d = 3, R = 3.5, and g = 2:

$$\text{PEG} = \frac{d}{(R-g)g} = \frac{3}{(3.5-2)2} = 1$$

What mistakes do you see in this researcher's analysis?

Answers

7.1 a. Shareholders receive dividends, not earnings. It is double-counting to count today's earnings plus the future earnings generated by reinvested earnings.

b. The discount rate should be an investor's required return, which takes into account the returns currently available on alternative investments (most importantly, Treasury bonds), risk, and anything else that matters to investors. When Treasury bonds pay double-digits, investors may require 20% on stocks. When Treasuries pay 3%, investors may settle for 7% on stocks. Even though investors may have earned an average of 10% on stocks in the past, they shouldn't discount the prospective cash flow from stocks by 10% if Treasuries are only paying 2% or are paying 15%.

7.2 A rational explanation for a strong stock market while the economy is weak is that declining interest rates reduce shareholders' required rates of return, thereby increasing the intrinsic value of a given cash flow.

7.3 A great company has an unattractive stock if the stock price is too high.

7.4 Logically, there is no compelling reason why each P/E should be constant. Mathematically, if each P/E is constant, both prices will increase by 1%! For example, suppose P/E = 10. If E = 10, then P = 100, if E increases by 1% to 10.1, then a constant P/E requires P to increase by 1%, to 101.

7.5 a. CAPE is Robert Shiller's cyclically adjusted price-earnings ratio, the ratio of the current S&P 500 price to average inflation-adjusted earnings over the previous 10 years.

b. Prices were historically high relative to earnings in 2020.

c. We should also consider interest rates, which were historically low in 2020.

7.6 CAPE is (a). For deciding whether stocks are currently cheap or expensive, it makes more sense to look at the current price, rather than prices over the past 10 years.

7.7 There is no good reason to assume that earnings will stay constant, particularly since one of the primary explanations of differences in P/E ratios is anticipated differences in growth rates. This is like analyzing differences in Treasury and junk bond yields and saying "assuming that there are no defaults." In addition, the time value of money is ignored and the years beyond the payback period are ignored.

7.8 Yes, it is possible. Bond prices are inversely related to interest rates, while stock prices are inversely related to interest rates and positively related to the strength of the economy. During times when there are little or no unexpected changes in the strength of the economy, bond and stock prices will be affected mainly by unexpected changes in interest rates and should be positively correlated. On the other hand, during times when unexpected changes in the economy happen to be positively correlated with unexpected changes in interest rates, bond and stock prices might be negatively correlated.

7.9 A stock is not necessarily undervalued if q is less than 1 or overvalued if q is greater than 1. Tobin's q should be less than 1 if the firm's profit rate is lower than the shareholders' required return, and greater than 1 if the reverse is true.

7.10 The equation doesn't make sense mathematically or logically. By the professor's reasoning, an astronomical P/E for NVDA (or any stock) means that "the upside is great" because the future P/E will almost certainly be lower—which, according to his valuation model, means that the future stock price will be higher than the current stock price. His implied conclusion: don't be frightened by high P/Es. Embrace them!

7.11 a. The price-earnings ratio is 11-to-12.

b. The "10-year" is the interest rate on 10-year Treasury bonds.

c. For a given level of earnings, an increase in interest rates will increase required returns and reduce stock prices and P/E ratios.

7.12 Unless the firm is going to be liquidated, its market value is the present value of the cash flow to investors, which depends on the profitability of its assets, not what it costs to acquire them. Using the logic of Tobin's q, the market value of a firm could be larger than the replacement cost of its assets if its return on assets is larger than shareholders' required rate of return.

7.13 In theory, Tobin's q (the ratio of market value to replacement cost) will be larger than, equal to, or smaller than 1 if the firm's profit rate is larger than, equal to, or smaller than the shareholders' required return.

7.14 In the constant-growth model, the firm's growth rate is equal to $(1 - d)\rho$, where $(1 - d)$ is the retention rate (the fraction of earnings reinvested in the firm) and ρ is the firm's rate of return on assets. Comparing Firm 1 (which retains 20% of earnings) and Firm 2 (which retains 100%):

$$\frac{g_1}{g_2} = \frac{.2\rho_1}{1.0\rho_2} > 1 \text{ if } \rho_1 > 5\rho_2$$

7.15 A stock's attractiveness depends on its price; for example, its price in relation to its dividends, earnings, cash flow. In addition, a company may have high earnings per share simply because it has few shares.

7.16 A 10-year 44% earnings growth rate is pretty optimistic. However, even if earnings were to grow by 44% annually, Goldstein assumes that the stock's price is constant for 10 years. Because the stock pays no dividends, shareholders would then have a 0% return for 10 years. Siegel assumes that investors in such a risky stock require a 15% return, which they can only get from the stock's price increasing 15% a year. Siegel's approach makes more sense. (JDS Uniphase turned out to be a terrible investment.)

7.17 Earnings are $E = \rho A = .20(\$35) = \$7$. A \$3.50 dividend represents a .5 payout: $d = D/E = \$3.50/\$7.00 = .5$.

a. Analyst 1 looks at the dividend yield $D/P = \$3.50/\$70 = .05$ and ignores the retained earnings, which will increase future earnings and dividends. Analyst 2 looks at the firm's 20% profits and ignores its payout/plowback policy. Analyst 3 does not take into account the price of the stock!

b. Another approach is to estimate the growth rate as $g = (1 - d)\rho = .50(.20) = .10$ and to estimate the shareholders' return as

$$R = \frac{D}{P} + g = \frac{\$3.50}{\$7.00} + .10 = .15$$

c. Tobin's q = (market value/assets = \$70/\$35 = 2.0.

d. Since $q > 1$, the stock market values this firm's assets at more than their cost (apparently $\rho > R$), and the retention of earnings to finance expansion should raise the firm's stock price.

7.18 Retaining earnings increase a company's growth rate, but do not benefit shareholders more than a dividend if the retained earnings are invested at a rate of return that is lower than the shareholders' required return. Consider a company with \$100 in assets, a 5% return on assets, no debt, and a 10% shareholder required rate of return. If the company has a 0% retention rate, the growth rate is $(1 - d).05 = .0(.05) = .0$, and the value of the company is

$$P = \frac{D}{R-g} = \frac{d\rho A}{R-(1-d)\rho} = \frac{1.0(.05)100}{1.10-(1-1.0).05} = 50$$

If the company instead has a 50% retention rate, the growth rate increases from 0% to 2.5% ($(1 - d).05 = .50(.05) = .025$), but the value of the company falls from \$50 to \$33.33:

$$P = \frac{D}{R-g} = \frac{d\rho A}{R-(1-d)\rho} = \frac{.5(.05)100}{.10-(1-.5).05} = 33.33$$

7.19 They do command a risk premium. The high required return reduces the price relative to the firm's current earnings.

7.20 a. For a given value of E, the value of P would have to be (15.7/24.6) (current P) = .64(current P), or 36% lower. (The S&P 500 would have had to be 57% lower for the dividend yield to equal its historical average.)

b. Hulbert neglects interest rates. The 10-year Treasury yield was 2.22%, which was 52% below its historical average of 4.58%.

7.21 One possibility is that interest rates were relatively low in 2022, compared to their historical average. (In fact, interest rates were at historic lows in 2022.)

7.22 a. The earnings yield is just the inverse of the P/E ratio. Fundamental analysis says that the price that investors are willing to pay for a company with a certain level of earnings per share should depend on (among other things) their required rate of return, which is strongly influenced by interest rates.

b. In theory, the earnings yield should be more closely related to the real Treasury rate than to the nominal Treasury rate. Since the United States experienced inflation over this time period, the real Treasury rate is lower than the nominal rate shown in the figure.

7.23 The company with the high dividend payout (Company 1) is fueling its growth with its high rate of return on equity, rather than, as with Company 2, retained earnings and diminished dividends—which makes Company 1 more valuable.

Mathematically, using subscripts 1 and 2 for the two companies, and remembering that they have the same growth rate g:

$g = (1 - d_1)\rho_1$

$g = (1 - d_2)\rho_2$

$d_1 > d_2$ implies $(1 - d_1) < (1 - d_2)$ implies $\rho_1 > \rho_2$

If shareholders apply the same required return R to both companies, the first is more valuable, relative to its assets:

$$P = \frac{D}{R-g} = \frac{d\rho A}{R-g}$$

$$\frac{P}{A} = \frac{d\rho}{R-g}$$

$$\frac{P_1}{A_1} = \frac{d_1\rho_1}{R-g} > \frac{P_2}{A_2} = \frac{d_2\rho_2}{R-g}$$

7.24 If L and M have the same return on assets ρ and their stocks are priced using the same required return R, then their different price-earnings ratios may be attributed to their different payout/retention policies. If $\rho > R$, as seems likely with $\rho = .20$, a firm that retains more of its earnings makes shareholders better off. Therefore, M, with the higher price-earnings ratio, probably has a lower payout ratio.

7.25 Answer (b) is correct. If $\rho = R$, then there would be no economic value added, and P = K. Only (b) and (c) have this property, and (c) ignores profits and the required return. The economic value added each period is the profits ρK minus the cost of capital, RK: EVA = $(\rho - R)K$. Using the present value of a perpetuity, the value of the firm is

$$P = K + \frac{(\rho - R)K}{R}$$

7.26 The appropriate discount rate depends on current interest rates (which fluctuate considerably) and risk (which depends on uncertainty about future oil prices and reserves, and can vary considerably from oil field to oil field).

7.27 $P = D/(R - g)$ implies $P/E = d/(R - g)$. Therefore, P/E is

a. positively related to the firm's growth rate of dividends and earnings.

b. negatively related to Treasury bond rates.

c. positively related to the firm's payout ratio d, and inversely related to the plowback ratio $1 - d$. Holding g constant, a firm that needs a high plowback ratio to grow is worth less.

7.28 The equation P = Eg is related to Peter Lynch's argument that a fairly priced stock has a PEG ratio (the ratio of its P/E to its percentage growth rate) of 1. It is true that the value of a stock should be higher if earnings are higher and if the growth rate of earnings is higher, but there is no logical basis for this specific equation.

Using the constant-dividend-growth model,

$$P = \frac{D}{R - g} = \frac{dE}{R - g}$$

we can see that P is positively related to E and g, but not by the simple Yahoo equation P = Eg. We can also see that P depends on the dividend payout ratio d and, most importantly, the required return R. Any valuation model that ignores interest rates must be fatally flawed.

Consider a hypothetical company with D = 10, E = 20, g = .10 (10%), and R = .125. Its intrinsic value is

$$P = \frac{D}{R - g} = \frac{10}{.125 - .10} = 400$$

$$\frac{P}{E} = \frac{400}{20} = 20$$

Its P/E of 20 is far above its 10% growth rate, but it is fairly valued at a price of \$400.

(At the time, long-term Treasury rates were below 2% and Apple's dividend yield was close to 1%, A growth rate of 11.47% makes Apple look pretty attractive. Apple split 4-for-1 in August 2020, so its split-adjusted price at the time of the Yahoo valuation was \$336/4 = \$84.)

7.29 Tobin's q will be above or below 1 when the profit rate ρ is larger/smaller than the shareholders' required return R.

7.30 Tobin's q depends on firm profit rates relative to shareholders' required returns.

a. When interest rates (and shareholder required returns) decrease, the value of Tobin's q should increase.

b. If businesses assess expansion plans by seeing if the profit rate is larger than shareholders' required return (or, equivalently, seeing whether Tobin's q is greater than 1), then the drop in interest rates and rise in Tobin's q encourage business investment.

c. Such a stimulus could well be explained by the decline in interest rates (and shareholder required rates of return), even if the economy and profit expectations are unchanged.

7.31 Because there is no change in the number of shares, earnings per share will increase as long as the new capital makes a profit ($\rho > 0$); however, shareholders will not be better off unless this profit rate is larger than their required rate of return.

7.32 Not unless the profit rate on these acquisitions and expanded operations exceed the shareholders' required rate of return.

7.33 The growth rate is $g = (1 - d)\rho = .6(.10) = .06$. Using the constant-growth model, the present value of the dividend stream is 200:

$$P = \frac{D}{R-g} = \frac{\$4}{.08-.06} = \$200$$

Tobin's q is (market value)/(book value) = 200/100 = 2.

7.34 With 40-1 leverage, the percentage return on equity is 40 times the return on assets. Therefore, a 2.5% loss on their assets would result in a –100% return on equity.

7.35 Using the constant-growth dividend-discount model,

$$P = \frac{D}{R-g} = \frac{d\rho A}{R-(1-d)\rho} = \frac{(2/3)(.15)100}{.10-.05} = 200$$

Tobin's q is 200/100 = 2. Using the fact that assets grow by 5% a year, the EVA model gives the same valuation as the dividend discount model.

$$
\begin{aligned}
V &= A_0 \frac{(\rho - R)A_0}{(1-R)^1} + \frac{(\rho - R)A_1}{(1-R)^2} + \ldots \\
&= 100 + \frac{(.15-.10)100}{(1+.10)^1} + \frac{(.15-.10)100(1+.05)}{(1+.10)^2} + \ldots \\
&= 100 + \frac{5}{(1+.10)^1} + \frac{5(1+.05)}{(1+.10)^2} \\
&= 100 + \frac{5}{.10-.05} \\
&= 100 + 100 \\
&= 200
\end{aligned}
$$

7.36 a. The table:

year	assets at the beginning of year ($)	profits during year ($)	dividends paid at end of year ($)
1	100	30	0
2	130	39	0
3	169	16.9	16.9
4	169	16.9	16.9

b. The value of the firm is the dividends discounted by the stockholders' 10% required return:

$$
\begin{aligned}
V &= \frac{16.9}{1.10^3} + \frac{16.9}{1.10^4} + \ldots \\
&= \frac{1}{1.10^2}\left(\frac{16.9}{1.10^1} + \frac{16.9}{1.10^2} + \ldots\right) \\
&= \frac{1}{1.10^2}\left(\frac{16.9}{.10}\right) = 139.67
\end{aligned}
$$

c. Not surprisingly, the EVA model gives the same answer as the dividend-discount model:

$$
\begin{aligned}
V &= A_0 + \frac{(\rho - R)A_0}{(1+R)^1} + \frac{(\rho - R)A_1}{(1+R)^2} + \ldots \\
&= 100 + \frac{(.3-.1)(100)}{1.10^1} + \frac{(.3-.1)(130)}{1.10^2} + \frac{(.1-.1)(169)}{1.10^3} + \frac{(.1-.1)(169)}{1.10^4} + \ldots \\
&= 100 + \frac{20}{1.10^1} + \frac{26}{1.10^2} \\
&= 139.67
\end{aligned}
$$

7.37 Here are the calculations:

firm	plowback rate	growth rate	price	dividend yield	P/E	shareholder return
1	.40	.08	\$85.71	.07	8.57	.15
2	.70	.14	\$300.00	.01	30.00	.15
3	.40	.14	\$600.00	.01	60.00	.15

Where plowback rate 1 – d = 1 – D/E; growth rate g = (1 – d) ρ; price P = D/(R – g); dividend yield = D/P; and shareholder return R = D/P + g.

The price-earnings ratios are higher for the low-yield, high-growth stocks than for the high-yield, low-growth stocks because the high profit rates fuel high growth rates, which require high prices to keep the return at 15%. All three stocks are priced to give shareholders a 15% return.

7.38 Using the constant-growth dividend-discount model with a 20% shareholder required return,

$$P = \frac{D}{R-g} = \frac{dE}{R-(1-d)\rho} = \frac{.5(4)}{.2-(1-.5).2} = \frac{2}{.2-.1} = 20$$

So, D/P = 2/20 = .10, E/P = 4/20 = .20, and P/E = 20/4 = 5. Increasing the plowback rate to .60 reduces the dividend yield and increases the growth rate, but has no effect on the price because the profit rate is equal to the shareholder's required return:

$$\frac{P/E}{100g} = \frac{d/(100g)}{R-g} = \frac{.5/(100(.05))}{.20-.05} = \frac{.5/5}{.15} = .667$$

$$P = \frac{D}{R-g} = \frac{dE}{R-(1-d)\rho} = \frac{.4(4)}{.2-(1-.4).2} = \frac{1.6}{.2-.12} = 20$$

D/P = 1.6/20 = .08, E/P = 4/20 = .20, and P/E = 20/4 = 5.

With a 14% required return,

$$P = \frac{D}{R-g} = \frac{dE}{R-(1-d)\rho} = \frac{.5(4)}{.14-(1-.5).2} = \frac{2}{.14-.1} = 50$$

So, D/P = 2/50 = .04, E/P = 4/50 = .08, and P/E = 50/4 = 12.5. Increasing the plowback rate to .60 increases the price because the profit rate is greater than the shareholder's required return:

$$P = \frac{D}{R-g} = \frac{dE}{R-(1-d)\rho} = \frac{.4(4)}{.14-(1-.4).2} = \frac{1.6}{.14-.12} = 80$$

D/P = 1.6/80 = .02, E/P = 4/80 = .05, and P/E = 80/4 = 20.

7.39 A high growth rate is good; so is a low P/E. So a low (P/E)/g is good. However, using the constant-dividend growth model (and remembering that PEG divides the P/E ratio by the percentage growth rate

$$P = \frac{D}{R - g}$$

$$P/E = \frac{D/E}{R - g} = \frac{d}{R - g}$$

$$\frac{P/E}{100g} = \frac{d/(100g)}{R - g}$$

There is no simple relationship between the PEG and the underlying parameters. Most glaringly, the PEG ignores R. In an era of high interest rates, R will be high and PEGs may be low—signaling that all stocks are attractive, when they are not necessarily so.

For the specific case of d = .5 and ρ = .10, g = .05 and (P/E)/(100g) = .667 if R = .20:

$$\frac{P/E}{100g} = \frac{d/(100g)}{R - g} = \frac{.5/(100(.05))}{.20 - .05} = \frac{.5/5}{.15} = .667$$

The PEG = .667, but this stock is fairly priced, not an immediate buy.

7.40 The values for R and g seem low, but a much bigger problem is that the units for R and g in the dividend discount model P = D/(R − g) should be fractions, R = .035 and g = .02 rather than percents R = 3.5, and g = 2. In addition, a dividend-payout ratio of 3 (dividends equal to three times earnings) is possible but extremely unusual. A typical value would be closer to .5.

A better set of assumptions would use values like these, letting G be the percent growth rate:

$$PEG = \frac{P/E}{G} = \frac{d}{(R - g)G} = \frac{.5}{(.15 - .10)10} = 1$$

8

Real Assets

8.1 Many Japanese firms have traditionally used a "yen in, yen out" rule for evaluating investments. By this criterion, an investment is attractive if the total amount of yen received (yen in) from the investment is greater than the total amount of yen spent on the investment (yen out), and an investment is more attractive the fewer the number of years it takes for the cumulative yen in to exceed the cumulative yen out. Explain why this criterion is flawed.

8.2 The Southeastern, Southwestern, and Western Power Associations are power companies owned and operated by the federal government. President Clinton proposed selling these power companies for $4.5 billion, which represents the present value (using a 7% discount rate) of their debt obligations to the U.S. Treasury. Explain why this price may be wildly unrealistic, using a hypothetical example to illustrate your reasoning.

8.3 In 1984, Pennzoil thought it had a deal to acquire three-sevenths of Getty Oil for $112.50 a share, but the entire company was instead sold to Texaco for $128 a share. Pennzoil sued Texaco and was awarded $7.5 billion plus punitive damages. The $7.5 billion figure was arrived at by estimating that it costs Pennzoil about $10.90 a barrel to find oil and that three-sevenths of Getty's oil reserves were 1 billion barrels. At $10.90 a barrel, it would have cost Pennzoil $10.9 billion to find this oil on its own; at $112.50 a share, it would have cost Pennzoil only $3.4 billion to acquire three-sevenths of Getty. The difference is $10.9 – $3.4 = $7.5 billion. Imagine that you are an economist hired by Texaco to defend against this suit. How might you attack their argument? (Hint: What if it costs Pennzoil $100 a barrel to find oil?)

8.4 In 1984, after paying $60 million for the Dallas Cowboys and $20 million for the Texas Stadium Corporation (which ran the stadium for the city of Irving, Texas), the new owner, H.R. (Bum) Bright, itemized the cost of replacing some of the upper-deck seats with 90 luxury boxes, which would be sold to the public for a total of $35 million. Bright itemized the cost of this project and concluded that, "It's a wash deal. Everybody understands that."

Fee to Irving, Texas (8% of $35,000,000)	$2,800,000
Cost of constructing the luxury boxes	$8,000,000
Annual lost ticket sales from removed seats	$400,000

 DOI: 10.1201/9781003630166-8

Annual interest on loan to buy the Cowboys	\$3,000,000
Cost of buying Texas Stadium Corporation	\$20,000,000
Total	\$34,200,000

Explain why it was not a wash deal, with the costs and benefits roughly balancing. How would you value the construction of luxury boxes?

8.5 In 2023, a newspaper reporter interviewed a finance professor about the Southern California real estate market. How would you answer each of these three questions?

a. "The stock market averages 10% a year. Shouldn't people rent instead of buying since home prices aren't going up 10% a year?"

b. "If you are going to buy real estate in an established community, isn't vacant land a better investment than developed real estate since there is less of it?"

c. "Isn't it better to be a landlord than a homeowner?"

8.6 Give persuasive counter-arguments to these arguments by prominent economists:

a. Indianapolis is a terrible place to buy a house, since housing prices only go up 2% to 3% a year.

b. The fact that housing prices have risen faster than construction costs shows that housing prices are too high.

c. The record level of the Case-Shiller index of housing prices shows that this is a bad time to buy a house.

8.7 Will Rogers once advised, "Buy land; they ain't making any more of it." Would a value investor agree?

8.8 An economist observed that, "Insurance companies tend to be leveraged at between 10 and 20 to 1 for life companies and 4 or 5 to 1 for casualty companies." If you were assigned to estimate the leverage ratio for a company, which of these data would you use and how: sales, before-tax profits, after-tax profits, assets, liabilities, net worth, stock price?

8.9 How much leverage would you have if you made a \$40,000 down payment and borrowed \$280,000 in order to buy a \$320,000 house?

8.10 The most popular way of determining whether a rental property is fairly priced is to calculate the property's capitalization rate ("cap rate"), which is the annual net after-tax income divided by the property's price. For example, a property priced at \$400,000 with \$40,000 net income would have a cap rate of 10%. A prospective buyer can then compare this property's cap rate to those for other properties and to interest rates. What absolutely crucial financial consideration is overlooked in this analysis. Give a numerical example to illustrate your argument.

8.11 Give a logical explanation for this observation by a respected radio and television financial editor: "Generally, the stock market does well when housing starts are up."

8.12 A *Wall Street Journal* writer made the following argument:

> Suppose, for a second, that two traders on a desert island had access to every statistic and piece of information in the world economy, except for the price of gold and of other precious metals. If asked to estimate the price of gold, they wouldn't have the slightest clue.... But equities are different. Two shipwrecked security analysts, stocked with information but isolated from the chatter of Wall Street, could put reasonable values on most stock prices most of the time.

Explain why investors can put a reasonable value on stocks but not on gold.

8.13 Charles de Vaulx, a self-described value investor, explained why 7% of his fund's assets were invested in gold bullion: "My final thought on gold is that we are value investors, after all, so why would we want to own something that has gone up sevenfold since July 2001? And I think the paradox with gold is that even though the price has gone up so much, it is still under-owned." What would a true value investor say in reply?

8.14 Why do you suppose Warren Buffett has never liked gold as an investment?

8.15 In 2022, a newly hired professor had to decide whether to rent or buy a house to live in. This professor expects to live in the house for the rest of her life. If she rents this house, the monthly rent is $3,000 and includes heat, electricity, and all utilities. If she buys this house, the price is $400,000. With a $100,000 down payment, the monthly mortgage payments are $2,201.29 on a 30-year 8% mortgage, and the monthly taxes, insurance, utilities, and maintenance are $1,000—giving a total monthly cost of $3,201.29. Thus, she concluded that she is better off renting. Identify three extremely important errors in this analysis (other than ignoring the tax deductibility of certain expenses).

8.16 Explain why you either agree or disagree with this advice from Peter Lynch, the legendary manager of Fidelity's Magellan Fund:

> Because of leverage, if you buy a $100,000 house for 20 percent down and the value of the house increases by five percent a year, you are making a 25 percent return on your down payment.

8.17 A widely circulated 2023 Zillow report concluded that the nationwide average "time it takes to make a profit on a home purchase" is 13.5 years. *Fortune* magazine's report on this conclusion was titled, "Housing market affordability is so bad that Zillow says it will take you 13.5 years to break even on a purchase from July onward." Zillow's "time it takes to make a profit" calculation is an estimate of the number of years required for homebuyers to sell their home for more than they paid for it, taking into account mortgage interest, maintenance, and closing costs. Why is this calculation a misleading gauge of the time it takes to make a profit on a home purchase?

8.18 On June 13, 2023, financial guru Grant Cardone said that, "Buying a home without a doubt is the WORST investment people can make." A Yahoo Finance news story explained:

> He gave the example of spending $576,000 on a home that you keep for 10 years. On top of that huge total, Cardone said you'd also have to pay the following fees over a decade:
>
> - 12%, or $69,120, in broker fees;
> - 10%, or $57,600, in maintenance fees;
> - 20%, or $115,200, in property taxes; and
> - 70%, or $403,200, in interest to the bank
>
> Those additional costs add up to $645,120 — and when added to the original price of the home ($576,000), brings the total to a staggering $1,221,120.
>
> "A $576,000 home will have to be sold for $1.2 million in 10 years—you're not going to sell it for that—to break even."

Cardone recommended that people instead rent and use the $100,000 they would have used for a down payment to invest in residential real estate that generates rental income.

Identify several problems with this analysis.

8.19 Ms. Anderson had been renting a house for $600/month, when her landlord offered to sell her the house for $90,000. She considered putting $20,000 down and borrowing $70,000 with a conventional 30-year, mortgage at 10%, giving her monthly payments of $641.30. Since this exceeded her monthly rent, she decided to continue renting. Explain why her approach, comparing the monthly mortgage payments with the rent, is flawed in that it can advise her to buy when she should rent, and vice versa. Suggest a better simple rule of thumb.

8.20 A *Fortune* article about renting versus buying a home gave this example:

> [The Olsons] crunched a few numbers. This time they decided to rent—and they're saving a bundle. For $2,350 a month, they have a four-bedroom, 2,100-square-foot home. If they were to purchase that same home today for $700,000 (the going rate for a similar home in the neighborhood), the monthly payment on a 30-year, $630,000 mortgage at 6.1% would run them more than $3,800."

What numbers would you crunch?

8.21 A seasoned investor gave a talk on investing in apartment buildings and used this example of an investment he had made: I want a 10% return on my investment. I have $800,000 to invest and will borrow

$3,640,760 at 8% for 25 years in order to buy a $4,440,760 apartment building with 20 units, each of which can be rented for $2,333 a month. My monthly mortgage payments will be $28,100, and my other monthly expenses will be $11,900. Therefore I will make $80,000 a year, which is a 10% return on my investment:

	Annual Income and Expenses
Rent (12x20x$2,333)	$560,000
Mortgage (12x$2,810)	–$337,200
Other expenses (12x$11,900)	–$142,800
Net	$80,000

Explain why, even neglecting tax considerations, the return is not 10%. Do you think that the actual return is more likely to be higher or lower than 10%? (You do not need to check any of the numbers.)

8.22 An analysis of the first-year income and expenses for a commercial real estate property that was purchased for $5 million in 2019 with a $1 million down payment found that the net profit was negative:

Rent	$540,000
Loan payments (15 years @ 6%)	–$405,048
Property Taxes (1% annually)	–50,000
Insurance	–40,000
Maintenance	–50,000
Total	–$5,048

Assuming that the property is never sold, why do you expect the net profit to turn positive in the future?

8.23 When a nationwide firm, like Century 21 or Coldwell Banker, acquires a local real estate company, it typically pays five times EBIDTA (earnings before interest, taxes, depreciation, and amortization), which is a measure of the company's cash flow. Suppose that reported EBIDTA is the correct and accurate measure of cash flow; specifically, EBIDTA hasn't been affected by accounting tricks or unusual events. Identify the most important reason why it isn't reasonable to use

a. a constant multiple over time
b. the same multiple for different firms even if they are equally risky.

8.24 In 1986, a columnist bemoaned the tax breaks that are given to real estate investments: "In general, generous tax breaks for rental and owner-occupied housing have not served to make housing more affordable or to increase the supply. Most of the value of these breaks has simply been capitalized into higher prices for land and existing structures." Explain why high market prices either should or should not influence housing construction.

8.25 An investor was interested in acquiring a commercial office building in 2014. She estimated that the annual after-tax cash flow was $800,000, and she predicted that this cash flow would increase by 5% annually forever. Using a 15% discount rate, she applied a "capitalization rate" of 10, giving the property a value of 10($800,000) = $8,000,000.

a. Where did the value 10 for the capitalization rate come from?

b. How would her valuation be affected if she planned on selling the property after 20 years?

8.26 An article in the *American Banker's Association Journal* discussed the estimation of commercial damages when one company's violation of a contract forces another to go out of business. Instead of trying to estimate the failed company's liquidation value, the author argued that a company with current net earnings of $50,000 growing at 5% a year would, at a 25% discount rate, have a "capitalization rate" of 5, giving it a value of 5($50,000) = $250,000. Where did the value 5 for the capitalization rate come from? The author went on to argue that, "It is common for appraisers in lawsuits to use a capitalization rate that is based on broad industry norms ... This method should be used with caution." Why?

8.27 A developer constructed an apartment building in 2015 based on these assumptions: construction cost = $12 million cash; annual net income = $800,000, growing at 5% a year; and 10% annual required rate of return. The developer calculated the net present value (NPV) two ways: (a) assuming that the building will be held forever and (b) assuming it will be sold after 10 years for a price reflecting a 10% required return. Which calculation gave a higher NPV? Assume, for simplicity, that the income is collected annually, beginning 1 year after the construction cost is paid.

8.28 When does an asset have two IRRs? (Be sure to define IRR.)

8.29 Explain the error in this passage in a textbook co-authored by two prominent finance professors, one an economics Nobel laureate. Use a realistic example to explain your reasoning:

> If the [IRR] is higher than the opportunity cost of capital [the required return], then we know that the NPV at the opportunity cost of capital itself must be positive.

8.30 The owner of a soccer team is considering converting hundreds of stadium seats to luxury boxes. The construction and sale of the luxury boxes will net a $100 million profit; however, the lost stadium seats will reduce future revenue by $12 million in the first year, growing by 8% annually. If the lost revenue is annual, beginning 1 year after the

$100 million profit from the construction and sale of the boxes, then the internal rate of return (IRR) is 20%. Show how the IRR was calculated. Does this mean that the project is profitable if the owner's IRR is less than 20%?

8.31 In 2010, $20 million was spent to refurbish the Empire State Building, including the replacement of 6,500 windows with energy-efficient windows. It was estimated that this refurbishing would reduce energy usage by 38% and save $4.4 million in energy costs in the year after the project was completed. Make a rough estimate of the long-run annual rate of return from this $20 million investment.

8.32 A professor noted that businesses are advised to gauge projects by discounting the dollar cash flow by nominal interest rates or, equivalently, by discounting the real cash flow by real interest rates. He argued that the latter option simplifies matters because real cash flows are easier to forecast than nominal flows (which depend on unknown rates of inflation) and real interest rates are approximately equal to zero. As evidence of the latter, he cited the fact that during the years 1948–1978, the average value of the long-term AAA corporate bond rate was approximately equal to the average annual rate of inflation. Why might you, as your business's chief financial officer, hesitate to follow this professor's advice?

8.33 Show mathematically:

a. The real, inflation-adjusted rate of return on an investment is approximately equal to the nominal rate of return minus the rate of inflation.

b. The present value of a payment of $1 a year from now, discounted by a nominal rate of return, is equal to the real value of that payment discounted by the real rate of return.

8.34 Project 1 has an initial cost of $100 and generates profits of $10 a year, forever, beginning 1 year from now. Project 2 has an initial cost of $200 and generates profits of $15 a year, forever, beginning 1 year from now.

a. What is Project 1's IRR?

b. What is Project 2's IRR?

c. Which project (if any) should you choose if your required rate of return is 3%?

8.35 In summer 1987, a group bought 13 acres with 1100 feet of beachfront on Martha's Vineyard, a Massachusetts island. This group sold shares for $25,000 each that enabled the purchaser to use this beach forever. If we let X be the annual fee that a person would pay to use the beach and assume that X increases by 5% a year, for what value of X does a price of $25,000 imply a 15% required return?

8.36 Consider a newly incorporated firm that spends $1 million to purchase a farm that yields $80,000 in profits each year, net of all expenses, including taxes. If the shareholders' required return is 12%, what is the size of the annual economic value added? If this annual economic value added is negative, is the value of the firm negative?

8.37 An accessory dwelling unit (ADU) is a secondary housing unit on a single-family residential lot. It might be a newly constructed detached structure, an addition to the main house, or a converted garage, basement, or other part of the house. In 2024, Newport Beach city officials estimated that an ADU would increase the value of a property by 100 times the monthly rent; for example, an ADU that rents for $1,500/month increases the property value by $150,000. How would you assess whether a Newport Beach ADU that rents for $3,000 a month is financially advantageous?

8.38 Consider two investments, A and B, each with a current price of $8. A will pay $4 every year, forever, beginning today; B will pay $6 every year, beginning 1 year from today. For each of these investment criteria, which investment is more attractive?

a. payback period
b. internal rate of return
c. net present value

8.39 Century-Minus-One Village is a complex of condominiums, which legally reverts back to the developer after 99 years. Assume that each unit yields its owner a constant real annual income of $2,000 (rent savings net of repairs and maintenance fees) beginning 1 year after purchase and is priced in the real estate market to yield a 5% real annual return. Roughly sketch the market price over the first 200 years.

8.40 In South Korea, people who rent property do not pay rent but instead pay a deposit called *jeonse* equal to from 50% to 90% of the property's value. At the end of the lease (typically two years), the landlord returns the deposit. How would you calculate the landlord's annual return, assuming that landlord pays cash for the property and rents it in a 1-year lease with a 70% deposit? (Assume that the tenant pays for utilities and maintenance expenses.) If there were no *jeonse*, what annual rent would the landlord have to charge in order to make the same rate of return?

Answers

8.1 This criterion ignores the time value of money and also ignores the cash flow beyond the payback period when the cumulative yen in covers the cumulative yen out.

8.2 The value of an enterprise is the present value of the cash flow it generates, not the present value of its debts. Is a company with no debt worthless? Is a company with no assets and \$1 billion in debt worth \$1 billion?

8.3 An asset is valued for its potential cash flow, not its cost. A tomato farm on Mount Everest may cost billions, but is worth pennies.

8.4 It is true that these five costs add up to almost \$35 million but there are two main problems that make this list a comparison of apples, oranges, and bananas. First, some items are one-time expenses and others are annual expenses. Second, the cost of buying the Texas Stadium Corporation and the interest on the money borrowed to buy the Cowboys are sunk costs that are irrelevant to an analysis of the luxury boxes.

When Bright first bought the team, he may have considered the possibility of putting in luxury boxes but, now that he has the team, all that matters for the luxury-box decision is the additional income and expenses.

We don't know the exact timing but let's assume that the sale of the boxes minus the cost, including the fee to Irving is immediate: \$35,000,000 – \$8,000,000 – \$2,800,000 = \$24,200,000 and that the \$400,000 lost ticket revenue begins a year later and grows at an annual rate g. The net present value (NPV) is

$$\text{NPV} = \$24,200,000 - \frac{\$400,000}{R-g}$$

$$> 0 \text{ if } R - g > \frac{\$400,000}{\$24,200,000} = .0165$$

This can be written as $g < R - .0165$ and is likely true. For example, $g < .0835$ if $R = .10$ and $g < .1335$ if $R = .15$.

8.5 Here are the answers that the finance professor gave:

a. Part (perhaps most) of the financial return from owning a home is the rent saving.

b. The intrinsic value of an asset is the cash it generates. Vacant land has a negative cash flow—property taxes. Vacant land is speculation, not value investing.

c. It might be better to be both! If you buy a home and must choose between living in it and renting it out, the tax laws are much more favorable for owner-occupied housing than for rental properties.

8.6 a. We should consider the rent savings, too.

b. Housing prices also depend on land values.

c. We need to take into account the rent savings and interest rates, which may also be at record levels.

8.7 No matter what the price? The value of an asset should be judged not by its scarcity, but by the cash and services it provides. Are beat-up soccer shoes that aren't being made anymore an attractive investment at $100,000 a pair?

8.8 The appropriate leverage estimate is the ratio of the firm's assets to its net worth.

8.9 Leverage = assets/equity = 320,000/40,000 = 8/1

8.10 As with stocks, the intrinsic value depends critically on the anticipated growth of the income. The example in the question is worth more if the income increases by 10% a year than if it increases by 5%, or doesn't increase at all.

8.11 The stock market and housing starts both depend on the same macroeconomic variables: interest rates and the strength of the economy.

8.12 As the author explains:

> Gold has value, due to its scarcity, beauty, durability and status as a historic currency-cum-inflation hedge, but the worth of those are indeterminate. Even if you knew how many people were likely to be fearful of inflation, that wouldn't tell you how much to pay for an ounce. And if people, including central bankers, wake up tomorrow and decide that it is overvalued, there is no court of appeal, no intrinsic yardstick, to fall back on. As an investment, it's sheer speculation.

He goes on to explain that, in contrast, a company's earnings can be used to estimate the intrinsic value of a share of stock.

8.13 Gold generates no income, so it has no intrinsic value. The argument that "it is still under-owned" sounds very much like the greater fool theory. (This interview took place right when gold was at a peak of $1,900/ounce. The price fell 40% over the next 3 years.)

8.14 Value investors don't like gold because it generates no income. Here is what Buffett said in a 1998 speech at Harvard: "It [gold] gets dug out of the ground in Africa, or someplace. Then we melt it down, dig another hole, bury it again and pay people to stand around guarding it. It has no utility. Anyone watching from Mars would be scratching their head."

8.15 This analysis ignores these four important points: the $100,000 down payment has an opportunity cost; the monthly mortgage payments include principal as well as interest; the mortgage payments will stop after 30 years, but the rent will not; and the rent and some expenses will grow over time.

8.16 The 25% return calculation ignores the interest on the mortgage. If you borrow at, say 5%, to invest at 5%, your rate of return is 5%. The calculation also ignores the fact that the house provides either rent or shelter.

8.17 Where are the rent savings? The biggest benefit from buying a home is that homeowners don't have to pay monthly rent. Housing affordability is all about whether it is cheaper to buy or rent a place to live—and Zillow completely ignores it.

8.18 He ignores the rent savings, mortgage payments, and the time value of money. Some of Cardone's assumptions are debatable; for example, 12% in broker fees (apparently 6% when buying and 6% when selling) and a 2% annual property tax. Also, because of tax laws, it is generally more profitable to buy a home to live in than to rent to others.

8.19 By her reasoning (comparing mortgage payments to rent), a house is always a good buy if you pay cash (and have no mortgage payments). She also ignores the tax deductibility of interest and the fact that rents will increase in the future. She should compare the present value of the cash flow (rent saving minus after-tax mortgage payments and other expenses) with the down payment. The constant-dividend-growth model $P = D/(R - g)$ suggests a rule of thumb: buy if $D/P + g > R$, where D is her initial net cash flow, P is her down payment, and R is her required rate of return.

8.20 The Olsons are ignoring the fact that rents will increase over time while mortgage payments will not and that the interest portion of their mortgage payment may be tax-deductible. They also left out property taxes, insurance, and maintenance expenses.

8.21 Rents will probably not be constant during the investment, and the building may also appreciate in value. Even if rents are constant and the value of the building does not change, the investor will make more than a 10% return because the mortgage payments include principal as well as interest. At the end of 25 years, the investor will own a \$4,440,760 building with no debt, in addition to the 10% annual income from the rent.

A reasonable way to calculate the implicit rate of return is to equate the present value of the cash flow to the initial \$800,000 investment. For simplicity, using annual amounts with rent paid at the beginning of each year, rent growing at a constant rate g, and the market value of the apartment building growing at a rate h:

$$\$800,000 = \$80,000 + \frac{\$80,000(1+g)^1}{(1+R)^1} + \frac{\$80,000(1+g)^2}{(1+R)^2} + \ldots + \frac{\$80,000(1+g)^{24}}{(1+R)^{24}} + \frac{\$4,440,760(1+h)^{25}}{(1+R)^{25}}$$

Even if g and h both equal 0, the implied rate of return is 13.2%, which is higher than 10%. Since g and h are both likely to be positive, the implied return is even higher.

8.22 Rent should increase over time, while mortgage payments are constant and will stop when the mortgage is paid off.

8.23 The valuation should depend on (a) interest rates and (b) how fast the cash flow is projected to grow.

8.24 As with Tobin's q, high market prices relative to construction costs make it profitable to build houses.

8.25 a. She is using the constant-dividend-growth model:

$$P = \frac{D}{R - g} = \frac{\$800{,}000}{.15 - .05} = 10(\$800{,}000) = \$8{,}000{,}000$$

The value of 10 for the capitalization rate comes from 1/(R – g) = 1/(.15 – .05) = 10.

b. The current value is not affected by her selling the property for an amount equal to the present value of the cash flow at the time she sells. If this is not true, the current value would be somewhat higher or lower.

8.26 Using the constant-growth dividend discount model,

$$P = \frac{D}{R - g} = \frac{\$50{,}000}{.25 - .05} = 5(\$50{,}000) = \$250{,}000$$

The capitalization rate comes from 1/(R – g) = 1/(.25 – .05) = 5. Cap rates should be used with caution because companies have different growth rates and are not equally risky.

8.27 The two approaches give the same NPV. The present-value model is internally consistent in that the value of the asset when it is sold is equal to the value of the asset if it is not sold. In general, holding an asset for k years:

$$V_0 = \frac{X_1}{(1+R)^1} + \frac{X_2}{(1+R)^2} + \ldots + \frac{X_k}{(1+R)^k} + \frac{X_{k+1}}{(1+R)^{k+1}} + \frac{X_{k+2}}{(1+R)^{k+2}} + \ldots$$

$$= \frac{X_1}{(1+R)^1} + \frac{X_2}{(1+R)^2} + \ldots + \frac{X_k}{(1+R)^k} + \left(\frac{1}{(1+R)^k}\right)\left[\frac{X_{k+1}}{(1+R)^1} + \frac{X_{k+2}}{(1+R)^2} + \ldots\right]$$

$$= \frac{X_1}{(1+R)^1} + \frac{X_2}{(1+R)^2} + \ldots + \frac{X_k}{(1+R)^k} + \left(\frac{1}{(1+R)^k}\right)V_k$$

The first line in the above equation is the present value of the asset if it is held forever. The third line is the present value if it is held for k years and then sold for a price V_k equal to the present value of the income that it will generate after year k. These are equal. The original owner might gain or lose from selling if the sale price is not equal to his or her present value of the future income. Here, V = D/(R – g) = \$800,000/(.10 – .05) = \$16,000,000, giving an NPV of \$16,000,000 – \$12,000,000 = \$4,000,000.

8.28 The IRR is the required return for which the net present value (NPV) equals 0. An asset can have two IRRs when there are two sign changes in the cash flow. For example, an asset that has this cash flow: –\$100 now, +\$100 after 1 year, +\$100 after 2 years, +\$100 after 3 years, and –\$225 after 4 years, has IRRs at 15.5% and 40.9%:

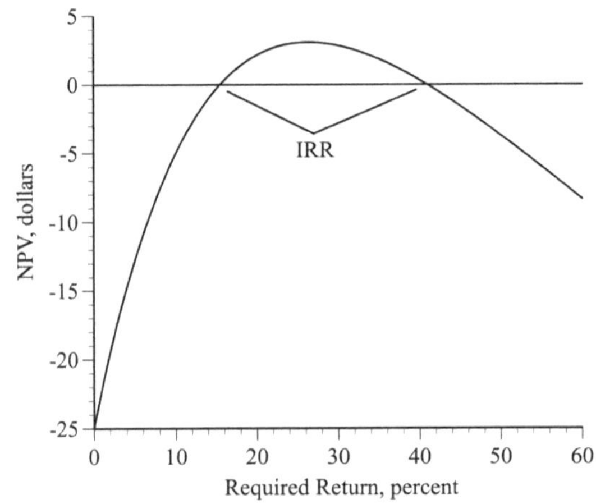

8.29 An IRR is a required return for which the net present value (NPV) is zero. It doesn't tell us if the NPV is positive or negative for other values of the required return. Consider, for example, an initial \$1,000,000 cash receipt, followed by payments of \$100,000 every year thereafter. This might be the sale of farmland that generates \$100,000 in profits each year. This has an IRR of 10%, but the NPV is negative for any required return less than 10%.

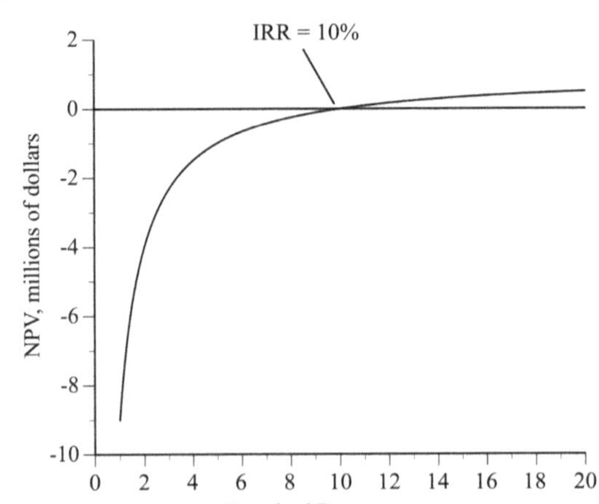

8.30 The IRR is the value of the required return for which the net present value (NPV) is equal to 0. Here,

$$0 = \$100 - \frac{\$12}{(1+R)} - \frac{\$12(1.08)}{(1+R)^2} - \frac{\$12(1.08)^2}{(1+R)^3} - \ldots$$

$$0 = \$100 - \frac{\$12}{R-.08}$$

$$R = .08 + \frac{\$12}{\$100}$$

$$R = .20$$

The IRR does not tell us whether the NPV is positive or negative for other required returns. Here, the NPV is *negative* for required returns that are less than the 20% IRR:

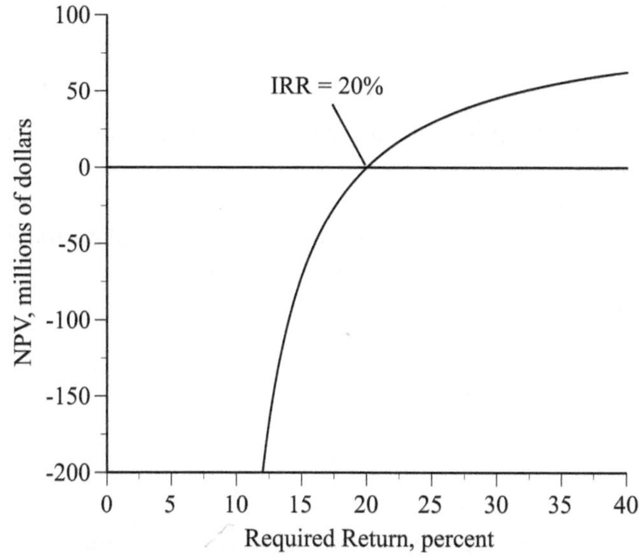

8.31 Using the constant-dividend-growth model, a reasonable return estimate is D/P + g = \$4.40/\$20 + g = .22 + g, where g is the long-run annual rate of growth of energy costs.

8.32 In deciding between investing in a project or corporate bonds, the appropriate real required return for the project depends on the real rates of return available now on corporate bonds, not some average of past returns.

8.33 Let P_0 = the current price level, P_1 = the price level a year from now, $\pi = (P_1 - P_0)/P_0$ = the rate of inflation, R = the nominal return, and r = the real return.

a. In nominal terms, an investment of X will grow to X(1 + R) 1 year from now. The real value of X(1 + R) is determined by deflating by the price level a year from now relative to the price level today. The real return is the relative increase in the real value of the investment:

$$\begin{aligned} r &= \frac{\dfrac{X(1+R)}{P_1/P_0} - X}{X} \\ &= \frac{1+R}{P_1/P_0} - 1 \\ &= \frac{1+R}{1+\pi} - 1 \\ &= R - \pi + \frac{\pi(\pi - R)}{1+\pi} \end{aligned}$$

The last term is close to zero for small values of π and $\pi - R$, leaving $r \approx R - \pi$.

b. Using some of the relationships in part (a), the real value of X, discounted by the real rate of return, is equal to the nominal value discounted by the nominal rate of return.

$$\frac{\left(\dfrac{X}{P_1/P_0}\right)}{1+r} = \frac{\left(\dfrac{X}{P_1/P_0}\right)}{\left(\dfrac{1+R}{P_1/P_0}\right)} = \frac{X}{1+R}$$

8.34 We can use the perpetuity formula, V = X/R, where V is the present value, X is the annual cash flow, and R is the annual required rate of return

a. 0 = –\$100 + \$10/IRR implies IRR = \$10/\$100 = .10 (10%)

b. 0 = –\$200 + \$15/IRR implies IRR = \$15/\$200 = .075 (7.5%)

c. NPV1 = –\$100 + \$10/.03 = \$233; NPV2 = –\$200 + \$15/.03 = \$300. The first project has the higher IRR but there is a crossover at R = 5%, where both NPVs are equal to 100, and the second project has the higher NPV at a 3% required return:

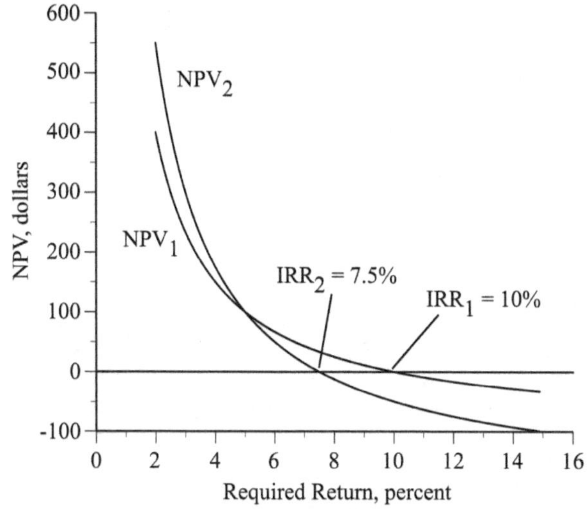

8.35 Using the constant-growth dividend-discount model: $V = X/(R - g)$ implies $X = V(R - g) = \$25,000/(.15 - .05) = \$2,500$.

8.36 The annual economic value added is $80,000 – .12($1,000,000) = –$40,000. If the annual economic value added is negative, then the firm's value is less than the cost of its assets ($1,000,000). Here, the economic value of the firm is $1,000,000 – $40,000/.12 = $666,666.

8.37 We need to list all the cash going in and out, starting with the cost of constructing the ADU. If the ADU costs $150,000 to build, for example, and generates $3,000 in monthly rent, the projected $300,000 increase in the property value is double the construction cost and would give a $150,000 profit if the property were sold immediately after the ADU is built. If the house is not sold, then we should compare the present value of the rent, net of expenses, to the $150,000 construction cost.

Working with annual numbers beginning 1 year from today, if the annual rent net of expenses is $15,000, growing at 3% a year, then the present value is $15,000/(R – .03). The breakeven required return is 13%. For any required return below 13%, the present value of the rental income exceeds the construction cost of the ADU.

8.38 Project A is better using the payback period and IRR criteria, but Project B is best using NPV for any required return less than 50%:

a. The payback periods are 1 year for A and 2 years for B

b. Using the perpetuity formula, $NPV_A = -8 + 4 + 4/R$ and A's IRR is 100%. For B, $NPV_B = -8 + 6/R$, and B's IRR is .75 (75%).

c. Using the NPVs in Part (b), $NPV_B > NPV_A$ if $R < .50$ (50%).

Here is a graph:

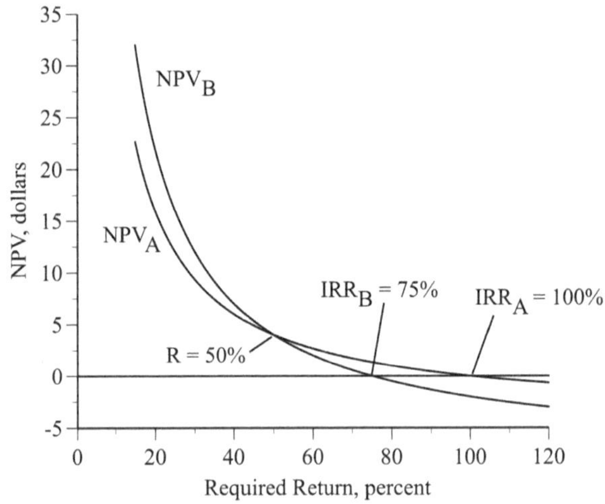

8.39 The present value during the first 99 years is equal to the real cash flow discounted by the real required return:

$$V = \frac{\$2,000}{1.05^1} + \frac{\$2,000}{1.05^2} + \ldots + \frac{\$2,000}{1.05^n}$$
$$= \frac{\$2,000}{.05}\left(1 - \frac{1}{1.05^n}\right)$$

where n is the number of years remaining until the condominium reverts back to the developer. After 99 years, the condo is a perpetuity with present value V = \$2,000/.05 = \$40,000. Here is a sketch:

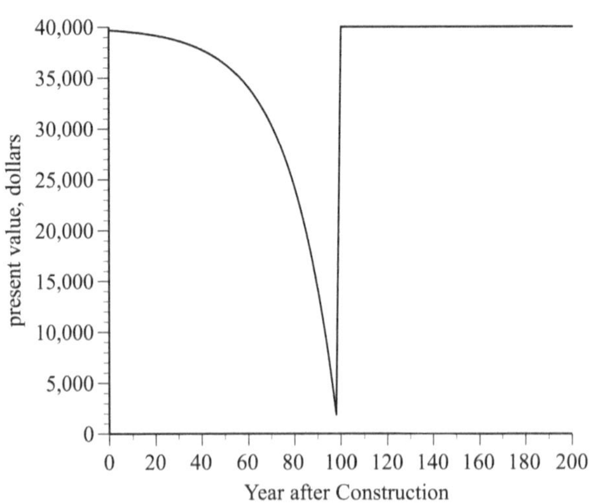

8.40 Let P = price of property, D = deposit = .7P, g = annual rate of increase in property's value, and R = annual rate of return on invested deposit. The landlord's future value after 1 year is P(1 + g) + D(1 + R) – D. The annual return S is:

$$P(1+S) = P(1+g) + D(1+R) - D$$

$$1+S = 1+g+\frac{D}{P}R$$

$$S = g + .7R$$

If the property were instead rented, the return would be the increase in the value of the property (g) plus the rent net of expenses. Therefore, the ratio of the annual net rent to the property's price would have to be .7R or higher. For example, with a $1,000,000 property, and a 5% return on the invested deposit, the net annual rent would have to be at least .7(.05)($1,000,000) = $35,000 ($2,917/month).

9

Conservation of Value

9.1 Critically evaluate this argument by a finance professor, writing in the *Harvard Business Review*, that stock dividends are real events and they are bad:

> What about stock dividends, which are theoretically used as a way of sharing profits while conserving cash? ... As I see it, the trouble with this approach is that shares outstanding increase at a compound rate. It's a 5% stock dividend this year, but next year it's 5% of 105, and so forth. This pattern holds down growth in earnings per share.

9.2 In the *Red Oaks* television show, one character gives a hot tip based on insider information to an employee who wants to make enough money in the stock market to buy a boat: "Rumor has it Galexa's stock is going to split by the end of the year, so you can get yourself a whole fleet of boats." Why are you skeptical?

9.3 Respond to this dialogue from the *Sopranos* television show. Carmela has been nagging Tony to buy a stock. Finally, Tony says, "Let's buy that stock." Carmela makes a face: "It split. It's too late, we missed it."

9.4 A *Business Week* article was entitled "How to Double Your Shares Without Spending a Dime." The secret was to buy a stock that splits 2-for-1. What's the catch?

9.5 The *Get Rich Investment Guide*, published by Consumers Digest, discusses the fact that an investor who buys a stock ex-dividend doesn't receive the latest dividend: "Obviously, one strategy is to know when the stock will go ex-dividend and buy a day or two before the cutoff. Then you can receive the dividends, and you can sell the shares as soon as you have [received the dividend]." What is the flaw in this strategy?

9.6 Explain the flaw in this investment strategy touted by a *Los Angeles Times* financial writer:

> Stockholders and investors often like to buy just before an ex-dividend date to capture an additional payment. For example, if you buy shares two days before an ex-dividend day and hold them for a year and one day, you should qualify for five dividend payments, not the four that holding shares for a year usually permits.

9.7 The only time Berkshire Hathaway paid a dividend was $.10/share in 1967, which Warren Buffett later described as "a terrible mistake." Yet, Berkshire repurchased $74 billion worth of its stock during the 5-year

 DOI: 10.1201/9781003630166-9

period, 2019–2023. How would you explain the fact that Berkshire repurchases its stock but is loath to pay dividends?

9.8 Legendary fund manager Peter Lynch wrote that, "If a company buys back half its shares and its overall earnings stay the same, the earnings per share have just doubled.".

a. Why don't all companies follow this advice and buy back half their shares?

b. Why don't all companies double their earnings per share by declaring 1-for-2 stock splits?

9.9 A *Washington Times* writer observed that

> The money center banks are highly profitable indeed. Bankers Trust's $371.2 million 1985 profit set a record, and for the seventh year in a row the bank was able to raise its cash dividend, then send its shareholders one share of stock for each one they owned.

Why does the bank's profitability have little to do with its ability to send shareholders one share of stock for each one they own? How much are these extra shares worth to stockholders?

9.10 Circle the correct words in each of the three bracketed parts of this quotation from a famed investor:

> Firms that commanded [high/low] price-to-earnings ratios could purchase firms with [higher/lower] P/Es because in an equity exchange the buyer's earnings per share increased. But the reverse transaction was anathema in the boardroom because it lowered earnings per share. This was the height of naiveté, since the combined firms were [worth more if the first firm did the acquiring/ worth more if the second firm did the acquiring/worth exactly the same no matter who did the acquiring].

9.11 A *Wall Street Journal* editorial criticized the myopic focus of many corporate executives on earnings per share:

> A lot of executives believe that if they can figure out a way to boost reported earnings, their stock prices will go up even if the higher earnings do not represent any underlying economic change. In other words, the executives think they are smart and the market is dumb.... The market is smart. Apparently the dumb one is the corporate executive caught up in the earnings-per-share mystique.

A management-consulting handbook printed this editorial and then stated that, "Unfortunately, our experience shows that many corporate managers still worship earnings per share, and thus are still betting that the market is dumb." Identify two different management policies that boost earnings per share, but should not increase (and may even decrease) shareholder wealth. (Do not use mindless speculation or fraudulent accounting as examples.) Explain your reasoning.

9.12 Explain the flaw in this financial writer's argument:

> Here's a sneaky one: A number of major corporations in recent years have announced programs for buying their own stocks, especially at times when the prices of those stocks were depressed.... Now, on the surface, an investor might think that this is a splendid confirmation of his own fine judgment; after all, if the corporation itself is buying its stock, it must augur great things to come, right? Well, maybe, but don't count on it. It could be a device to increase earnings per share. When those shares come into the company's treasury, there are that many fewer shares outstanding—so the same amount of earnings will produce higher earnings per share.

9.13 Critically evaluate this 2012 analysis by the finance blogger at Reuters,

> Buybacks are considered a good thing, on the stock market.... [T] hey reduce the number of shares outstanding, which means that the value of the remaining shares goes up: the company is worth the same amount, so the value per share is higher.

9.14 Explain why you either agree or disagree with this investment advisor's argument in a piece titled, "Share Repurchase vs. Dividend: It's a No Brainer," that dividends are better than share repurchases:

> Although some may think that a company paying dividends is a weakness, showing that the company needs to entice investors to invest in the company, dividend payments are much more profitable to investors than company buybacks are.... Dividends allow shareholders the opportunity to invest back into the company. Many long-term investors choose to automatically reinvest their dividends into additional company shares, and most major companies ... make this process easy.

9.15 On Monday, October 27, 2003, Bank of America agreed to buy FleetBoston Financial in an all-stock merger, with Fleet shareholders receiving .5553 BofA common shares for each of their shares. At the time, Fleet had 1.05 billion shares outstanding and BofA had 1.49 billion shares outstanding. The preceding Friday, FleetBoston stock closed at $31.80, and BofA stock closed at $81.86. On the day the merger was announced, FleetBoston stock closed at $39.2 and BofA stock closed at $73.57. Explain this observation by an analyst at CreditSights: "The market feels that BofA is overpaying and may be destroying more value than it creates through cost savings."

9.16 Company A's stock is selling for $60/share and Company B's stock is selling for $30/share. Company A acquires Company B by giving each B shareholder one share of A stock for two shares of B. Earnings are unaffected, in that earnings after the acquisition are equal to the sum of the two companies' pre-merger earnings, yet A's earnings/share drop after the acquisition. How did this happen?

9.17 Consider these two companies:

	Company A	Company B
Total revenue (millions)	25	50
Operating expenses (millions)	10	20
Taxes (millions)	5	10
Net after-tax income (millions)	10	20
Dividends (millions), D	4	8
Retained earnings (millions)	6	12
Rate of return on assets, ρ	10%	10%
Shareholders' required return, R	8%	10%
Shares outstanding (millions), n	20	10

Assume that each firm's dividends, earnings, and assets are all growing at a constant rate. Now the two companies merge, with Company A issuing 30 million shares to take over Company B. After the merger, the two companies operate exactly as before, with no synergies, economies of scale, or reorganization.

a. What are Company A's earnings per share before the merger and after the merger?

b. Who gains or loses from the merger?

9.18 Suppose two firms with no debt and these characteristics merge:

	Firm 1	Firm 2
Assets	100	200
Return on assets	20%	20%
Dividend payout	1/2	1/3
Shareholder required return	20%	20%

Explain why the theoretical total value of the post-merger company is or is not equal to 300.

9.19 Here is an excerpt from a case study of EG Corporation in a management consulting firm's handbook:

> What Ralph [the chief executive officer] found was disturbing—and revealing. EG's return to investors had indeed been below the market overall and below the returns for a roughly assembled set of 'comparable' companies. What also stood out from the analysis were a couple of events that had knocked down the value of EG relative to the market. In the period 1980 to 1985, EG had made several acquisitions to establish and build the Woodco furniture businesses. Ralph noticed a decline in EG's share price relative to comparables and the market around the date of each acquisition.

> In fact, when the team calculated the impact of these declines on EG's total value, they realized that the decline in EG's total value was about equal to the dollar amount of the premiums over market price EG had paid to acquire the companies.

a. Under what circumstances would an acquisition have this effect on the wealth of EG shareholders?

b. What do you think happened to the wealth of the target companies' shareholders?

9.20 Here is an excerpt from a case study of EG Corporation in a management consulting firm's handbook:

> EG had sizable and stable free cash flows that could support much higher debt. The Consumerco business, which generated the bulk of the cash, was recession-resistant.... [B]eing considered investment grade or not was irrelevant.... EG could raise $500 million in new debt in the next six months and use the proceeds to repurchase shares or pay a special dividend. This debt would be worth about $200 million in present value to EG's shareholders.

a. Why is it important that EG be recession-resistant?

b. How could shareholders possibly benefit from the issuance of debt that leads to a downgrading of the company's rating from investment grade?

c. How do you suppose the handbook calculated the $200 million additional value for shareholders? (Hint: Assume the debt is an interest-only perpetuity and the firm has a 40% tax rate.)

9.21 Critically evaluate this finance professor's advice (published in the *Harvard Business Review*) for firms wishing to increase earnings per share: "As simple as it seems, stock repurchase for publicly held concerns is another way for management to [increase] earnings per share."

9.22 Explain this argument by a Motley Fool writer about why many tech companies use stock buybacks instead of paying dividends:

> Tech companies have been reluctant to pay dividends for many reasons.... [A] selfish reason may have to do with tech company compensation, which has historically revolved around stock options.

9.23 In January 2020, a *Barron's* associate editor wrote that,

> During its latest fiscal year that ended in September, Apple bought back $67 billion in stock and paid out $14 billion in dividends. The shares, which rose $2.37, or .8%, to $299.80 on Monday, trade just below the record high of $300 set on Jan. 2....
>
> Apple could take a more-balanced approach and double its dividend while cutting back the annual buyback program by $15 billion to around $52 billion. That would result in a 2% dividend yield, in line with that of the S&P 500 index.

What disadvantages do you see from Apple increasing dividends and reducing buybacks?

9.24 It has been proposed that a company's risk exposure be assessed by calculating the ratio of its debt per share to its earnings per share—the higher the ratio, the greater the risk. What problem(s) do you see with this metric?

9.25 Here is an excerpt from a *Wall Street Journal* article:

> Stock buybacks, long a favorite tool for pleasing investors, could be developing some unpleasant side effects. The surge of announced buybacks since the fall has come at the same time that corporate America is issuing record amounts of debt. Some analysts now worry that with profits and sales flat, companies may find themselves ill prepared for an economic downturn.

a. Why do investors generally prefer stock buybacks to dividends?

b. The companies that are issuing debt might not be the same ones that are buying back stock. Would it ever be sensible for a company to issue debt and use the proceeds to buy back stock?

c. Why are flat profits and sales worrisome for such companies?

9.26 If executive compensation is based on how much the company's stock price increases during the next 12 months, rather than total shareholder return during the next 12 months, identify an action that a company's management might take that should make the stock price higher than it would otherwise be 12 months from now without improving shareholder return. (Do not use splits or reverse-splits.) Be sure to define total shareholder return.

9.27 Explain why you either agree or disagree with this answer by a co-manager of Federated Strategic Value Dividend Fund, to the question "Why isn't it better for companies to engage in stock buybacks [instead of paying dividends]?"

> A dollar of dividends, albeit highly taxed, is still a check in the mail. A share repurchase goes off into the ether and never benefits Main Street. It's just money that could've come to you that didn't.

9.28 A company has 50 million shares of common stock outstanding with a current market price of $20 a share. It decides to give its shareholders 50 million warrants, one for each outstanding share of common stock. The warrants have an exercise price of $20 a share; when a warrant is exercised, the warrant holder pays the exercise price to the company, and the company issues a new share of stock. In theory, what should the per-share value of the common stock be if these warrants are issued and immediately exercised? What should the per-share value of the common stock be if the warrants are issued with an exercise price of $10 and immediately exercised?

9.29 Explain the error(s) in this example from a best-selling corporate finance textbook:

Here are recent financial data on Pisa Construction Company:

stock price = \$40
number of shares = 10,000
book value = \$500,000
market value = \$400,000
return on investment = 8%
earnings per share = \$4

Pisa has not performed spectacularly to date. However, it wishes to issue new shares to obtain \$80,000 to finance expansion into a promising market. Pisa's financial advisers think a stock issue is a poor choice because "sale of a stock at a price below book value per share can only depress the stock price and decrease shareholder wealth." To prove this point, they construct the following example: "Suppose 2000 new shares are issued at \$40 and the proceeds invested. Then

$$\begin{aligned} \text{book net worth} &= \$580,000 \\ \text{total earnings} &= .08(\$580,000) = \$46,400 \\ \text{earnings per share} &= \frac{\$46,400}{12,000} = \$3.87 \end{aligned}$$

Thus, EPS declines, book value per share declines, and share price will decline proportionately to \$38.70.

9.30 Explain why you either agree or disagree with this logic in a best-selling corporate finance textbook:

Many companies use stock repurchase to increase earnings per share. For example, suppose that a company is in the following position:

net profit	\$10 million
number of shares	1 million
earnings per share	\$10
price-earnings ratio	20
share price	\$200

The company now repurchases 200,000 shares at \$200 a share. The number of shares declines to 800,000 shares and the earnings per share increase to \$12.50. Assuming the price-earnings ratio stays at 20, the share price must rise to \$250.

9.31 Explain the error(s) in this explanation of stock repurchases in a widely used corporate finance textbook:

[ADC] earned \$4.4 million in 1984, and 50% of that amount, or \$2.2 million, had been allocated for distribution to common shareholders. There were 1.1 million shares outstanding, and the market price was $20 a share. ADC felt that it could use the $2.2 million to repurchase 100,000 of its shares through a tender offer or could pay a cash dividend of $2 a share.

The effect of the repurchase on the EPS and the market price per share of the remaining stock can be determined in the following way:

$$\text{current EPS} = \frac{\text{total earnings}}{\text{number of shares}} = \frac{\$4.4 \text{ million}}{1.1 \text{ million}} = \$4$$

$$\text{P / E ratio} = \frac{\$20}{\$4} = 5$$

$$\text{EPS after repurchase} = \frac{\$4.4 \text{ million}}{1 \text{ million}} = \$4.40$$

$$\text{market price after repurchase} = \frac{\text{P}}{\text{E}}(\text{EPS after repurchase}) = \$22$$

It should be noticed from this example that investors would receive benefits of $2 per share in either case, either in the form of a $2 cash dividend or a $2 increase in the stock price.

9.32 Dividends are paid to those who own the company's shares on the "record date." For instance, the board of directors might declare a $2 dividend to be paid on March 1 to those who own stock on the record date of February 15. To allow for the processing of transactions, the NYSE and most other exchanges stocks use an *ex-dividend* (excluding dividend) date two business days before the record date; those who buy the stock ex-dividend do not receive the dividend.

CRSP has comprehensive data on daily returns for individual stocks. Why do you suppose they record an investor as having received the dividend on the day the stock goes ex-dividend, instead of the day that the investor is actually paid the dividend?

9.33 Since debt creates the possibility of bankruptcy, why do corporations ever borrow? Why not raise all the needed funds through the sale of additional shares of stock?

9.34 John Kenneth Galbraith observed that "all of the takeovers and all of the efforts to avoid takeovers have involved a substitution of debt for equity." How does a company substitute debt for equity? Is there any rational reason why such a substitution would make the company more valuable? What problems are created by the substitution of debt for equity?

9.35 CBA has 1,000,000 shares outstanding and three assets

1. $10,000,000 cash that generates $100,000 in after-tax revenue.
2. Division H with a book value of $10,000,000 that generates $2,000,000 in after-tax revenue.

3. Division L with a book value of $20,000,000 that generates $1,000,000 in after-tax revenue

All of its after-tax revenue is distributed as dividends to its shareholders. If Divisions H and L were stand-alone companies, their after-tax revenue would be discounted at a 10% required return.

a. By the conservation of value principle, what is the total value of CBA per share?
b. What would be the effect on shareholders if the $10,000,000 cash were distributed as a one-time special dividend?
c. What would be the effect on shareholders if Division H were sold for $20,000,000 and the proceeds were distributed as a one-time special dividend?
d. What would be the effect on shareholders if Division L were sold for $10,000,000 and the proceeds were distributed as a one-time special dividend?

9.36 Explain why you agree or disagree with this financial analyst's advice:

> A fast-growing company that can generate the bulk of the funds it needs internally is of course far more desirable than one that must rely heavily on outside borrowing or on the sale of stock, which would dilute the present shareholders' equity.

9.37 Explain why the following conclusion is or is not logically correct:

> If the Modigliani-Miller theorem is true, then monetary policy cannot influence the investment activity of modern American corporations, since the investment decision is independent of the method and hence the cost of financing.

9.38 *The Wall Street Journal* reported that many corporations were repurchasing their shares and noted that one money manager "cautions against buying the stocks of companies that are borrowing money to finance share repurchases." How can shareholders benefit when companies borrow money in order to repurchase their shares?

9.39 In 2014, Time-Warner planned a spin-off of Time, Inc., the publisher of *Time*, *Fortune*, *Sports Illustrated*, *People*, and several other magazines, giving the newly created shares of Time to the existing Time-Warner shareholders. Time's cash flow before interest and taxes was projected to be $524 million in 2014 and to fall by about 7% annually thereafter.

One question was what percentage of Time-Warner's current debt should be given to Time and what percentage should be retained by Time-Warner.

An analysis published in *Fortune* assumed that Time would keep its interest payments equal to a constant percentage (for example, 20%) of its cash flow, which implied that it would have to repay some of its debt as its cash flow declines. The problem, according to *Fortune*, is that the more debt that is given to Time, the more cash it will need to use to pay down its debt and the less it will have for investments in new projects. What is the most important flaw in this analysis?

9.40 Many companies have dividend-reinvestment plans that allow shareholders to specify that their dividends be used to purchase additional shares of stock, newly issued by the company. The shareholders avoid brokerage fees, and the company raises some cash without paying fees to an underwriter. Shareholders still pay taxes on their dividends. Carefully explain why shareholders who take advantage of a dividend-reinvestment plan would prefer that the firm eliminate its dividend altogether and instead repurchase shares.

For concreteness, consider a company with 100 million shares outstanding, valued at $5 apiece, that will either (a) pay a dividend of $1 a share, with half the shareholders reinvesting their dividend; or (b) spend $50 million repurchasing shares. Assume further that there are two shareholders, each owning 50 million shares. Stockholder 1 will participate fully in the dividend reinvestment plan and will not sell shares in the stock repurchase plan. Stockholder 2 will not participate in the dividend reinvestment plan and will sell shares in the stock repurchase plan. Compare how these policies affect each shareholder's wealth and stake in the company.

Answers

9.1 The conservation-of-value principle guides us to the truth. A stock dividend is a nonevent, increasing the number of shares by 5% and reducing the value of each share by 5%. The increase in the number of shares does reduce earnings per share, but has no effect on earnings per shareholder.

9.2 In theory, stock splits are nonevents. If the number of shares doubles, the value of each share is halved.

9.3 If stock splits are so great for shareholders, why don't all companies split their stock? The answer is that stock splits do nothing at all for shareholders beyond possible signaling management confidence in the company. A stock split increases the number of shares, true enough, but it reduces the value of each share proportionately.

9.4 If a stock splits two for one, its price per share will be (approximately) halved.

9.5 As the stock goes ex-dividend, the price of the stock will drop by (approximately) the size of the dividend.

9.6 After the stock goes ex-dividend, the stock's price will drop (approximately) by the size of the dividend.

9.7 Repurchases are a more tax-efficient way to distribute cash to shareholders. Dividends are fully taxable income to shareholders, while repurchases are only taxable for shareholders who choose to sell—and then only taxable to the extent there are realized capital gains.

9.8 a. If a company uses half its assets to buy back half its shares, it is unlikely that its earnings will stay the same. One good reason for not liquidating a company's assets is that they are sufficiently profitable (profit rate greater than shareholders' required return) so that shareholders prefer the company investing on their behalf to receiving funds that they can invest on their own.

b. The conservation-of-value principle implies that a 1-for-2 stock split will, by halving the number of shares, double earnings per share and double the market value of each share; but since each shareholder will have half as many of these twice-as-valuable shares, they are not made any better (or worse off) by this purely cosmetic action.

9.9 A company can always split its stock, regardless of its profitability. According to the conservation of value principle, stockholders do not benefit: they have twice as many shares, but each share is worth half as much as previously.

9.10 The correct quotation is:

> Firms that commanded [high] price-to-earnings ratios could purchase firms with [lower] P/Es because in an equity exchange the buyer's earnings per share increased. But the reverse transaction was anathema in the boardroom because it lowered earnings per share. This was the height of naiveté, since the combined firms were [worth exactly the same no matter who did the acquiring].

9.11 Reinvesting earnings when the profit rate is positive, but less than shareholders' required return boosts earnings (and thus earnings per share), but reduces shareholder wealth. A reverse stock split reduces the number of shares outstanding and so increases earnings per share; however, there is no effect on shareholder wealth, except for the negative effect of the cost of this transaction. Buying a low-P/E company boosts earnings per share; again, there is no effect on shareholder wealth, except for the decrease caused by the cost of the transaction.

9.12 It is unlikely that earnings will be unaffected by the firm liquidating assets to raise cash to buy back shares.

9.13 How could the company be worth the same amount if it has disbursed cash to buy back shares?

9.14 In theory, dividends and share purchases are equally attractive ways of giving cash to shareholders—except that dividends incur higher taxes.

Shareholders who receive dividends and use the money to buy shares are worse off because of the taxes paid on the dividends.

9.15 On Friday, the total market value of the two banks was (1.05 billion)($31.80) + (1.49 billion)($81.86) = $155.36 billion. On Monday, the total market value was (1.05 billion)($39.20) + (1.49 billion)($73.57) = $150.78 billion, a decrease of $4.58 billion.

BofA's .5553 offer was substantially above the Friday price ratio: $31.80/$81.86 = .388. The price of Fleet stock went up, and the price of BofA stock went down because investors believed that BofA overpaid.

9.16 A had a lower P/E than B.

9.17 Each firm retains 60% of earnings and has a growth rate of 6%: $(1-d)\rho = .6(0.10) = .06$. The aggregate market values and per-share prices are:

$$n_A P_A = \frac{D_A}{R_A - g} = \frac{\$4}{.08 - .06} = \$200 \Rightarrow P_A = \frac{\$200}{20} = \$10$$

$$n_B P_B = \frac{D_B}{R_B - g} = \frac{\$8}{.10 - .06} = \$200 \Rightarrow P_B = \frac{\$200}{10} = \$20$$

If firm A issues 30 million shares to take over Firm B, then the new price P is

$$P = \frac{\$200 + \$200}{20 + 30} = \$8$$

The initial and new earnings per share are:

$$E_A = \frac{\$10}{20} = \$.50$$

$$E_B = \frac{\$20}{10} = \$2.00$$

$$E = \frac{\$10}{20} + \frac{\$20}{30} = \$.60$$

a. Company A's earnings per share were $.50 before the merger and $.60 after the merger.

b. Company A's shareholders lose because the stock price drops from $10 to $8. Company B's shareholders gain because they get 3 shares worth $8 each for 1 share worth $20.

9.18 Since each firm's return on assets is equal to the shareholders' required rate of return, each firm's market value is equal to its assets, 100 for Firm 1 and 200 for Firm 2. The conservation-of-value principle tells us that the total value of the merged firms is equal to the sum of the pre-merger values: 100 + 200 = 300.

9.19 a. The handbook explained that, "Evidently, the stock market did not believe that EG would add any value to the acquired business." The conservation-of-value principle implies that a merger that does not create more aggregate cash flow than the two separate companies had before the merger does not increase shareholder wealth. Wealth, therefore, declines by the size of the premium paid.

b. If the acquiring company pays a premium over the market price to acquire a company, then the acquiring company's shareholder wealth drops by the size of the premium. In contrast, the wealth of the shareholders of the target company increases by the size of the premium.

9.20 This exercise has to do with the profitable use of debt as a tax shield.

a. For EG to take on new debt, it is important that the company be recession-resistant so that it is not thrown into bankruptcy by a sudden drop in its cash flow.

b. The issuance of debt, even if it leads to a downgrading of the company's debt rating, can benefit shareholders by shielding a larger portion of the company's profits from taxation.

c. At an interest rate R and a 40% tax rate, an interest-only perpetuity would generate .4(R)($500 million) in annual tax savings. Discounted by R, the present value of these annual tax savings is .4(R)($500 million)/R = $200 million.

9.21 By reducing the number of shares without altering current earnings, the firm does increase current earnings per share, but the cost of the stock repurchase reduces the firm's assets and, therefore, reduces its future earnings. If shares, assets, and earnings decline proportionately, there is no effect on future earnings per share. More generally, the conservation-of-value principle says that firms cannot make shareholders better off by buying stock for what it is worth.

9.22 According to the conservation of value principle, a stock buyback has no effect on a stock's price, while a dividend reduces the price of the stock by the size of the dividend—which would be bad for executives holding stock options.

9.23 Dividends are involuntary, generally taxable events, while buybacks are voluntary and lightly taxed.

9.24 It would be better to compare the ratio of the required debt payments (say, over a year) to the earnings. More generally, the burden of the debt depends on the interest rate on the debt: high-interest debt is worse than low-interest debt. Also, debt is not unambiguously bad in that it can provide a tax shield.

9.25 a. Dividend payments compel shareholders to pay income taxes on the funds distributed by the company. With share repurchases, investors are not compelled to sell and, if they do sell, they will only pay capital gains taxes on the capital gains, if any. Some who sell may even benefit from the favorable tax implications of realizing capital losses.

b. Debt can be an effective tax shield that reduces corporate taxes and consequently increases the funds available for expansion or distribution to the firm's bondholders and stockholders.

c. They may be forced into an expensive bankruptcy if they cannot pay the larger interest payments due on their increased debt.

9.26 The total shareholder return is the dividend yield plus the capital gain

$$\frac{D}{P_0} + \frac{P_1 - P_0}{P_0}$$

The conservation of value principle tells us that dividend payments reduce a stock's price, without affecting total shareholder return. If the firm reduces its dividends, the stock's price should be higher than it would otherwise be, with no change in shareholder return.

9.27 The conservation of value principle says that these are equivalent ways of distributing cash to shareholders, except for tax issues or information asymmetries. The problem with dividends is that shareholders must pay taxes on the dividends. With repurchases, you only have to pay taxes if you sell, and you only pay taxes on the capital gains, not the entire amount of cash received.

9.28 We can use the conservation of value principle. The total market value of the company before the warrant issue is $20(50 million) = $1 billion. If 50 million warrants are issued and exercised at $20 each, the company will receive $1 billion in cash, doubling its assets. Since the number of outstanding shares has doubled, too, there is no change in the per-share value of the stock. If, instead, 50 million warrants are exercised at $10, the company only receives $.5 billion, increasing its assets to $1.5 billion. With 100 million shares outstanding, the value of each falls to ($1.5 billion)/(100 million) = $15.

9.29 The conservation-of-value principle implies that selling shares for their market value is a nonevent. With the infusion of $40(2,000) = $80,000 in cash, the total market value of the company should increase from $400,000 to $480,000—implying a per-share market value of $480,000/12,000 = $40 as before. If they invest this $80,000 in ventures as unattractive as their current operations (with a q of .8), the $80,000 in cash will be converted into a project worth only .8($80,000) = $64,000. In this case, the total market value will be $464,000 and the value per share will be \$464,000/12,000 = \$38.67. However, if they use the \$80,000 to expand into "a promising market," they may be able to convert \$80,000 in cash into a project worth more than \$80,000.

9.30 According to the conservation of value principle, total value after repurchase = \$200 million − \$200(200,000) = \$160 million and the value per share = (\$160 million)/800,000 = \$200. (If the share price rises to \$250, then the total value of the company stays at \$200 million, even though the company has \$40 million less cash.)

9.31 Let's see what the conservation of value says. The total market value is (\$20/share)(1.1 million shares) = \$22 million. If the firm distributes \$2.2 million to shareholders, its total market value will fall to \$22 million − \$2.2 million = \$19.8 million. If the cash is distributed as a dividend, the number of shares is constant. So, the shareholders get a \$2 dividend and the value of their stock falls by \$2 to \$18: \$19.8 million/(1.1 million shares) = \$18. If the cash is distributed as a share repurchase of 100,000 shares at \$22/share, the number of shares falls to 1 million, each with a market value of (\$19.8 million)/(1 million shares) = \$19.8. The firm paid \$2/share(100,000 shares) = \$200,000 more than the shares were worth, and value of the remaining shares dropped by \$200,000/(1 million shares) = \$.20, from \$20 to \$19.80.

It is not true that "investors would receive benefits of \$2 per share in either case, either in the form of a \$2 cash dividend or a \$2 increase in the stock price." With a dividend, shareholders get no benefit—a \$2 dividend, offset by a \$2 price decline. With a share repurchase, shareholders lose because the company paid more than the shares are worth.

The textbook's mistake was to assume that earnings per share and the P/E ratio are both constant.

9.32 The stock price can be expected to drop on the ex-dividend date by the size of the dividend. It would be misleading to show a negative return on that date and a positive return later, when the dividend is paid.

9.33 Debt creates a valuable tax shield. With less taxes paid to the government, there is more cash to distribute to the firm's bondholders and stockholders. Those stockholders who dislike the increased leverage can unlever by buying the firm's debt and equity.

9.34 Firms substitute debt for equity when they issue debt and use the proceeds to buy a target company's shares. The debt creates a tax shield; however, if the company cannot make its debt payments, it will be forced into bankruptcy and lawyers will receive some of the company's assets.

9.35 a. The total value is \$10,000,000 + \$2,000,000/.10 + \$1,000,000/.10 = \$10,000,000 + \$20,000,000 + \$10,000,000 = \$40,000,000. The value per share is \$40,000,000/1,000,000 = \$40.

b. By the conservation-of-value principle, this is a nonevent. Each share receives a $10 dividend but the company's assets fall by $10 million and the price per share falls by $10.

c. By the conservation-of-value principle, this is a nonevent. Each share receives a $20 dividend but the company's assets fall by $20 million and the price per share falls by $20.

d. By the conservation-of-value principle, this is a nonevent. Each share receives a $10 dividend but the company's assets fall by $10 million, and the price per share falls by $10.

9.36 One advantage of outside borrowing is that the tax-deductible interest creates a tax shield, reducing the firm's tax liability. A stock sale doesn't necessarily dilute shareholder equity. If the funds that are raised are invested in sufficiently profitable ventures, the firm's stock price may increase. It is true that there are tax reasons for paying less dividends and retaining more earnings rather than selling stock to raise cash that is used to pay dividends.

9.37 If the Modigliani-Miller theorem is true, the investment decision is independent of the method of financing, but required returns on debt and equity still depend on interest rates. For instance, the Modigliani-Miller theorem implies that the total value of a levered firm would be the same if it were unlevered. Thus, a firm can judge an investment project by asking whether shareholders would value the project at more than its cost—whether, if it were equity financed, the firm could sell enough stock to pay for the cost of the project. These considerations depend critically on shareholders' required rates of return, which are strongly influenced by interest rates and, hence, monetary policy.

9.38 An increase in the debt-equity ratio can create a valuable tax shield.

9.39 By the conservation of value principle, the value of the two separate companies should equal the value of the combined company unless the spin-off of Time changes the total cash flow. More debt for Time means less debt for Time-Warner. Less cash flow for Time after interest, taxes, and debt repayment means more for Time-Warner. Shifting assets or liabilities between these two companies does not directly benefit shareholders.

Perhaps the key issue is whether Time or Time-Warner will have more attractive opportunities for investing this cash flow in new projects.

9.40 A dividend-reinvestment plan forces shareholders to pay taxes on their dividends; a share repurchase does not. A company with 100 million shares outstanding, valued at $5 apiece, has an aggregate market value of $500 million. A $1 dividend will reduce the firm's assets by $100 million, to $400 million, implying a per-share value of $400,000,000/100,000,000 = $4. In place of a share worth $5, stockholders have a share worth $4 plus $1 in dividends, on which they must pay taxes.

If stockholder 1 participates in the dividend-reinvestment plan, the company's assets will increase by $50 million (to $450 million), and the number of shares outstanding will increase by $50,000,000/$4 = 12,500,000, to 112,500,000, implying a per share value of $450,000,000/112,500,000 = $4. These are all nonevents, except for the taxes. Stockholder 1 will own a slightly larger share (62,500,000/112,500,000 = .556) of a somewhat smaller company. Stockholder 2 will have $50 million in cash and own a slightly smaller share of a somewhat smaller company.

If, instead, the firm uses $50 million to repurchase 10 million shares, it will have $450 million in assets (the same as in case (a), with each share worth $450,000,000/9,000,000 = $5, a nonevent. Stockholder 1 does not sell shares and now owns a slightly larger share (50,000,000/90,000,000 = .556) of a somewhat smaller company. Stockholder 2 has $50 million in cash and owns a slightly smaller share of a somewhat smaller company.

10

Technical Analysis

10.1 The Boston Snow (B.S.) indicator uses the presence or absence of snow in Boston on Christmas Eve to predict the direction the stock market will go the following year: "the average gain following snow on the ground was about 80% greater than for years in which there was no snow." How would you explain the success of the B.S. indicator?

10.2 In 1987, the director of economic analysis for the National Association of Realtors said,

> If the rates for fixed-rate loans were to rise to the threshold level of 12% or above, as was the case in 1985, you'd see an extreme shift in behavior. The market buyer psychology would be altered and ARMs [adjustable rate mortgages] would storm back in alarming numbers.

Do you interpret such behavior as a momentum or reaction approach to predicting interest rates?

10.3 Fidelity offers a variety of sector mutual funds, each investing in stocks in only one industry. An independent investment advisory service that specializes in selecting the most attractive of these Fidelity sector funds wrote:

> Our switch rules are simple. Invest in that fund that has been the strongest over the last 39 weeks. Stay with that strongest fund until it falls a full dollar below its 39- week weighted moving average, or more than two funds outrank it by a dollar or more. Then switch to the new strongest fund.

Would you say that this advisory service is a believer in momentum or reaction? Why are you skeptical?

10.4 One of 10 technical indicators regularly reported on the public television show, *Wall Street Week*, gave a buy signal when most stocks had prices that were below their average price over the preceding 10 and 30 weeks. Explain why this is a momentum or reaction interpretation of such data.

10.5 A computer program was advertised that had picked 14 NYSE stocks, 13 of which went up, for a 30% return in 4 months:

> Each disk is valid for only four months. You pay only $199 for the program ... and purchasing the disk entitles you to renew the disk every four months thereafter for the same $199 per disk....

DOI: 10.1201/9781003630166-10

> Our guarantee of satisfaction is very compelling. If, after the four months, you are not satisfied with the program or have not seen it pay for itself many times over, please return it and get a full refund of your $199 investment. You can't lose.

Is it true that this money-back guarantee ensures that you can't lose? Why do you suppose that the disk must be renewed every 4 months? How might an unscrupulous company write a very simple computer program guaranteeing that half of its subscribers will be satisfied during each 4-month period?

10.6 Burton Crane, *New York Times* stock market columnist for 35 years, advised, "Buy stocks when they are making new highs and attracting attention, not when they are down at the bottom and nobody loves them." Is this advice more consistent with the momentum or reaction school?

10.7 Investors sometimes place a "buy stop order" to buy a stock now trading for, say, $26.50 when the market price rises above $30. Why would they want to buy later at $30 when they could buy now at $26.50?

10.8 A JP Morgan study concluded that Donald Trump tweets containing the words *China, billion, products, Democrats,* or *great* had statistically significant effects on 2-year and 5-year Treasury rates. How would you interpret this?

10.9 Believing that changes in the money supply have an effect on the stock market, a prominent monetarist economist (and former chair of the Council of Economic Advisers) found that, neglecting brokerage fees, the following strategy would have given an average capital gain of 6% a year between 1918 and 1964, while simply buying and holding stocks would have yielded 5.5% a year:

a. Keep track of the average growth rate of the seasonally adjusted money supply over the preceding 6 months.
b. Buy stocks 2 months after a trough in this moving average.
c. Sell stocks 15 months after a peak in this moving average.

Why are you skeptical of this strategy?

10.10 Here is an explanation of "statistics-based technical analysis."

> Statistics-based technical analysis utilizes the known probabilities associated with a bell curve; for example, that there is only a 2.5% chance of getting an observation that is two standard deviations above the mean. Suppose that a stock's price over the past 100 days has a mean of $10 with a standard deviation of $5. If the price on Day 100 is $20, there is only 2.5% chance the price will go even higher, above $20. This is an obvious sell situation.

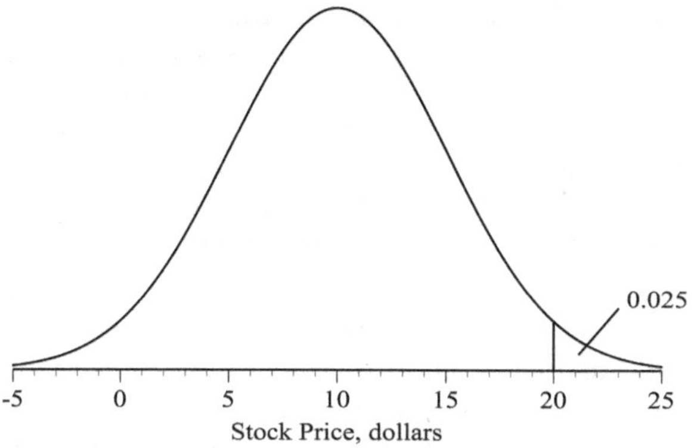

a. What is the logical error in this reasoning?

b. How would you describe statistics-based technical analysis, for example, "fundamental analysis using Tobin's q."

10.11 Filter systems monitor price movements, looking for stocks that have changed direction. Users adopt a rule of buying whenever a stock has risen x% from a previous low and selling whenever a stock has fallen x% from a previous high.

a. How can sell-stop and buy-stop orders be used to implement this strategy?

b. What is the implicit assumption underlying this strategy?

c. If this assumption is correct, what is the disadvantage of using a large value of x?

d. What is the disadvantage of using a small value of x?

10.12 Explain why the following evidence does or does not persuade you that Dragon years are especially good years to buy stocks:

> Trying to discern any sort of seasonality in stock market movements may be a futile exercise. Perhaps the most ingenious "analysis" was done by the Rothschild firm, which noted that February begins the Year of the Dragon in the Chinese calendar.... During the 20th century ... there were twice as many up Dragon years (4) as down Dragon years (2).

10.13 What advantages and disadvantages do you see for this investment strategy?

> [We use] an investment strategy entirely run by a proprietary and adaptive artificial intelligence system that analyzes data and extracts patterns.... The machine learning process underpinning MIND's investment strategy is known as Deep Neural Network Learning—which is a construct of artificial neural networks that enable the A.I. system to recognize patterns and make its own decisions, much like how the human brain works, but at hyper-fast speeds.

10.14 In January 2018, Wealthfront, an automated investment manager that used "rules-based strategy" rather than subjective judgment, reported that, although it had underperformed the market during its first 4 months of operation, this was "just noise." Wealthfront had developed its strategy using decades of data and concluded that it generated a "very attractive risk-adjusted, long-term rate of return," which "speaks much more loudly to us than any one month." Why are you skeptical?

10.15 After a year of underperformance that was a "complete disappointment," the Chief Executive Officer (CEO) of Horizons artificial intelligence (AI) Canadian exchange-traded fund (ETF) announced that,

> The Horizons Active A.I. Global Equity ETF (MIND), which uses a proprietary AI-directed selection process to invest in major global equity indexes through a basket of ETFs, has trailed the market over the past year, down 1.04 per cent on a return basis, versus a positive total return, in Canadian dollar terms, of 5.76 per cent for the MSCI World Index….
>
> "To the extent that they may have underperformed today, there is a strong possibility that they can outperform in the future," Mr. Hawkins [Horizons CEO] said.

Explain Hawkins' reasoning and why you either agree or disagree with it.

10.16 A Yale economics professor and graduate student looked at bitcoin prices from January 1, 2011 to May 31, 2018 (as far back as there are reliable data). Among their findings:

1. When bitcoin's price increased, it tended to keep increasing; so they offered this trading rule: "buy bitcoin if its price increases more than 20 percent the previous week."
2. Bitcoin's price tended to increase after surges in Google searches for the word *bitcoin* and decline after a surge in Google searches for the phrase *bitcoin hack.*
3. They calculated correlations between bitcoin returns and hundreds of other financial variables, and found that bitcoin returns were positively correlated with stock returns in the consumer goods and health care industries and negatively correlated with stock returns in the fabricated products and metal mining industries.

Why are you skeptical of the usefulness of these three findings?

10.17 Here is the Motley Fool's "Foolish Four" investment strategy. At the beginning of January each year:

a. Identify the 10 Dow Jones Industrial Average stocks with the highest dividend yields (dividend/price).
b. Of these 10, identify the five stocks with the lowest prices.
c. Drop the stock with the lowest price.

d. Invest 40% of your wealth in the second-to-lowest priced stock and 20% each in the other three stocks.

Explain why each of these four criteria either does or does not make sense.

The Motley Fool's leaders, Tom and David Gardner, reported that during the 20-year period, 1973–1993, the Foolish Four strategy returned an annual average return of 25% and that it "should grant its fans the same 25 percent annualized returns going forward that it has served up in the past." Why are you skeptical?

10.18 The Wall Street expression "Don't fight the tape" means don't buy stocks if prices are falling and don't sell if prices are rising. Would you characterize this as a momentum or reaction theory?

10.19 Some investors hold on to stocks that have gone up in price and sell the stocks they own that have gone down in price. Is this anything more than momentum investing?

10.20 Some analysts monitor data on the fraction of mutual fund assets invested in cash (Treasury bills and other short-term bonds). A buy signal might be given when the cash ratio exceeds 10% and a sell signal when mutual fund cash drops below 5%. Give two possible logical explanations.

10.21 The long-time host of the popular public television show, *Wall Street Week*, began one of his newspaper columns with, "Wonderful news: the experts are getting pessimistic about the stock market." Why would anyone think that this news is bullish?

10.22 In 1987, a year with 3 Friday the 13ths, the chief economist at a Philadelphia bank reported that in the past 40 years, there had been 6 other years with 3 Friday the 13ths, and a recession started in 3 of those 6 years. Explain why you do or do not find this evidence persuasive.

10.23 Explain the following observation:

> There have always been a considerable number of pathetic people who busy themselves examining the last thousand numbers which have appeared on a roulette wheel, in search of some repeating pattern. Sadly enough, they have usually found it.

10.24 Explain the success of the following stock market theory, advanced by a Tijuana brokerage firm, based on the clothes worn by television personality Vanna White: "If she sports a white, strapless dress, a 'buy' program appears to follow. 'Sell' programs are initiated if she wears neck-high garments."

10.25 "As January goes, so goes the year" is an old stock market adage. The idea is that if the market goes up from January 1 to January 31, then it will go up for the entire year, January 1 to December 31. If the market drops in January, then it will be a bad year. *Newsweek* cited this theory and reported that "this rule of thumb has proved correct in 20 of the past 24 years." Explain why you are skeptical about this evidence.

10.26 While playing bridge recently, Ira Rate picked up his 13-card hand and found that it contained no spades. He promptly threw his cards down and declared that the deal had not been random. He read in a statistics textbook that (a) the probability of being dealt a hand with no spades is less than 5% and (b) this low a probability is sufficient evidence to show that the deal was not fair. What is the error in his reasoning? Why are technical analysts prone to making the same error?

10.27 A letter to *Sports Illustrated* reported that the winning team in all five college football games played on January 2 that year started the game going right to left on the writer's television screen. If the direction makes no difference, the probability of the right-to-left team winning all five games is .0312, which is below the .05 level considered to be statistically significant. How would you explain this pattern? What has this got to do with technical analysis?

10.28 A *Fortune* magazine article discussed a company selling a computer program for forecasting the stock market 80 days ahead. The company selling this program claimed to have found a pattern in stock prices that would have enabled a user to make a 72.1% profit over the preceding 3 years, while the stock market as a whole went down 6.1%. A *Fortune* editor ordered the program and used it for 80 days. Every single day during this 80-day period, the computer program advised selling stocks. However, stock prices soared in one of the strongest advances in stock market history. How do you explain this gap between advertised and actual performance, even assuming that the company's reported 72.1% profit was true?

10.29 As of October 2024, 10 publicly traded mutual funds had been launched that made stock selections based entirely on artificial intelligence computer algorithms with no human intervention. Every one of these funds did worse than the S&P 500. Their average annual return was 10 percentage points worse than the S&P 500. How do you explain this dismal performance?

10.30 Why are you skeptical of the Telephone Switch Newsletter's investment philosophy?

> Let us assume that the stock market can be divided into ten different segments.... For example,... blue chip stocks, energy-related stocks, stocks which concentrate in gold mining companies, bonds, utilities, and a cash position.... Reviewing the past shows that no matter what the economic or political situation has been during the past 100 years, there has always been at least one of the segments of the stock market where you could make money....
>
> So what does our individual investment counselor actually do? He determines which segments of the market at present are in an

> uptrend and invests his money into mutual funds that specialize in these segments. During the allotted one hour per week he gives to monitoring his plan, he sees whether the segment he is using is still in an uptrend. As long as the uptrend is still in place, he stays with the investment. When the trend is broken, funds are taken out of that segment and moved to a segment that is currently in an uptrend. If none of the segments being monitored are in an uptrend, he then goes to cash.... Once we realize that we are in control no matter what economic situation develops here or abroad, we know that there will always be some investment that will offer growth for our capital. The important word here is always.

Answers

10.1 Snow in Boston on Christmas Eve surely has nothing to do with the performance of the stock market the following year. This is most likely a data-mined coincidence.

10.2 Homebuyers flock to ARMs if they expect interest rates to go down in the future, so this is a reaction approach: If mortgage rates go very high, they expect them to come back down.

10.3 Switching to a sector fund that has done well recently is a momentum strategy. The 39-week rule reeks of data mining.

10.4 If the current price is below the past average price, then the price has fallen. A buy signal is a reaction strategy.

10.5 You can lose by buying the stocks that the program recommends. It might be renewed every 4 months because they are constantly revising the algorithm after failures; also, they can keep charging buyers every 4 months. An unscrupulous company could send buy recommendations to half of its customers and sell recommendations to the other half.

10.6 This advice is more consistent with the momentum school.

10.7 These investors belong to the momentum school. If the price rises to 30, this signals that the price will continue to rise and that they should buy the stock. If the price doesn't rise to 30, then it has no momentum and is of no interest.

10.8 This sure sounds like data mining, which is good at identifying past patterns that are unreliable guides to the future. Why these words? Why 2-year and 5-year Treasury rates? Because they happened to be coincidentally correlated.

10.9 This recommendation is so complicated that it could only have been concocted after looking at the data. We should be skeptical of theories derived from data.

10.10 a. When observations are drawn from a normal distribution with a mean of 10 and a standard deviation of 5, each selection is independent of previous selections and has a .95 probability of being between 0 and 20. Stock prices are different. Tomorrow's price is *not* independent of today's price. If the price on Day 100 is 20, the price on Day 101 is far more likely to be near 20 than near 10.

b. Statistics-based technical analysis is a reaction strategy. When the price is high relative to its average price over the past 100 days, it predicts the price will fall.

10.11 a. A sell-stop order (also called a stop-loss order) triggers a sale when the price drops to a specified level. A buy-stop order triggers a buy when the price rises to a specified level.

b. This is a momentum strategy: what has gone up will continue going up; what has gone down will keep going down.

c. A large value of x will result in few transactions (and few profits, even if there is momentum.

d. A small value of x will result in many transactions and transaction costs, including bid-ask spreads.

10.12 The Chinese calendar surely has nothing to do with how well the stock market does. The fact that they picked one of 12 Chinese zodiac signs and only have 6 years of data signals a data-mined coincidence.

10.13 The algorithm may spot useful patterns, but it is more likely to identify useless coincidences.

10.14 With backtesting, it is always possible to find strategies that fit past data remarkably well; the real test is how it does with fresh data. Wealthfront has underperformed the S&P 500.

10.15 Data-mined backtesting is unreliable, and this argument is the fallacious law of averages. From its 2017 launch until the spring of 2022, MIND investors had a –10% return while those who invested in an S&P 500 index fund had a +63% return. With MIND on life support, Horizons pulled the plug and terminated the fund on May 20, 2022.

10.16 There is no theoretical way to value bitcoin since it yields no income. These patterns are surely useless data-mining.

10.17 a. This is plausible. Stocks with high dividend yields are appealing. The basic idea is that contrarian investors should buck the trend by buying out-of-favor stocks that have low prices and high dividend yields.

b. Illogical. The price of one share of stock depends on how many shares the company has outstanding.

c. Illogical. Why, after selecting the five stocks with the lowest price, as if it is good to have a low price, would we cross out the stock with the lowest price?

d. Illogical. Why invest twice as much money in the next lowest priced stock?

We should be skeptical because of the obvious data mining. (Only 1 year after the introduction of the Foolish Four, the Gardners tweaked their system and renamed it the UV4. Their explanation confirms their data mining: "Why the switch? History shows that the UV4 has actually done better than the old Foolish Four." It is hardly surprising that a data-mined strategy doesn't do as well outside the years used to concoct the theory. The Gardners admitted as much when the Motley Fool stopped recommending both the Foolish Four and UV4 strategies.)

10.18 This is a momentum strategy: buy when prices are rising, sell when prices are falling.

10.19 Yes, it is profitable tax-harvesting—selling stocks that have gone down in price so that the losses can be claimed (with limitations) on their tax returns.

10.20 Mutual funds have a lot of cash when they are bearish on the market. A contrarian strategy is to do the opposite. A second argument is that the funds have lots of buying power when they decide to get back in the market.

10.21 Contrarians do the opposite of what the experts do.

10.22 Friday the 13ths surely have nothing to do with economic recessions. Six observations are a very small sample, and we don't know how often recessions started in years that didn't have three Friday the 13ths. This is just data-mining. (There was no recession in 1987.)

10.23 Data mining will discover patterns, even in coin flips and roulette spins, that are coincidental and useless.

10.24 This is obviously useless data mining.

10.25 This feels like data mining. In addition, a core problem is that the "entire year" includes January. If the market goes up in January, then it is already partway to an up year. Also, the market usually goes up, regardless of what happens in January. They should have compared the market in January (good or bad) to the other 11 months of the year. (There is, in fact, no correlation.)

10.26 The probability calculation assumes that the event (a hand with no spades) is specified before the hand is dealt. After a hand is dealt, there will inevitably be something unusual about the hand related to the absence or presence of certain cards. The identification of such unusual features is easy and useless. The same is true of technical analysis that searches for unusual features in past data.

10.27 This is surely a coincidence that was discovered after the games had been played. There were no doubt other coincidental patterns related to the color of the uniforms, names of the teams, names of the quarterbacks, and so on. In the same way, technical analysts will surely find patterns in events that have already occurred. The more relevant (and difficult) task is making predictions about things that have not yet happened.

10.28 Just like the coin flips, it is easy to find profitable patterns in past stock prices, even if the stock market—like coin flips—is completely random.

10.29 The AI funds evidently traded based on discovered patterns in historical data—which turned out to be coincidental. It is remarkable how badly they did since we might expect them to vary randomly from the performance of the S&P 500. Perhaps they had high expenses and traded excessively, incurring large transaction costs, including bid-ask spreads.

10.30 Yes, "there will always be some investment that will offer growth for our capital." The problem is identifying the investment ahead of time. This switch strategy is just a momentum strategy. Whether some sector has done well in the past is a poor guide to whether it will do well in the future.

11

The Efficient-Market Hypothesis

11.1 Explain why this advice from a long-time financial columnist for the *New York Times* is logical, but not very helpful:

> It is obviously good sense to buy bonds when the Federal Reserve Banks start lowering interest rates. It is just as obviously bad sense to buy them at any time when, two or three or four months hence, the Fed is certain to start raising money rates and lowering the prices of outstanding bonds.

11.2 Explain why this advice from a long-time financial columnist for the *New York Times* is not very helpful:

> Since we know stocks are going to fall as well as rise, we might as well get a little traffic out of them. A man who buys a stock at 10 and sells it at 20 makes 100 per cent. But a man who buys it at 10, sells it at 14 1/2, buys it back at 12 and sells it at 18, buys it back at 15 and sells it at 20, makes 188 per cent.

11.3 Explain why you won't get rich following this advice in Consumer Digest's *Get Rich Investment Guide*:

> The ability to track interest rates as they pertain to bonds is made easier by following the path of the Prime Rate (the rate of interest charged by banks to their top clients). If the consensus shown in top business journals indicates that rates are going up, this means that bonds will go down in price. Therefore, when it seems that rates are moving up, an investor should wait until some "peaking" of rates is foreseen.

11.4 Respond to this argument by a Wall Street analyst:

> It is widely expected that income tax rates will go up when Democrats regain control of the federal government. Even if it is certain that within the next 10 to 20 years, those currently paying a 25% tax on interest income and a 15% tax on dividend income will have to pay a 35% tax on interest income, while retaining a 15% tax on dividends, this will have no immediate effect on stock prices because: (a) the 15% tax on dividends will not change; and (b) nothing will change for at least 10 years.

11.5 A *Wall Street Journal* article advised:

> The long-term investor can make his decisions based on information easily available in his morning newspaper. Indeed, Thom Brown, managing director of the Philadelphia investment firm of Rutherford, Brown & Catherwood, advises investors to simply read a daily newspaper. "Look for anything that suggests the direction

DOI: 10.1201/9781003630166-11

> of the economy," he says. "Auto sales, for example, give you an idea about how willing consumers are to part with their money." An expanding economy usually means rising stock prices.

Write a letter to the editor of the *Journal*, refuting this advice.

11.6 A CEO once told a group of Wall Street analysts that, "We give investors a chance to sleep at night knowing that you're going to get consistency and visibility and, over every economic cycle, performance that surpasses the S&P 500." What would an efficient-market believer say about this CEO's assertion that his company's stock will always surpass the S&P 500?

11.7 Explain this observation by a veteran stock market analyst:

> You can do a pretty good job of predicting the economy using prior changes in stock prices, but predicting stock prices from the economic forecasts works almost not at all.

11.8 In 1996, Morningstar, an independent mutual fund rating service, began rating mutual funds on their annual performance, even though in 1995 Morningstar's president said that was "the dumbest thing imaginable." What do you suppose he meant by this?

11.9 After the close of trading on July 19, 2022, Netflix (the video streaming company) announced that it had lost 970,000 subscribers in the second quarter of 2022. The company did not indicate any change in its future plans, yet in after-hours trading, the price of Netflix stock jumped 7.85%, from $201.63 at the close of trading to $217.46. What is your most compelling explanation for this price jump?

11.10 Answer the question at the end of this quotation from Louis Rukeyser, who was the long-time host of the popular public television show, *Wall Street Week*:

> There are many who regard the stock market as wholly perverse ... How else, they demand, can one explain a situation in which a company announces increased earnings—and sees its stock decline? What is the justification for a day on which all the news is bad—and the market rises?

11.11 In November 1985, financial advisor Edward Yardeni said, "We still like stocks not so much because we foresee better-than-expected profits, but because we foresee lower than-expected interest rates." Why are high profits and low interest rates good for stock prices? Explain why Yardeni said "better-than-expected profits" and "lower-than-expected interest rates" instead of "higher profits" and "lower interest rates."

11.12 A Harvard Business School professor wrote that, "The vast scientific evidence on the [on the unpredictability of changes in stock prices] indicates that, in the absence of inside information, a security's market price represents the best available estimate of its true value." The argument is that if stock prices are always equal to true values, then stock prices will only change because of new information—which is unpredictable. Why, even if this argument is true, does evidence indicating it is difficult to predict changes in stock prices not prove that a stock's price is always equal to its true value?

11.13 Explain the fallacy in this finance professor's argument:

> In an efficient market with stocks always priced to give investors their market-equilibrium required rates of return, taking into account all available information, actual returns that are higher or lower than these required returns are due solely to new information which, by definition, is unpredictable. The empirical fact that it is nearly impossible to predict whether actual stock returns will be abnormally high or low proves that the efficient market hypothesis is correct.

11.14 During the 1988 presidential election campaign, it was widely believed that the stock market would benefit more from a George Bush presidency than from a Michael Dukakis presidency. Yet on Friday, January 20, 1989, the day of George Bush's inauguration as president, stock prices fell slightly, with the Dow down 3.75 points to 2235.36. How would the efficient-market hypothesis explain this apparent contradiction?

11.15 A *Wall Street Journal* columnist wrote that, "the only reason to invest in the market is because you think you know something others don't." If everyone had exactly the same information, would anyone buy stocks?

11.16 Explain why you either agree or disagree with this reasoning in *Confessions of a Wall Street Insider*:

> The stock market is built on an absolutely necessary foundation of error. The market depends on error for its very existence. If people weren't wrong, there could be no stock market.
>
> Suppose everybody knew the future perfectly. Suppose everybody knew with absolute certainty, for example, that the fortunes of a certain company were about to improve. Nobody would then want to sell that company's stock. There would a world full of buyers but no sellers. And when the shape of the future changed, when everybody knew for sure that the company was heading for trouble, there would be a world of sellers but no buyers. There would be no stock market. There could be none.

11.17 A *Los Angeles Times* article about the stock market was titled, "Even the Experts Disagree on the Market's Direction." How can the stock market be efficient if the experts can't agree on whether stock prices are going up or down?

11.18 The stock market went up sharply the day before the Presidential election on November 6, 2012. Some commentators said that stock prices went up because, although it was very uncertain whether Obama or Romney would win, investors don't like uncertainty. As one analyst said: "Regardless of who wins the U.S. election, uncertainty declines." Why is this explanation of the pre-election bump unconvincing?

11.19 Former Federal Reserve Chair Alan Greenspan was notoriously vague and cryptic. (It was reported that when he proposed marriage to Andrea Mitchell, she did not realize that he was asking her to marry him.) Suppose that Greenspan had decided to adhere to rigid interest rate targets, announcing that the Fed would reduce the federal funds rate by 25 basis points on March 28, another 25 points on April 25, and another 25 points on May 30. Do you think that such interest rate reductions will raise or lower bond prices? If you are 100% certain the Fed will do this, can you ensure large profits by buying/selling bonds (a) on March 27, April 24, and May 29? (b) On March 29, April 26, and May 31?

11.20 An economics professor said that he/she will wait to refinance his/her home mortgage until after the next Federal Open Market Committee meeting, since everyone expects the Fed to vote at this meeting to reduce short-term interest rates. What would you advise?

11.21 Starting with $1,000 in 1978, Hillary Clinton made nearly a $100,000 profit investing in cattle futures while her husband, Bill, was Governor of Arkansas. Although she had no experience trading futures contracts, she said that the reason for her success was that she read *The Wall Street Journal*. Why would you be skeptical of anyone making such a claim?

11.22 What do you think Vanguard founder Jack Bogle meant when he said: "If everybody indexed, the only word you could use is chaos, catastrophe."

11.23 On Thursday, November 11, 2010, TheStreet.com posted an article titled "How Nokia's Stock Price Could Double." Three days later, on Sunday, November 14, 2010, Seeking Alpha posted an article titled "Nokia is Still Overvalued," arguing that a "more realistic" value would be half of its current price. Nothing substantive happened between November 11 and November 14. How could these two influential websites have such dramatically different views of Nokia's stock price? Doesn't the efficient market hypothesis imply that the market price is the correct price?

11.24 The Federal Home Loan Bank System argued that one advantage of Freddie Mac for savings & loan associations (S&Ls) is that, "When interest rates are rising, [S&Ls] can sell off their older, low-interest loans [to Freddie Mac] and reinvest in mortgages at higher interest rates." What is the implicit assumption?

11.25 On May 7, 2020, the U.S. government reported that the national unemployment rate had jumped from 4.4% in March to 14.8% in April. Yet, the Dow Jones Average went up .89% that day and 1.91% the next day. How would you explain this apparent paradox?

11.26 Explain the error in this commentary: "It is widely expected that the Fed will cut interest rates at its next meeting. Investors should therefore buy long-term bonds immediately and wait to buy stocks until after the Fed meets."

11.27 Explain why you either agree or disagree with this advice from MSN Money Central:

> Let's say you've found two stocks that you're weighing as potential buys. Both are projected to grow earnings by a very impressive 39% over the next 12 months, and after doing your own due diligence, you agree with those calculations. The stocks are in pretty much the same industry and trade at the same price-to-earnings ratio. But you've got only enough cash to buy one. Which do you buy?
>
> Obviously, the one with earnings momentum. A stock with a 39% annual earnings growth composed of a +10% quarter, followed by a +9% quarter, a +8% quarter and a +7% quarter, is likely to trace a downhill price path over the course of the year. A stock that has started with a +7% quarter-to-quarter growth, and moved successively up to 8%, 9% and 10% growth quarters, is likely to end the period well above where it began. It's only logical that a stock showing accelerating growth is a better buy than one where the rate of growth is declining.

11.28 Explain why you either agree or disagree with this reasoning by the author of *Happiness Is a Stock That Doubles in One Year*:

> Using common sense, you don't have to be a professional Wall Street analyst to pick winners.
>
> Your first step is to decide what industries are in an uptrend. That's not too difficult. For example, there's a fuel crisis. Accordingly, even quite small companies that are successful in exploration and production of oil and natural gas or possess extensive coal reserves should increase their profits....
>
> Choose a stock in a sound company whose profits are growing by 15-20 percent a year, and you'll probably make money. Also there's money to be made in companies likely to be bought out. In the past year stockholders in Sea World, Koehring, Milgo Electronics, and S. and S. Corporation (a maker of coal-mining machinery) have all gained 50 percent or more by "buy out" offers for their holdings.
>
> On the Amex [last year] there were 200 stocks that doubled. The standout performer, Resort International; "B," rose from 2 5/8 to 22 1/2. Look for stocks like these.

11.29 A widely respected finance professor wrote that,

> In an efficient market, all prices are "fair"—meaning that they equate to their intrinsic values (which are usually not directly observable) and investors can "beat the market" only through luck or random variation around market benchmarks.

Explain why you either agree or disagree with the argument that evidence that investors can beat the market only through luck implies that market prices are equal to intrinsic values.

11.30 A graduate student once appealed to the random walk hypothesis in arguing that population growth follows a random walk. What economic forces that imply a random walk of stock prices might not apply to birth rates?

11.31 Oil prices are declining. You reason that oil prices will reduce inflation and nominal interest rates, increasing bond prices. Lower oil prices should also be good for airlines, which have large fuel expenses. On the other hand, falling oil prices are bad for companies with large oil reserves and for banks that have lent money to such oil-rich companies. You decide to sell oil and bank stocks and buy bonds and airline stocks. Why might your reasoning, even if correct, not be profitable?

11.32 A study of annual earnings reports found that these reports had no effect on stock prices. How can we reconcile this conclusion with economic theory, which says that stock prices depend crucially on a corporation's economic health, in particular, its dividends and earnings?

11.33 Explain why you either agree or disagree with this argument in Burton Malkiel's classic book, *A Random Walk Down Wall Street*:

> Efficient market theory... [is] built on the premise that stock-market investors are rational because they make reasonable estimates of the present value of stocks, and their buying and selling ensures that the prices of stocks fairly represent their future prospects.

11.34 A man gives inspirational lectures on how to make a fortune in real estate by buying "bargain properties." For example, "if you buy a $100,000 house for $80,000 you've got a $20,000 profit right off the bat." If so, is the real estate market efficient? If the real estate market is reasonably efficient, what is the flaw in his advice?

11.35 In May 1932, with stock prices at their lowest level in this century, Dean Witter sent a memo to his company's brokers and management saying,

> All of our customers with money must some day put it to work—into some revenue- producing investment. Why not invest it now, when securities are cheap? Some people say they want to wait for a clearer view of the future. But when the future is again clear, the present bargains will have vanished. In fact, does anyone think that today's prices will prevail once full confidence has been restored?

Explain why you either agree or disagree with his logic.

11.36 Explain the error in this analyst's predicted increase in the price of Timberland stock, a leading maker of premium footwear and outdoor clothing. "The coming of winter is likely to spark sales of jackets and boots."

11.37 Explain why you would or would not expect stock prices to exhibit a

a. long-run trend

b. seasonal pattern

11.38 Would the following, *if true*, be evidence against the strong form of the efficient-market hypothesis?

a. A well-known investment strategy consistently earns a return greater than zero.

b. When the stock market goes down in January, it usually goes down during the next 11 months.

c. The stock market almost always goes up at least 20% in the 9 months preceding presidential elections and goes down 20% during the 12 months following elections.

d. Interest rates are higher on AAA Corporate bonds than on AAA municipal bonds.

11.39 Briefly explain why each of the following events is or is not a persuasive reason to buy stock:

a. Consolidated Water hasn't missed a dividend payment in 120 years.

b. CoolTech has a Tobin's q of 2.3.

c. Yesterday, the Fed reported a $2.5 billion increase in the money supply last week.

d. The term structure is downward sloping, indicating that financial experts expect interest rates to fall.

11.40 Briefly explain why the following allegations, if true, either would or would not provide evidence against the strong form of the efficient-market hypothesis:

a. When a company announces a stock split, its stock price generally goes up substantially the day before the split is announced.

b. When a company announces a stock split, its stock price generally goes up substantially the day *after* the split is announced.

c. The stock market almost always goes down on Friday the 13th.

Answers

11.1 It is true that bond prices rise when interest rates fall (and fall when interest rates rise) but if the Fed is certain to do something, then this anticipated action will surely already be reflected in bond prices (more specifically, in the term structure, so that no strategy makes abnormal profits).

11.2 This nimble trading would be very profitable, but how do we know when a rising or falling price is about to go in the opposite direction?

11.3 Widely held views will surely already be reflected in market prices.

11.4 The higher tax rate on interest income will lower the required return on stocks, making them more valuable. Since there will be an immediate effect on the present value of future dividends, the effect should be immediate.

11.5 This readily available information is surely already reflected in stock prices.

11.6 The efficient market theory says that stocks only do unusually well or poorly because of unpredictable events. Unless this stock is especially risky, there is no logical reason why it will be priced in an efficient market to consistently give a higher return than the average stock.

11.7 To the extent that stock analysts can predict changes in the economy, stock prices will change before the economy does. (Or perhaps changes in stock prices cause changes in the economy.) On the other hand, to the extent that the stock market is efficient, stock prices can't be predicted from well-known economic forecasts. People won't sell if it is easy to predict that stock prices will soon rise, and they won't buy if price declines are easily foretold.

11.8 Past performance is not a reliable predictor of future performance.

11.9 Analysts had expected them to lose far more subscribers (2 million).

11.10 Most likely, the bad news was not as bad as had been expected.

11.11 He assumed that profit and interest rate expectations are already embedded in stock prices. The relevant question is not how today differs from yesterday or how tomorrow differs from today, but how his expectations of tomorrow differ from other's expectations.

11.12 Logically, A implies B does not mean that B implies A. It may be difficult to predict changes in stock prices, not because the market price is the correct price, but because changes in market prices are due to unpredictable swings in human emotions.

11.13 Logically, A implies B does not mean that B implies A. Abnormally high or low stock returns could be due, for example, to unpredictable swings in investor psychology ("animal spirits").

11.14 The fact that George Bush was going to be inaugurated on January 20, 1989, was surely known to investors well before that date and already incorporated in stock prices.

11.15 Stocks do pay dividends, which grow with the firm. Even if there were no uncertainty about a stock's return, it would still be priced to yield the same as other risk-free investments, and people would still invest, just as they do with Treasury bills, savings accounts, and other risk-free investments.

11.16 There would still be a stock market just as there is a thriving market for Treasury bonds, even though everyone knows what the coupons will be. If future dividends, interest rates, and stock prices were certain, there would still be buyers and sellers, with stocks priced so that there is a balance between the two. Some people who have savings to invest would buy stocks, just as they now buy Treasury bills or deposit money in banks. Those who sell stocks would do so to raise cash for spending or to invest elsewhere, just as some people today sell their Treasury bills and withdraw money from banks.

11.17 The market would *not* be efficient if experts agreed that stock prices will soon rise or fall by a considerable amount, because then stocks would be clearly mispriced.

11.18 If stock prices were going to increase no matter who won, they would have increased long before the election. Investors didn't wake up on November 5, surprised that the election would be the next day. If stock prices increased sharply on November 5, it must have been because of a revised assessment of the probability that Obama or Romney would win.

11.19 If other investors are as confident as you are, these anticipated reductions will be fully embedded in the term structure, so that no excess profits could be made with either strategy.

11.20 If everyone expects the rate cut, it should already be reflected in long-term interest rates. Also, a cut in a very short-term rate won't affect long-term rates much if the rate cut is expected to be short-lived. The delay gives her less time to benefit from refinancing at a lower rate.

11.21 Stories in the *Journal* are surely old news, already reflected in futures prices. A study by three economists concluded that the odds of an honest trader making a $100,000 profit on a $1,000 investment during this time period were less than 1 in 31 trillion. An alternative explanation was disguised bribery.

11.22 If everyone indexed, making no attempt to assess whether stocks are fairly valued, stock prices could become wildly disconnected from fundamental values.

11.23 The efficient market hypothesis is that one cannot consistently realize above-average risk-adjusted returns because all available information is already taken into account by investors and consequently already reflected in market prices. It could still be the case that, because of their differing interpretations of available information, investors disagree about whether a stock is cheap or expensive at the current market price—so bulls buy from bears.

11.24 The implicit assumption is that Freddie Mac will pay more than these old low-interest loans are worth. If these loans are fairly priced to give rates of return comparable to new loans, there is no advantage to selling the old loans and making new ones.

11.25 Investors may have anticipated an even larger increase in the unemployment rate, or there may have been offsetting good news. As Ian Shepherdson, an economist at Pantheon Macroeconomics, said: "Terrible, but not really news."

11.26 If this rate cut is widely expected, it will already be reflected in (higher) bond and stock prices.

11.27 If widely expected, this will already be reflected in the prices.

11.28 Common sense and readily available information should already be embedded in stock prices. Common sense and easy information couldn't have predicted that Resorts International would soon rise from 2 5/8 to 22 1/2. If such an increase was readily apparent, people would not have sold at 2 5/8. At that price, there must have been considerably disagreement about whether the price was going to rise or fall.

11.29 It may be difficult to beat the market because market prices are buffeted by unpredictable news events and animal spirits, even though market prices are far from intrinsic value.

11.30 The random walk hypothesis says that future stock price changes cannot be predicted from past prices because, otherwise, the stock market would be leaving $100 bills on the sidewalk. There are no $100 bills to be had from predicting population growth.

11.31 Maybe other, equally well-informed but more well-financed, investors have already reasoned this way and bid prices to levels that reflect this information.

11.32 The market evidently knew what was going to be in the earnings reports before they were published. Even if these are surprises, the average effect on stock prices will be close to zero if the market's expectations are unbiased.

11.33 There is a crucial difference between stock-price changes being unpredictable and stock prices being good estimates of intrinsic values.

11.34 If you can buy a house for $80,000 and then sell it for $100,000, the real estate market is not very efficient. If the market were efficient, there wouldn't be $20,000 bills on the sidewalk.

11.35 May 1932 may not have been the absolutely best time to buy stocks, but it is surely true that stock prices will be much higher when full confidence has been restored.

11.36 Surely, the coming of winter is anticipated and already embedded in the price of Timberland stock.

11.37 a. Yes, stock prices should rise in the long run along with corporate dividends, earnings, and assets.

b. No, because a regular seasonal pattern could be exploited profitably. Who will buy in July if we know that prices will fall in August?

11.38 a. No, even bank accounts pay more than zero.

b. Yes, this would be a way to earn abnormal returns.

c. Yes, this would be a way to earn abnormal returns.

d. No, municipal bonds are tax advantaged.

11.39 None of these are persuasive reasons to buy stock because they are presumably already well-known and reflected in stock prices.

11.40 a. Yes, because insiders evidently know about the split before it is announced to the public.

b. Yes, because investors could make money buying the stock on the day the split is announced.

c. Yes, because investors could make money selling the day before a Friday the 13th.

12

The Human Factor in Investments

12.1 After 32-year-old Albert Pujols signed a $250 million 10-year contract with the Los Angeles Angels in 2011, an ESPN commentator said that it made economic sense for the Angels because the owner, Arturo Moreno, bought the team in 2005 for a bargain price. Explain why you either agree or disagree with this logic. What would be similar reasoning by stock market investors?

12.2 Fans paid thousands of dollars for seats right behind home plate for the deciding game 7 of the 2023 American League Championship game between the Houston Astros and the Texas Rangers. When the Rangers took a 10-2 lead in the sixth inning, thousands of fans headed for the exits, including some who had paid for seats behind home plate.

One of many similar comments on social media: "If I'm paying for those seats at a game 7, I don't care what the score is. I am not leaving until it's over."

Explain why this reasoning is an example of diminishing marginal returns, law of averages, regression toward the mean, or sunk-cost fallacy. What would be a similar flawed reasoning by stock market investors?

12.3 In his book, *Against the Gods,* Peter Bernstein gave this example of regression toward the mean:

> The track records of professional investment managers are also subject to regression to the mean. There is a strong probability that the hot manager of today will be the cold manager of tomorrow, or at least the day after tomorrow, and vice versa.... The wisest strategy is to dismiss the manager with the best track record and to transfer one's assets to the manager who has been doing the worst.

Explain why you either agree or disagree.

12.4 In his book, *Against the Gods,* Peter Bernstein gave this example of regression toward the mean: "Joseph had this preordained sequence of events in mind when he predicted that seven years of famine would follow seven years of plenty." Why is this example flawed?

12.5 In his book, *Against the Gods,* Peter Bernstein gave this example of regression toward the mean: "Regression to the mean ... is what motivates the gambler's dream that a long string of losses is bound to give way to a long string of winnings." Why is this example flawed?

DOI: 10.1201/9781003630166-12

12.6 An investment textbook written by a Nobel laureate states that, "Multistage dividend discount models assume that, ultimately, economic forces will force the convergence of the profitability and growth rates of different firms." To support this assumption, the book looked at the 20% of firms with the highest profit rates in 1966 and the 20% with the lowest profit rates that year. Fourteen years later, in 1980, the profit rates of both were more nearly average: "convergence ... is apparent ... the phenomenon is undoubtedly real." Explain why the explanation might be statistical rather than economic.

12.7 Two distinguished finance professors—one a Nobel laureate—found that corporate profits tend to decline for the most profitable firms and increase for the least profitable ones, a pattern they attributed to competitive forces:

> In a competitive environment, profitability is mean reverting within as well as across industries. Other firms eventually mimic innovative products and technologies that produce above normal profitability for a firm. And the prospect of failure or takeover gives firms with low profitability incentives to allocate assets to more productive uses.

Provide an alternative, purely statistical explanation for this pattern in corporate profits.

12.8 Explain why you either agree or disagree with this statement by the author of *What are the Chances*: "only if everyone has the same information will price changes reflect a stock's true value."

12.9 Daniel Kahneman, a psychologist who won a Nobel prize in economics, once told Israeli flight instructors that their trainees would progress faster if they were praised instead of punished. A senior instructor strongly objected:

> On many occasions I have praised flight cadets for clean execution of some aerobatic maneuver, and in general when they try it again, they do worse. On the other hand, I have often screamed at cadets for bad execution, and in general they do better the next time. So please don't tell us that reinforcement works and punishment does not, because the opposite is the case.

What would you have said in response?

12.10 Explain why you either agree or disagree with this money manager's explanation of regression toward the mean that was published in the *Financial Analysts Journal*:

> There is a phenomenon in nature called 'reversion to the mean,' which asserts that, over time, properties of members of groups tend to converge to the average value for the group as a whole. This concept is widely applicable in situations where economic forces tend to move things toward equilibrium.... Over time, company results have a tendency to regress to the mean as underlying

economic forces attract new entrants to attractive markets and encourage participants to leave low-return businesses. Because of this tendency, companies that have been "good" performers in the past may prove to be inferior investments, while "poor" companies frequently provide superior investment returns in the future.

12.11 Explain why you either agree or disagree with this bank trust investment officer's explanation of regression toward the mean that was published in the *Financial Analysts Journal*:

> [The] key financial ratios of companies tend, over time, to revert to the mean for the market as a whole. The thesis is easily defended. High returns eventually invite new entrants, driving down profitability, while poor returns cause the exit of competitors, leaving a more profitable industry for the survivors."

12.12 A McKinsey study separated the companies in the S&P 500 into quintiles based on their return on invested capital (ROIC), a measure of a firm's profitability. For the 100 firms with the highest initial ROICs, the average ROIC over the next 15 years decreased. For the 100 firms with the lowest initial ROICs, the average ROIC over the next 15 years increased. Provide a persuasive explanation other than that successful companies slack off while unsuccessful companies are energized.

12.13 A Credit Suisse study looked at the annual Cash Flow Return on Investment (CFROI) for more than 6,000 companies. The study separated the companies into quintiles based on their CFROI in 2015, with the companies in Quintile 1 having the highest CFROI, Quintile 2 the second highest, and so on. The study then calculated the average CFROI for the companies in each 2015 quintile, every year from 2015 back to 2005. Explain the results below, using language that an ordinary investor would understand.

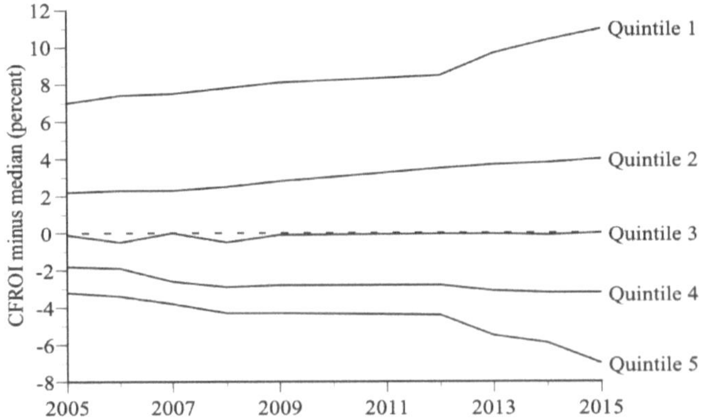

12.14 The 30 firms in the Dow Jones Industrial average are intended to be "substantial companies—renowned for the quality and wide acceptance of their products or services—with strong histories of successful growth." Substitutions are made periodically, replacing recently less successful companies with more successful ones. Do you think that after a substitution is made, the stocks that are added to the Dow generally do better or worse than the stocks they replace? Explain your reasoning.

12.15 Does regression toward the mean in corporate profits imply that all companies will soon earn the same profits?

12.16 Many argue that company performance is enhanced by having a "moat" that protects it from competition. In 2002, Morningstar assigned moat ratings to thousands of companies: wide moat, narrow moat, no moat. The wide-moat companies had the largest, most stable profits. Morningstar then tracked the performance of three portfolios composed of stocks in these three categories and found that the portfolio consisting of the wide-most stocks underperformed the other two portfolios. How would you explain this underperformance?

12.17 A 2016 *Sports Illustrated* article noted that the Chicago Cubs had won 24 of their first 30 Major League Baseball games, and that only 13 teams had done so well in the modern baseball era. What patterns do you see in these data, and how would you explain them?

	First 30 Games			Rest of Season		
	Wins	Losses	%	Wins	Losses	%
1905 Giants	24	6	80.0	81	42	65.9
1907 Cubs	24	6	80.0	83	39	68.0
1907 Giants	25	5	83.3	57	66	46.3
1911 Tigers	25	5	83.3	64	60	51.6
1921 Pirates	24	6	80.0	66	57	53.7
1928 Yankees	24	6	80.0	77	47	62.1
1939 Yankees	24	6	80.0	82	39	67.8
1946 Red Sox	24	6	80.0	80	44	64.5
1955 Dodgers	25	5	83.3	73	50	59.3
1958 Yankees	24	6	80.0	68	56	54.8
1977 Dodgers	24	6	80.0	74	58	56.1
1981 A's	24	6	80.0	40	39	50.6
1984 Tigers	26	4	86.7	78	54	59.1

12.18 Of those major league baseball teams that win more than 100 out of 162 games in a season, 90% win fewer games the following season. How would you explain this statistical pattern?

12.19 A study of stock analysts' earnings forecasts found that stocks of companies with the most optimistic forecasts tended to do worse than the stocks of companies with the most pessimistic forecasts.

a. A reviewer wrote, "There is no explicit theoretical model of the mechanism or the intuition that connects the analyst forecast errors and price reversal." Discuss a possible theoretical model that is consistent with this pattern. Explain in sufficient detail for a layperson to understand your reasoning.

b. The reviewer also wrote, "What is the direction of the causality? Does analyst error cause price reversal? Or does price reversal cause analyst error? The paper seems to suggest the former but it will be interesting to also check the possibility of the latter." What do you think?

12.20 Data on the profits (return on assets) of 100 firms were grouped into quartiles based on their 1930 profits: the top 25, the second 25, the third 25, and the bottom 25. The average profits in 1930 and 1920 were then calculated for the firms in these 1930 quartiles. How would you explain the graph?

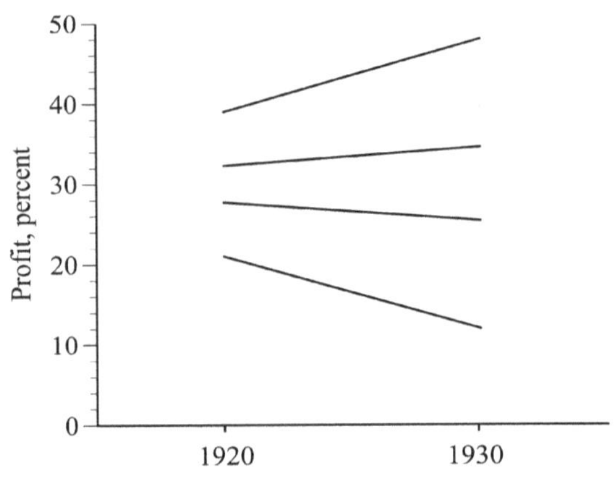

12.21 Students going to Harvey Mudd College (HMC) used to be given a Graduate Records Examination (GRE) test when they arrived as first-year students and when they graduated 4 years later. The faculty were dismayed to discover that the students who had the highest first-year GRE scores generally did not do as well when they took the test 4 years later. Reassure these professors that these students did not necessarily unlearn while at HMC. Explain your answer in language that a lay person can understand.

12.22 The International Bank of Roseau made this offer: For $300, you can receive a short course on international banking and earn the right to sign others up for this course. If you sign up six people, you receive a $1000 "loan" from the bank that does not have to be repaid. Let's say that you sign up six people and each of these sign up six people and so on eight more times. How many people (including yourself) will have taken this course? How much money will the bank have taken in and paid out? Why do you think the Florida attorney general shut down this bank?

12.23 J. David & Co. sent a memo to a bank that had lent it money stating that J. David's cash flow problems were temporary, because its investor requests for withdrawals could soon be satisfied by the arrival of funds from new investors. Why might such a memo suggest fraud? Why might a legitimate business do the same thing, with no fraud whatsoever? If you were a bank officer, how would you tell the difference between a fraud and a legitimate business?

12.24 After the U.S. stock market fell more than 50% between October 2008 and March 2009, Mr. Jones told his investment manager to sell all his stocks and to get back into the stock market after the economic recession had ended. What flaw do you see in this strategy?

12.25 In the early 1980s, a famous Yale professor boasted that he had made 25% a year during the terrible bear market in the 1970s. Surely, another professor asked, you must have bought some stocks that went down? The Yale professor replied, "Yes, but I haven't sold them yet." Explain why you either agree or disagree with the Yale professor's reasoning.

12.26 A *Businessweek* 2013 article reported that Warren Buffett's Berkshire Hathaway had underperformed the S&P500 for 4 months in a row, June, July, August, and September, and noted that only once before in its history had Berkshire underperformed the S&P for more than 4 months in a row (5 months in 2011). The article concluded that "past performance would suggest that Berkshire stock is due for a comeback vs. the S&P." Explain why you either agree or disagree with this reasoning.

12.27 An institutional investor who had been buying before the market crash on October 19, 1987, said that although he believed stocks were overpriced, "we followed the 'trend is your friend' philosophy." What did he mean by this? Why is this strategy risky?

12.28 A study of Treasury bond traders found that they are much more likely to take large risks in the afternoon if they had losses in the morning. How would you explain this behavior? How does it apply to stock market investors?

12.29 A study of high-stakes poker players found that they tended to bet more aggressively after losing a big pot. How would you explain this behavior? How does it apply to stock market investors?

12.30 Explain why you either agree or disagree with this argument:

> The many are smarter than the few. Any single person's prediction of a stock's price next year may be much too high or much too low, but the average prediction of a large number of people will almost certainly be close to the true expected value. Here's a proof. If there are n investors and each investor's prediction has a standard deviation of σ, then we know from statistics that the standard deviation of the average prediction has a standard deviation equal to $\sigma/\sqrt{n}$, which approaches 0 as n increases.

Answers

12.1 The 2005 purchase price is a sunk cost. The relevant question in 2011 is whether the marginal benefit of signing Pujols exceeded the cost. In the stock market, investors might pay too much for a stock, rationalizing the purchase by the fact that they had bought the stock in the past at a much lower price.

12.2 This is the sunk cost fallacy—people think they must do something because they paid for it, even though the payment is a sunk cost that cannot be recouped. In the stock market, investors might buy a stock that drops dramatically in price and say that they are not going to sell until the price comes back to what they paid for the stock.

12.3 This is the fallacious law of averages. The regression-toward-the-mean argument in this context is that managers who have been hot recently have probably had some good luck. If so, their future performance is likely to be closer to the average performance of managers, not worse than average. If they are skilled, not entirely lucky, then they are likely to continue with their above-average performance, and investors should not dismiss them.

12.4 This is the fallacious law of averages. The regression-toward-the-mean argument in this context is that 7 years of famine is unusually extreme. Unless there has been a permanent climate change (in which case, more famine can be expected), the future is likely to be closer to the long-run frequency of famine/feast.

12.5 This is the fallacious law of averages. The regression-toward-the-mean argument in this context is that a long string of losses is unusually extreme. Unless the game is crooked (in which case, more losses can be expected), the future is likely to be closer to the long-run frequency of wins and losses.

12.6 A plausible statistical explanation is regression toward the mean. Those firms with the highest observed profit rates are more likely to be experiencing an unusually good year than an unusually bad year. Those with the lowest profit rates are, on average, experiencing unusually bad years.

12.7 The regression toward the mean explanation is that the most profitable firms tended to have benefited from some good luck, while the least profitable firms tended to have experienced bad luck. If such luck does not persist, their profits will be closer to average.

12.8 We don't need everyone to have the same information, just enough people to arbitrage away any obvious mispricing. On the other hand, even if everyone has the same information, contagious bubbles and panics could cause prices to depart significantly from true values.

12.9 The senior instructor was fooled by regression toward the mean. The pilots who performed poorly were more likely to have had bad luck than good luck and are consequently likely to do better next time, even if the instructor says nothing at all.

12.10 Economic forces may well cause profits to decrease or increase in high-profit and low-profit industries, but regression toward the mean is the purely statistical argument that unusually high or low profits exaggerate how far a company is from the average.

12.11 Regression toward the mean does not assume that competition affects financial ratios. Regression is based on the fact that measurements of an underlying trait that are far from the mean are probably farther from the mean than are the traits.

12.12 Regression toward the mean. The top-quintile companies most likely had more good luck than bad, while the opposite was true of the bottom-quintile companies.

12.13 This is regression toward the mean. Those companies that did the best in 2015 most likely benefited from good luck in 2015 and did not do as well in earlier years because they were not as lucky in those years.

12.14 Regression toward the mean suggests that the companies being replaced may not be in as dire straits as their recent performance suggests, and the companies that replace them may not be as stellar as they appear. Investors who are unaware of regression toward the mean are likely to underestimate the strength of companies doing poorly and overestimate the strength of companies doing well, causing market prices to be too low for the former and too high for the latter relative to long-run fundamental values. When the performance of companies that had been doing poorly regresses to the mean, their stock prices will correct upward; and when companies that had been doing well regress toward the mean, their prices will fall. Therefore, the stocks being replaced can be expected to do better than the stocks that replace them (and they generally do).

12.15 No, every year some above-average companies will have some good luck, followed by somewhat lower profits, while some below-average companies will have some bad luck, followed by somewhat higher profits. Their places at the top and bottom of the profit distribution will be taken by other firms.

12.16 Maybe the 2002 stock prices of the wide-moat companies were too high because investors did not appreciate the fact that their profits were likely to regress toward the mean.

12.17 This is clear evidence of regression toward the mean. These 13 teams generally won more than half their games the remainder of the season (they were above-average teams), but none of them did as well after the first 30 games as they did during the first 30 games.

12.18 This sounds like regression toward the mean: those teams that won more than 100 games were more likely to have been lucky than unlucky that year (with regard to injuries, close calls, etc.).

12.19 a. If analysts are, on average, excessively optimistic about the companies that they predict will have the largest earnings increases in earnings and overly pessimistic about the companies predicted to have the smallest increases, stock prices may be too high for the former and too low for the latter—mistakes that will be corrected when earnings regress toward the mean relative to these forecasts. If so, stocks with relatively pessimistic earnings forecasts may outperform stocks with relatively optimistic predictions.

b. It is hard to see how analyst earnings forecasts could be affected by subsequent stock price changes. Even if forecasts of price changes affected earnings forecasts, why would a predicted stock price decline lead to more optimistic earnings forecasts?

12.20 A firm's profits fluctuate about its average profit. Regression toward the mean occurs because firms with observed profits that are far from the mean tend to have average profits that are closer to the mean. Thus, their profits in any other year will be closer to the mean.

12.21 There was regression toward the mean here; those students with the highest first-year scores are more likely to have scored above their ability than below and will consequently probably not do as well on another test.

12.22 The total number of people taking the course is $1 + 6 + 6^2 + 6^3 + \ldots + 6^8 = 2{,}015{,}539$. The bank will take in $300($2,015,539) = $604,661,700 and loan out $1,000($2,015,539/6) = $335,923,000. The attorney general recognized that this was a Ponzi scheme.

12.23 It sounds like a Ponzi scheme: money from new investors is needed to pay off old investors. On the other hand, a legitimate business might have a mismatch between payments and receipts. A bank officer could investigate whether the business is making and selling anything, or just shuffling dollars.

12.24 By the time the recession is over, stock prices will surely have recovered. Selling low and buying back high will just lock in his losses.

12.25 The professor who asked the question nearly fell out of his seat laughing, until he realized that the Yale professor was not trying to be funny. The professor's losses were not erased by a refusal to sell at a loss. Going forward, the relevant question is whether the stocks are worth buying at their current prices, not what their prices were when the professor bought them.

12.26 It is the fallacious law of averages to think that the below-average performance of Berkshire (or any other investor) makes above-average performance more likely. Unless Berkshire has lost its magic touch, it is likely to do better in the future than it has done in the recent past, but not necessarily above-average.

12.27 This is a momentum strategy—buy stocks when their prices are rising. Since the investor believed stocks were overpriced, he/she was essentially following the greater fool theory, which can fuel bubbles.

12.28 They evidently take larger risks in the afternoon because they remember their morning losses and are eager to win back what they lost. Stock investors may well behave the same way, taking larger risks after losing money.

12.29 Instead of thinking of the best strategy going forward, they remember the money they lost and try to win it back. In the same way, investors who lose money may trade more aggressively, trying to recoup their losses.

12.30 This argument and calculation assume that the estimates are unbiased and independent. In the stock market, investor opinions are not formed independently and are not free of systematic biases. They are influenced by the opinions of widely followed pundits and are shaped by cognitive errors. Stock prices are buffeted by fads, fancies, greed, and gloom—what Keynes called animal spirits—and this contagious mass psychology can cause speculative bubbles and unwarranted panics.

13

Mean-Variance Analysis

13.1 Explain what is incorrect about this description of a Markowitz frontier from a book based on the Public Broadcasting System series *Beyond Wall Street*:

> The curves illustrate maximum return at the various levels of risk that an investor is willing to assume. Investments above the curve have too much risk. Below the curve, the returns are too low. Goldilocks would say that the risk along the curve is not too hot and not too cold; it's just right.

13.2 Explain why you either agree or disagree: "Mean-variance analysis is fine on paper, but it assumes an efficient stock market and there is plenty of evidence of bubbles and busts that cause stock prices to be irrationally high or low."

13.3 Mean-variance analysis was recently used to assess the opportunities available for investors dividing all of their wealth among these three asset classes: 1-year T-bills, 20-year Treasury zeros, and an S&P 500 index fund. The analyst worked with nominal returns and assumed that the investments would be made for 1 year with no changes during the year. Explain the major conceptual error in this argument: "We should not assume that T-bills are safe, since their returns vary from year to year. From 1962 through 2022, the return on 1-year T-bills had a mean of 6.2% and a standard deviation of 2.4%."

13.4 Explain why this statement from *The Prudent Investor's Guide to Beating Wall Street at its Own Game* is incorrect: "When two assets have a +1.000 correlation, they move up and down at the same time, with the same magnitude."

13.5 Identify the errors in this mean-variance analysis with a 1-year horizon of a portfolio allocation among 1-year Treasury bills, 10-year Treasury bonds, and the S&P 500. (Do not use the same error for multiple answers.)

a. The mean return on Treasury bills was set equal to average Treasury bill return since 1926.

b. The standard deviation of the return on 10-year Treasury bonds was set equal to the standard deviation of the yield to maturity on 10-year Treasury bonds since 1926.

c. The mean return on the S&P 500 was set equal to the average percentage price change in the S&P 500 since 1926.

 DOI: 10.1201/9781003630166-13

d. The correlation between the returns on 10-year Treasury bonds and the S&P 500 was set equal to –.5 because stock prices generally fall when interest rates go up.

13.6 Mr. Jones is a new investment manager who wants to use modern portfolio theory to manage his clients' money. He is starting with three asset classes (1-year Treasury bills, 20-year Treasury zeros, and a Vanguard S&P 500 index fund) and wants to identify the Markowitz frontier for a 1-year investment horizon. He collected annual data over the past 20 years on the interest rate B on 1-year Treasury bills, the interest rate Z on 20-year Treasury zeros, and the annual price change S in the S&P 500. He then calculated the historical means, standard deviations, and correlations as a starting point, to be adjusted based on current market conditions. Explains his mistakes:

a. He estimated the mean stock return from the average value of S.

b. He estimated the correlation between Treasury-zeros and stocks from the correlation between Z and S.

c. He estimated the Treasury-bill standard deviation from the standard deviation of B.

13.7 Harry Markowitz proposed measuring risk by the semi-variance of a set of stock returns, $R_1, R_2, \ldots, R_n$:

$$\bar{R} = \sum \frac{R_i}{n}$$

$$SV = \sum \frac{\left(R_i - \bar{R}\right)^2}{m}, \quad \text{if } R_i < \bar{R}$$

where the mean is calculated using all n observations, but the semi-variance SV only uses those m values of R_i that are less than the mean. What advantage do see in using the semi-variance instead of the variance?

13.8 Explain carefully why the standard deviation of an asset return used in mean-variance analysis is conceptually different from the historical standard deviation of this asset's annual returns.

13.9 David Swensen used mean-variance analysis to manage Yale's endowment portfolio. Here are some assumptions he used at one point about the real returns from three assets:

	U.S. Bonds	U.S. Stocks	Absolute Return
Expected value (%)	2	6	7
Standard Deviation (%)	10	20	15

Explain why you either agree or disagree with this critique: "These assumptions are inconsistent with mean-variance analysis. In a risk-averse world, no one would hold U.S. stocks if their expected return was smaller and their standard deviation larger than those on absolute-return assets. Clearly the market doesn't think that U.S. stocks have a lower expected return and higher standard deviation than absolute-return assets."

13.10 Which of these uncertainties is the most important for a John-Burr-Williams value investor: future dividends, future interest rates, or future stock prices? Explain your reasoning.

13.11 On November 24, 2022, a website reported the following summary statistics, using stock return data for the preceding 10 years for Coca-Cola and Johnson & Johnson (JNJ):

	Mean	**Std Dev**	**Correlation**
Coca-Cola	8.67%	7.53%	.950
JNJ	12.90%	9.24%	

Identify the apparently incorrect number.

13.12 Vanguard showed a graph of R-squared for the equation B = a + bS + e, where B is the monthly return for the Lehman Aggregate Bond Index and S is the monthly return for the S&P 500. (The R-squared for each month was based on the previous 5 years' data.)

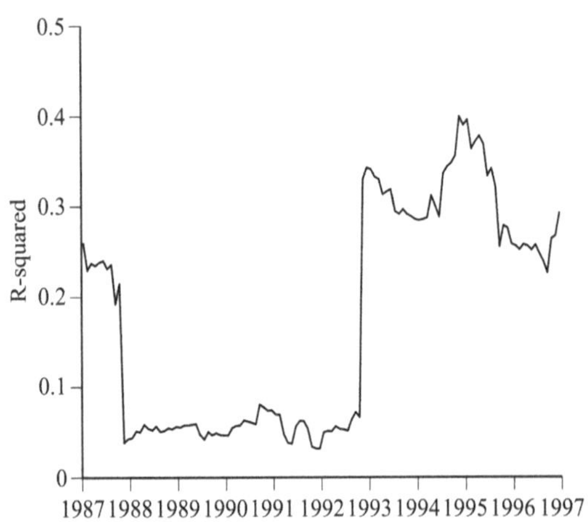

a. Provide a logical explanation for the empirical fact that R-squared is sometimes near 0% and sometimes near 40%.

b. This figure was used to support an argument for either: adding bonds to a stock portfolio or excluding bonds from a stock portfolio. Which and why?

13.13 A bank estimated that the return from a portfolio of Mexican bonds has an expected value of 18% and a standard deviation of 20% and that the return from a portfolio of U.S. corporate bonds has an expected return of 8% and a standard deviation of 10%. A senior officer argued that, because the bank is risk averse, it should invest in both. Is this argument more persuasive if the returns on the U.S. and Mexican bonds are positively correlated or negatively correlated? Why?

13.14 "Tobin's separation theorem is crazy. Why would the young, the elderly, the cautious, and the bold all hold the same stock portfolio? Clearly this guy has never been outside his Ivory tower." Describe Tobin's separation theorem and explain how investors with different risk preferences can satisfy their taste for risk while holding the same stock portfolio.

13.15 In November 1990, Edward Yardeni, Director of Economics and Fixed Income Research for Prudential-Bache Securities, wrote that

> For well over two years now, we have argued that rolling recessions [hitting specific regions of the country] were more likely than an economy-wide recession. We hedged our bet by adding that if the economy ever did start to slide into an economy-wide recession, the Fed would probably lower interest rates quickly to revive growth.... the Fed doesn't want a recession.

If Yardeni were using mean-variance analysis to decide how much to invest in long-term bonds and how much in stocks, does his reasoning imply that stock and bond returns are strongly positively correlated, strongly negatively correlated, or essentially uncorrelated?

13.16 Identify each of these probability distributions as positively skewed, negatively skewed, or symmetrical:

a. the normal distribution

b. a Superfecta bet, where correctly picking the first four finishers in a horse race wins a large amount of money

c. the purchase of a junk bond.

13.17 An investor will use mean-variance analysis to allocate her wealth among Treasury bills, a long-term Treasury bond fund, and an S&P 500 stock fund, with expected returns of 1.5%, 3%, and 7%, respectively. Which of these two scenarios do you predict will lead to a higher ratio of stocks to bonds in the optimal portfolio? Be sure to explain your reasoning.

a. There is little uncertainty about the economy and considerable uncertainty about interest rates.

b. There is little uncertainty about interest rates and considerable uncertainty about the economy.

13.18 A computer program identified these three portfolios as being on the Markowitz frontier. Carefully explain why there must be an error in this program.

Portfolio	Expected Return	Standard Deviation
1	5	8
2	10	15
3	15	18

13.19 Explain (a) the logic behind the Sharpe ratio and (b) how it is used.

13.20 Explain the theoretical rationale and weakness of judging mutual fund performance by the Sharpe ratio: (M – R)/S. Be sure to define M, R, and S.

13.21 William F. Sharpe's 1966 seminal study of the performance of 34 mutual funds over the 10-year period (1954–1963) calculated the risk-adjusted performance by taking the difference between each fund's average annual rate of return and the annual return on a safe asset, and dividing this difference by the standard deviation of the fund's annual rate of return. What is this calculation now called? For the annual return on a safe asset, he used the average interest rate on 10-year Treasury bonds in 1953. What is problematic about this choice?

13.22 Consider two risky investments, the first with an expected return of –5% and a standard deviation of 15%, and the second with an expected return of +5% and a standard deviation of 10%. A safe asset has a return of 0%. Would a risk-averse investor using mean-variance analysis to allocate her money among these three assets ever invest anything in the first asset?

13.23 A global asset management company used monthly data to estimate the correlation coefficients among the returns from three different types of assets: S&P 500 stock index, Lehman Brothers Treasury bond index, and TCW's high-yield bond index. The correlation coefficient between stocks and Treasury bonds was .2; the correlation coefficient between stocks and high-yield bonds was .5; and the correlation coefficient between Treasuries and high-yield bonds was .4. Explain the following:

a. why Treasuries and high-yields are positively correlated.
b. why Treasuries and stocks are positively correlated.
c. why the correlation between Treasuries and stocks is far from perfect.
d. why high-yield bonds are more closely correlated with stocks than with Treasury bonds.

13.24 A global asset management company used these assumptions for S&P 500 stocks, Treasury bonds, and high-yield (junk) bonds to construct this mean-variance opportunity locus:

			Correlations		
	Mean	**Std Dev**	**Stocks**	**Treasuries**	**Junk**
Stocks	12	20	1.00	.2	.5
Treasuries	6	10	.2	1.00	.4
Junk bonds	8	10	.5	.4	1.00

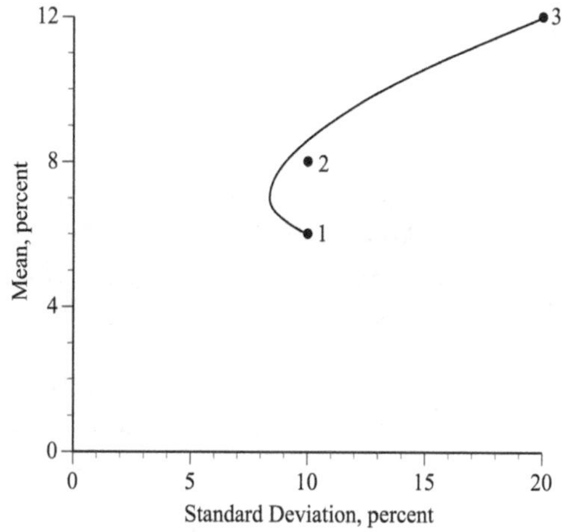

a. Which asset is labeled 2 in the graph?

b. Explain why Asset 2 is not on the opportunity locus.

c. What portfolio would a risk-neutral investor choose?

13.25 A retired person has all of her money invested in Treasury bills paying 5%. A financial adviser is trying to persuade her to invest some of her money in one of these diversified mutual funds:

Mutual Fund	**Average Return**	**Standard Deviation**
A	7%	7%
B	12%	12%
C	15%	15%

Using mean-variance analysis and assuming these to be the appropriate means and standard deviations looking forward, which one should she choose? Explain why her choice does not depend on her risk preferences.

13.26 A college endowment will divide its money among three groups of assets: T-bills paying 5%, a bundle of long-term bonds with an expected return of 8% and a standard deviation of 10%, and a bundle of stocks with an expected return of 15% and a standard deviation of 20%. What can you say about the ratio of long-term bonds to stocks that the endowment should hold in its portfolio if there is no uncertainty about the economy and considerable uncertainty about interest rates, so that the correlation coefficient between the returns on stocks and long-term bonds is 1.0? Would it make any difference if there was considerable uncertainty about the economy?

13.27 Which of the following does mean-variance analysis assume?

a. The probability distribution of returns is skewed.

b. Investor preferences depend only on the mean and variance of returns.

c. There is a safe asset.

d. The probability distribution of stock returns is uniform.

13.28 In 1996, Warren Buffett's Berkshire Hathaway signed an agreement with the California Earthquake Authority that took effect on April 1, 1997. The Authority paid Berkshire $590 million. In return, if an earthquake during the next 4 years resulted in homeowner claims that exceeded $7 billion, Berkshire would pay the next $1.5 billion in claims. The Earthquake Authority estimated that there was a .05 probability that there would be an earthquake during these 4 years that would cause claims to exceed $7 billion. Using this probability, calculate the expected value of Berkshire obligation. (Ignore the time value of money and assume that Berkshire will either have to pay $1.5 billion or nothing.)

13.29 Before Muhammad Ali's 1965 boxing rematch with Sonny Liston, rumors circulated that Ali would be murdered by Liston's gangster friends. Shortly before the match, the fight's closed-circuit-television promoter paid $1,000 for a three-day $1 million life insurance policy for Ali. For what probability P of Ali's death is the expected value of this policy less than its $1,000 cost?

13.30 What is the expected value of the payoff from this game? A fair coin will be flipped until it lands tails. Then the game ends. If it lands tails on the first flip, the player wins $1. The player wins $2 if it takes 2 flips, $4 if it takes 3 flips, and so on, with the prize doubling with every additional flip.

13.31 The 1-year return from Stock 1 has a mean of 10% and a standard deviation of 15%. The 1-year return from Stock 2 has a mean of 20% and a standard deviation of 20%. If both returns are normally distributed, which stock has a higher probability of a negative return?

13.32 A *Financial Analysts Journal* article showed a hypothetical scatter diagram of the expected returns and standard deviations for several stocks. The authors made the following "important observation":

> There are many stocks at each level of risk, but only one has the highest return. (It is all too easy to take high risks without getting commensurate rewards, especially in the short run.)

Explain the difference between the expected return and the highest return. Explain why it can be perfectly rational for someone to invest some money in a stock that has the same standard deviation and a lower expected return than another stock.

13.33 What is wrong with this Markowitz Frontier?

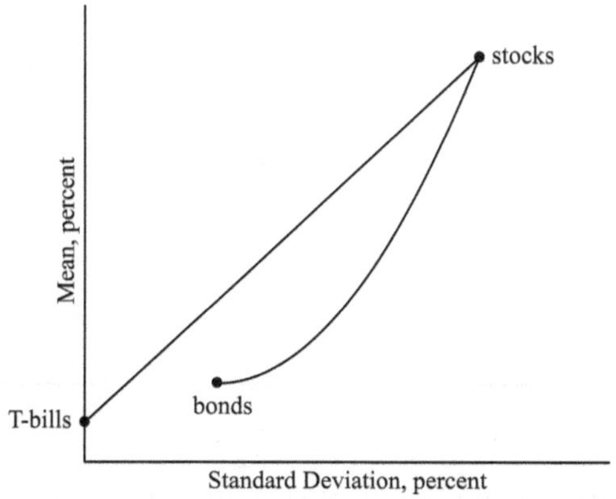

13.34 Mean-variance analysis provides a theoretical basis for holding diversified portfolios. Why, in practice, does the use of historical data to estimate mean-variance parameters often lead to extremely undiversified portfolios?

13.35 In his 1959 book, *Portfolio Selection: Efficient Diversification of Investments,* Harry Markowitz draws the mean-variance graph with the mean on the horizontal axis and the variance on the vertical axis. Which of these Markowitz frontiers for two risky assets assumes that the correlation between the returns is .0 and which assumes the correlation is .5?

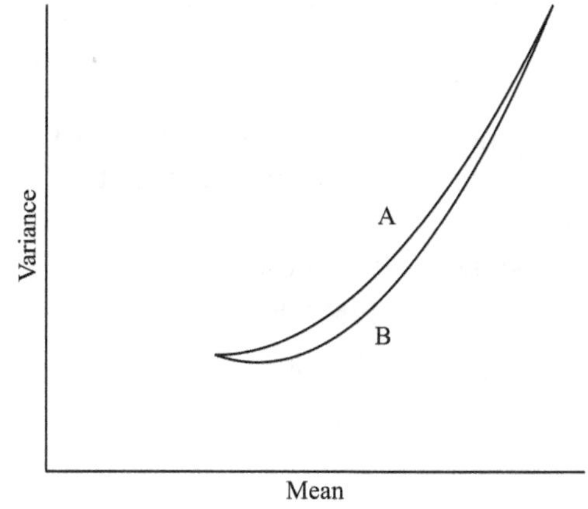

13.36 In his 1959 book, *Portfolio Selection: Efficient Diversification of Investments*, Harry Markowitz draws the mean-variance graph with the mean on the horizontal axis and the variance on the vertical axis:

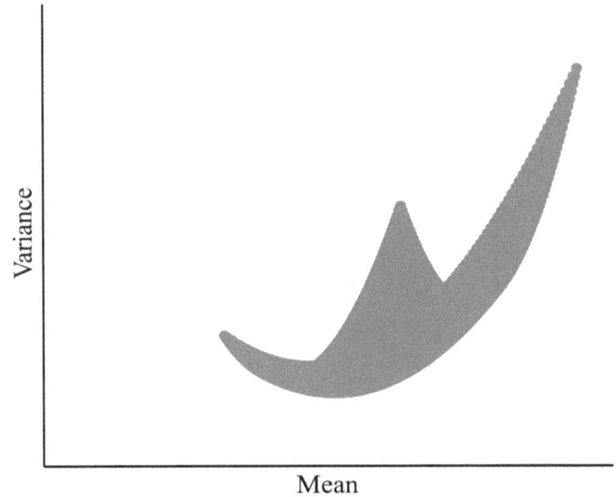

Draw the Markowitz Frontier in this graph. What is Tobin's Separation Theorem? Does it still hold?

13.37 The website efficientfrontier.app says that, "The Efficient Frontier is the set of optimal portfolios that offer the highest expected return for a defined level of risk." On November 17, 2022, using historical data for the previous year, the app estimated the following parameters:

			Correlations		
	Mean	**Std Dev**	**Apple**	**Google**	**IBM**
Apple	−5.20	7.96	1.00	.79	−.28
Google	−34.32	13.71	.79	1.00	−.44
IBM	30.10	5.55	−.28	−.44	1.00

The accompanying opportunity locus showed the means and standard deviations for all possible combinations of portfolios in 10% increments; for example

Apple 0%, Google 0%, IBM 100%

Apple 0%, Google 10%, IBM 90%

Apple 0%, Google 20%, IBM 80%

...

Apple 10%, Google 0%, IBM 90%

Apple 10%, Google 10%, IBM 80%

...

Apple 90%, Google 10%, IBM 0%

Apple 100%, Google 0%, IBM 0%

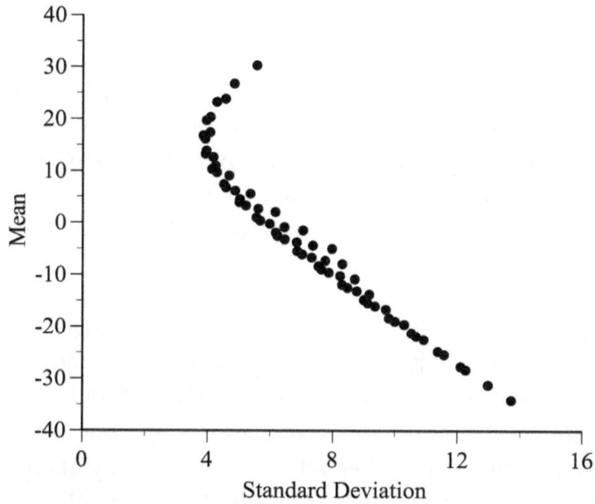

Using the same means, standard deviations, and correlations in the above table, a mean-variance software program gave this figure:

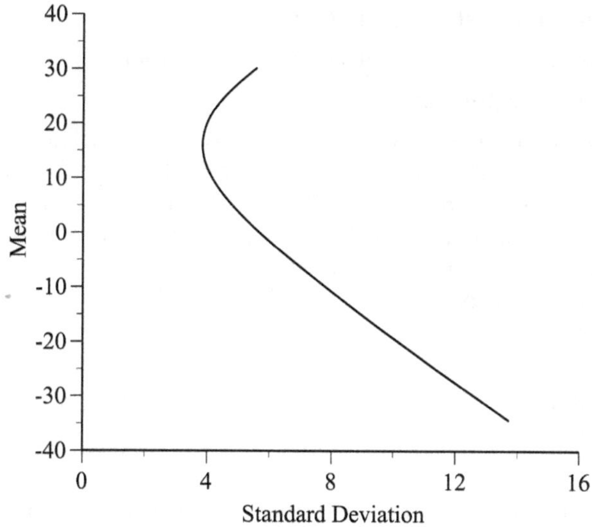

Explain why these graphs look so different.

13.38 The historical annual percentage returns for stocks and corporate bonds gave these estimates:

	Stocks	Bonds
Average	11.2	3.4
Standard deviation	22.2	5.7

Assuming these numbers to be the expected returns and standard deviation for the coming year, what portfolio of stocks and safe T-bills paying 2.5% dominates corporate bonds (has the same standard deviation as corporate bonds, but a higher expected return)? If so, why would any rational investor buy corporate bonds?

13.39 You are considering two tax-exempt assets, one with a guaranteed 0% return and the other with an expected return of 10% and a standard deviation of 20%. Considering the risk and return, you have decided to invest 60% in the risky asset and 40% in the safe asset. Use mean-variance analysis to show whether you will hold more or less of the risky asset if the government levies a 25% tax on both asset returns.

13.40 An investor is considering two tax-exempt assets, one with a guaranteed 0% return and the other with a return that is equally likely to be +25% or −5%. The investor decides to invest half of their wealth in each asset.

a. What is the expected % return on the first asset?

b. What is the expected % return on the second asset?

c. What is the expected % return on my portfolio?

d. What is the first asset's standard deviation?

e. What is the second asset's standard deviation?

f. What is the portfolio standard deviation?

A 20% tax has been levied on these investments. The first asset continues to yield a 0% after-tax return, while the second is equally likely to have an after-tax return of +20% or −4%. (The government gives a tax credit in the case of a loss.) Should the investor put more or less of their wealth in the risky asset? Use mean-variance analysis and explain your reasoning carefully.

Answers

13.1 The Markowitz Frontier describes opportunities, not preferences. It is not true that "Investments above the curve have too much risk." Investments above the curve are not possible, as the curve gives those portfolios that have the maximum expected return for any given level of risk.

13.2 Mean-variance analysis doesn't assume efficient stock markets. It can be used during bubbles and busts, with investors setting the values of mean, standard deviations, and correlation coefficients to reflect their beliefs.

13.3 For a horizon of 1-year, the purchase of a 1-year T-bill is a perfectly safe investment, with a rate of return equal to the current rate of return on a 1-year T-bill.

13.4 When the correlations between two returns is +1, there is a perfect positive relationship between the two returns in that either return can be predicted perfectly from the other, and the returns move in the same direction. It is not true that the magnitudes of the change in returns are the same.

13.5 All these calculations are flawed by the complete reliance on historical data but the same error is not supposed to be used for multiple answers.

a. We should use the current Treasury-bill return, not the historical average.

b. The standard deviation of the return on 10-year Treasury bonds measures uncertainty about the total return (coupons plus capital gains), not the volatility of the yield to maturity.

c. The expected value of the return on the S&P 500 should include dividends as well as price changes.

d. This is an argument for a positive correlation between stock and bond returns. (In addition, stock returns are affected by the economy.)

13.6 a. The total return from stocks should include dividends.

b. He should use the return on zeros, not the interest rate.

c. Looking forward, over a 1-year horizon, 1-year T-bills are risk-free.

13.7 The variance measures uncertainty by treating deviations above or below the mean equally. The semi-variance measures downside risk by only considered returns below the mean. (Markowitz proposed looking at the deviations not only below the mean, but below 0, or any other target return.)

13.8 The standard deviation used in mean-variance analysis is a measure of how certain we are about the return from an asset during the next year (or whatever horizon is being used). The historical standard deviation gauges the variation in the return from year to year. One-year T-bills, for example, have no uncertainty about their return during the next year, but may have considerable year-to-year variability.

13.9 U.S. stocks will still be held if they are sufficiently uncorrelated with the other assets. In practice, Swensen estimated that the correlations were .45 between U.S. stocks and U.S. bonds, .30 between U.S. stocks and absolute return assets, and .35 between U.S. bonds and absolute return assets.

13.10 Future dividends. The John Burr Williams valuation model is the present value of future dividends, discounted by required returns. Future stock prices are not considered and the required returns depend on *current* interest rates.

13.11 The correlation between the returns is surely not so close to 1.

13.12 a. Fluctuations in interest rates have similar effects on bond and stock returns; however, stock returns are also affected by the strength of the economy and investor psychology, which lowers the correlation between bond and stock returns—sometimes to near zero.

b. The empirical observation that the correlation between bond and stock returns was far from 1 was used to argue that bonds should be added to a stock portfolio for diversification.

13.13 The argument for diversification is stronger if the returns are negatively correlated because, in this case, diversification reduces the portfolio's standard deviation more.

13.14 In mean-variance analysis, if there is a safe asset, then Tobin's Separation Theorem states that there is an optimal risky portfolio on the Markowitz frontier that can be determined without regard to risk preferences. Those who are especially risk averse should put most of their wealth in the safe asset and relatively little in this risky bundle. Those who are less risk averse should invest larger amounts in the risky bundle, borrowing if necessary to leverage themselves.

13.15 His 1990 reasoning suggests that the macro economy is likely to be stable, but that there is considerable uncertainty about interest rates—which strongly affect both stocks and long-term bonds in the same direction. Therefore, stock and bond returns would be strongly positively correlated. If the Fed lowers interest rates to avoid a recession, both stock and bond prices will increase—making stocks and bonds positively correlated.

13.16 a. The normal distribution is symmetrical.

b. The return on a Superfecta bet is positively skewed.

c. The return on a junk bond is negatively skewed.

13.17 Scenario (a) favors a larger ratio of stocks to bonds in the portfolio; scenario (b) favors a smaller ratio. In scenario (a), stock and bond returns have large standard deviations and are strongly positively correlated, which argues against the inclusion of a lot of bonds in the portfolio. In scenario (b), Treasury bonds have little risk, stocks have considerable risk, and the returns are largely uncorrelated, which favors the inclusion of more bonds in the portfolio despite the relatively low expected return.

13.18 If the returns on Portfolios 1 and 3 were perfectly positively correlated, the opportunity locus between the two portfolios would be a straight line. One point on the line would be halfway between these two portfolios with an expected return of 10% and a standard deviation of 13%. This is to the left of Portfolio 2—the same expected return with a lower standard deviation! If the returns from Portfolios 1 and 3 are not perfectly positively correlated, then the opportunity locus is curved to the left. Thus, Portfolio 2 cannot be on the Markowitz frontier:

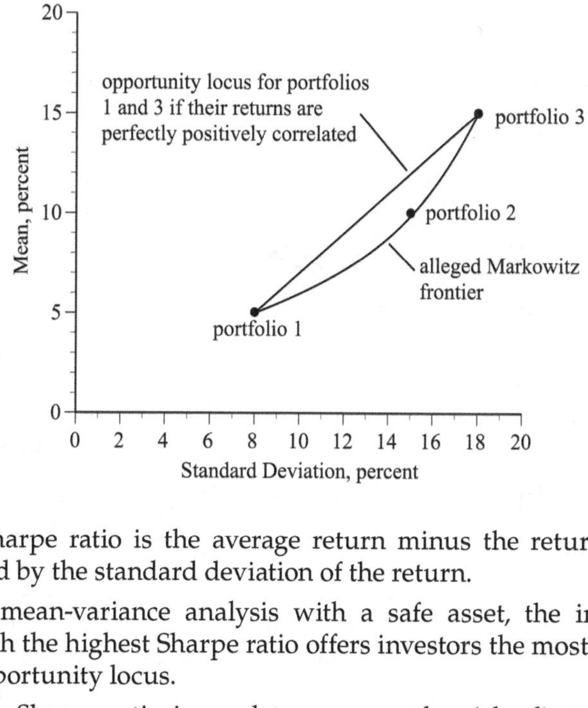

13.19 The Sharpe ratio is the average return minus the return on T-bills, divided by the standard deviation of the return.

a. In mean-variance analysis with a safe asset, the investment with the highest Sharpe ratio offers investors the most attractive opportunity locus.

b. The Sharpe ratio is used to compare the risk-adjusted performance of different investments, for example, mutual funds.

13.20 The symbol M stands for the fund's mean return, S for its standard deviation, and R for the return on safe T-bills. Using a mean-standard deviation diagram with investors allocating their money between safe T-bills and a single mutual fund, it can be seen that a fund with a high Sharpe ratio offers investors an opportunity locus that lies above the opportunity locus of funds with lower Sharpe ratios. Thus, an investor choosing between funds should select the fund with the highest Sharpe ratio. (On the other hand, if investors can allocate their money among safe T-bills and more than one mutual fund, the Jensen ratio (M – R/ beta is more appropriate).

13.21 It is called the Sharpe ratio. The means and standard deviations of the annual returns assume that investors have a 1-year horizon but the average 1953 interest rate on 10-year Treasury bonds is not a safe return over a 1-year horizon because fluctuations in interest rates will cause capital gains and losses on the bond. The standard deviation of the returns from 10-year Treasury bonds is not zero. Sharpe should have used the return on a 1-year Treasury bond, which is safe over a 1-year horizon. The problem is that the 1-year Treasury rate fluctuated greatly over the 10-year period (1954–1963), and there is no compelling reason for choosing which year's rate to use. So, Sharpe used a 10-year rate—even though different rates might have given somewhat different conclusions.

13.22 Yes, if the correlation coefficient is sufficiently negative. For example, with a correlation of –.9:

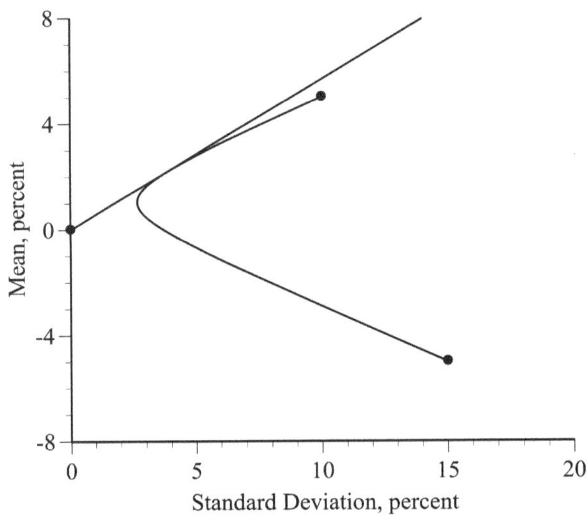

13.23 High-yield bonds are junk bonds.

a. Treasuries and high-yields are both bonds with promised future coupons and principal; the present values (and market prices) decline when market interest rates go up and rise when market interest rates fall.

b. Stocks, too, have a future cash flow (dividends), with a present value that is inversely related to interest rates.

c. The correlation between Treasuries and stocks is far from perfect because, unlike Treasuries with their fixed coupons, the future cash flow from stocks is uncertain and fluctuates with the strength of the economy.

d. High-yields are evidently more closely correlated with stocks than with Treasuries because their returns are sensitive to the strength of the economy in the same direction as stocks. This makes sense because a strong economy will not only increase stock earnings and dividends but also make it more likely that junk-bond issuers will be able to pay their promised coupons and principal.

13.24 a. Asset 2 is junk bonds.

b. By itself, junk bonds are not mean-variance efficient.

c. A risk-neutral investor maximizes expected return and would invest 100% in stocks.

13.25 A sketch of each opportunity locus for combining the safe asset with a mutual fund shows that Fund C wins in that it offers the highest mean for any standard deviation. (The opportunity locus for combining all three funds would likely offer even better options.)

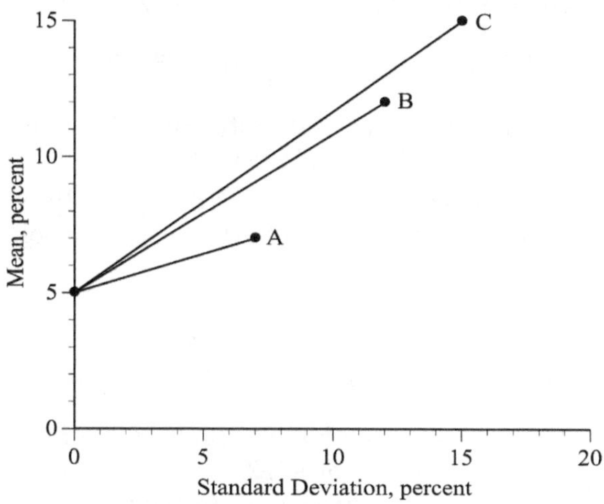

13.26 If the correlation between stocks and long-term bonds is 1.0, the opportunity locus for these two risky assets is a straight line. The figure shows that a combination of T-bills with stocks dominates any portfolio of bonds and stocks (or any portfolio that includes T-bills, bonds, and stocks). However, if there were considerable uncertainty about the economy, so that the bond-stock correlation is substantially less than 1, the bond-stock opportunity locus would be curved, and it might be desirable to hold bonds to diversify the portfolio.

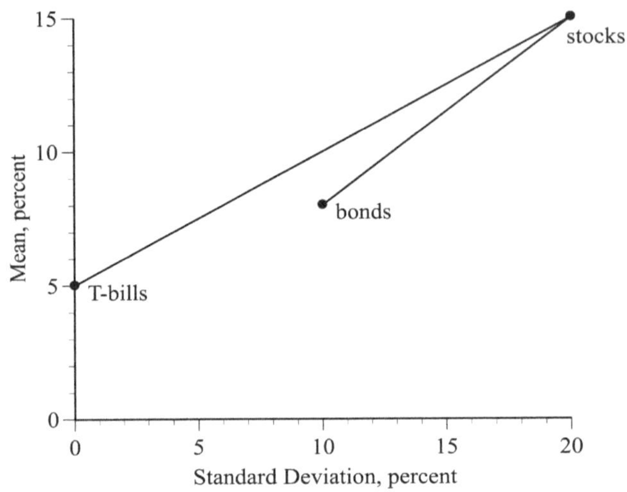

13.27 Mean-variance analysis assumes (b) that investor preferences depend only on the mean and variance of returns.

13.28 The expected value of Berkshire's liability is \$75 million:

$$(\$1.5 \text{ billion})(.05)+(\$0)(.95)=\$75 \text{ million}$$

The California Earthquake Authority paid \$590 million to avoid a gamble with an expected value of \$75 million.

13.29 Letting P be the probability of Ali's death during the three days covered by the policy, the expected value of the life insurance policy is less than \$1,000 if P < .001:

$$\mu=\$1,000,000(\mathrm{P})+\$0(1-\mathrm{P})$$
$$<\$1,000 \text{ if } \mathrm{P}<\$1,000/\$1,000,000=.001$$

13.30 This is the St Petersburg paradox. The probability of the game ending after 1 flip (tails on the first flip) is 1/2; the probability of the game ending after two flips (a HT sequence) is 1/4; the probability of the game ending after three flips (a HHT sequence) is 1/8; and so on. The expected value of the payoff is infinite, but few people would pay more than a few dollars to play, demonstrating that people do not simply maximize expected return.

$$\text{expected value}=\$1\left(\frac{1}{2}\right)+\$2\left(\frac{1}{4}\right)+\$4\left(\frac{1}{8}\right)+\ldots$$
$$=\left(\frac{1}{2}\right)+\left(\frac{1}{2}\right)+\left(\frac{1}{2}\right)+\ldots=\infty$$

13.31 Converting to standardized Z values, Stock 1 is more likely to have a negative return:

$$\text{Stock 1: } P[X<0]=P\left[\frac{X-\mu}{\sigma}<\frac{0-10}{15}\right]=P\left[Z<-\frac{2}{3}\right]$$

$$\text{Stock 2: } P[X<0]=P\left[\frac{X-\mu}{\sigma}<\frac{0-20}{20}\right]=P[Z<-1]$$

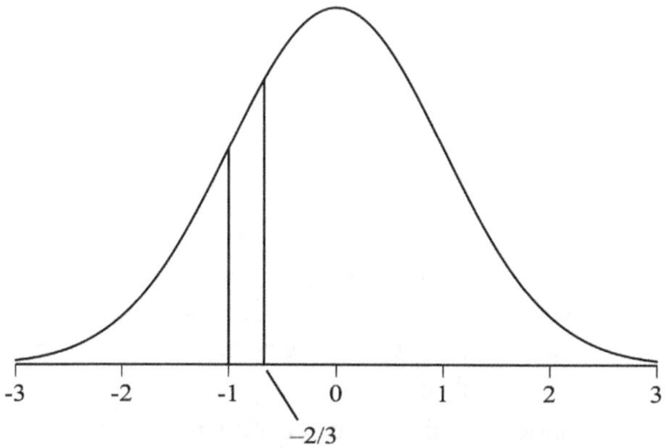

13.32 The expected return is the anticipated long-run average return; even if the probabilities that underlie these expected returns are accurate, there is no assurance that the investment with the highest expected value will turn out to have the highest actual return. Someone might invest in a stock with the same standard deviation and a lower expected return than another stock if it has a low enough correlation with other stocks to provide diversification:

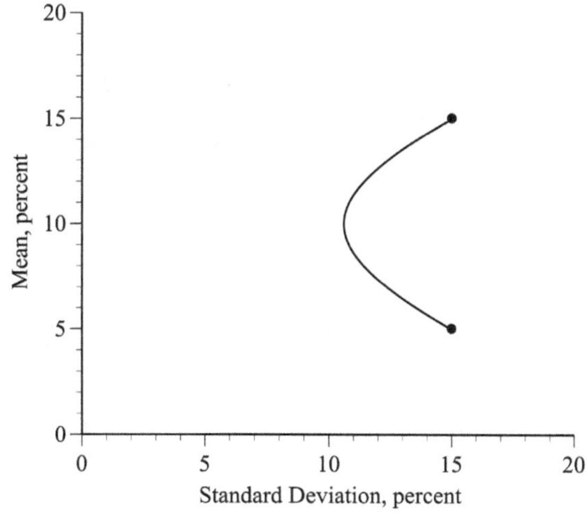

13.33 The stock-bond frontier is bowed in the wrong direction. It should be something like this:

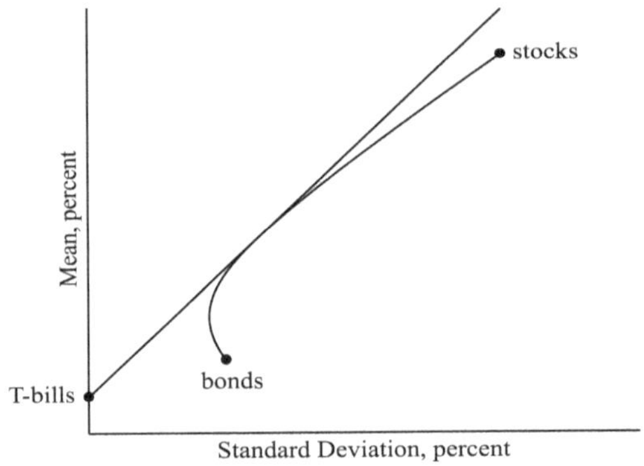

13.34 Often, one or two risky assets happen to have done much better than the other assets being considered. If these abnormally high returns are used as expected values going forward, mean-variance analysis is likely to recommend investing very heavily in the best-performing assets and almost nothing in the other assets.

13.35 A smaller correlation implies a greater reduction in variance for any given expected return. So, B is the Markowitz frontier for a correlation of .0.

13.36 The Markowitz Frontier is the minimum variance for any mean, but it doesn't go left of the minimum variance because for those points on the curve, it is possible to have a higher mean for the same variance:

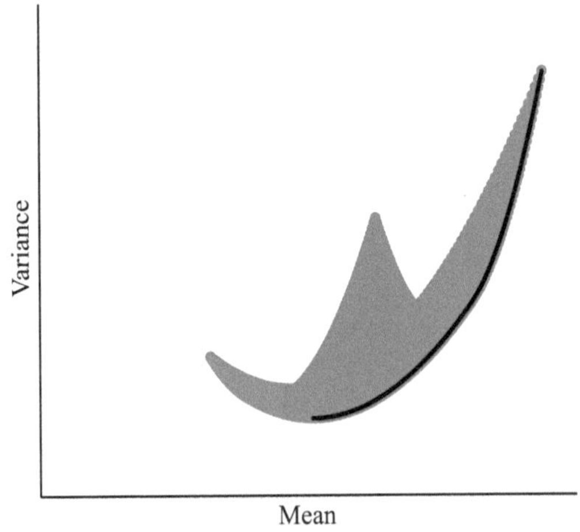

Tobin's Separation Theorem is that the optimal risky portfolio doesn't depend on preferences. It still holds, because this theorem doesn't depend on how the opportunity locus is graphed.

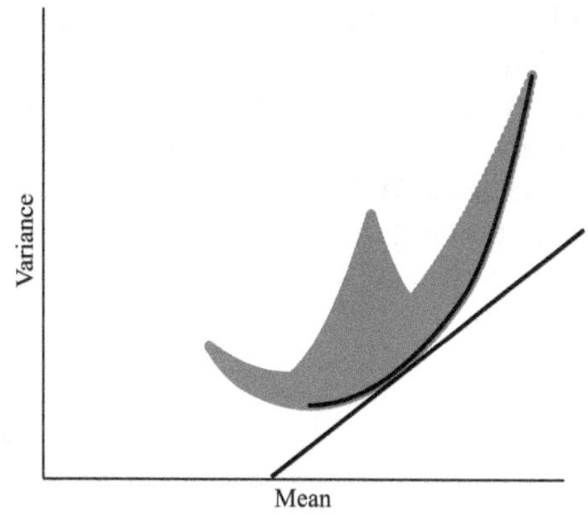

13.37 The efficientfrontier.app does not give the efficient Markowitz frontier, just the means and standard deviations for various portfolios, most of which are not mean-variance efficient.

13.38 The expected return and standard deviation for a portfolio with a fraction α of wealth invested in stocks and (1 – α) invested in safe T-bills are

$$\text{Mean} = \alpha(11.2) + (1-\alpha)2.5$$
$$\text{Std. dev.} = \alpha(22.2)$$

The portfolio standard deviation is equal to 5.7 (which is the standard deviation of bonds) if α is 5.7/22.7 = .251. The mean for this portfolio is .251(11.2) + (1 – .251)(2.5) = 4.68, which is larger than the 3.4 bond mean return. This portfolio dominates corporate bonds in that it has a higher expected return with the same standard deviation.

A rational mean-variance investor would not buy corporate bonds alone, but might include corporate bonds in a portfolio that also contains Treasury bills and stocks if the bond and stock returns are sufficiently uncorrelated.

Graphically:

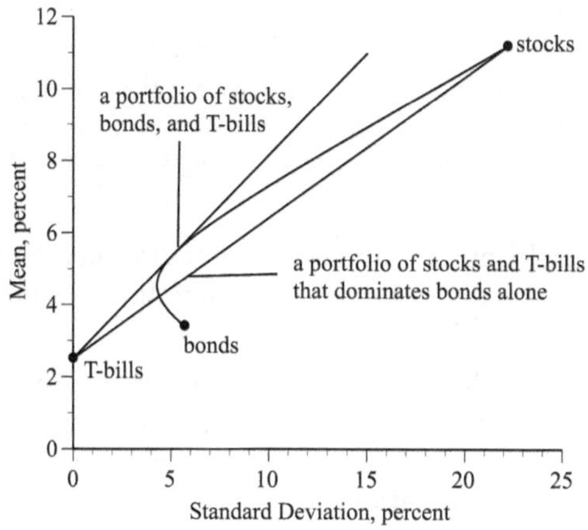

13.39 The 25% tax reduces the expected value of the after-tax return on the risky asset to .75(10%) = 7.5% and reduces the standard deviation to .75(20%) = 15%. This shrinks the opportunity locus toward the origin. If you had a tangency before with a 60-40 division giving an expected return of 6% and a standard deviation of 12%, you will continue to have a tangency at that point but now you will have to invest 75% in the risky asset to get a 6% expected return and 12% standard deviation.

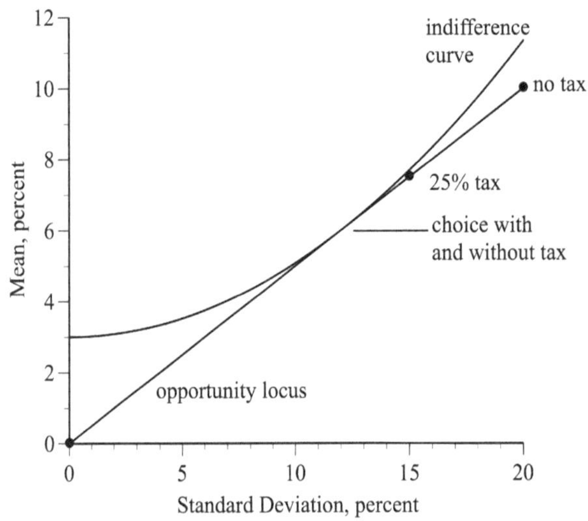

13.40 a. The expected return equals the guaranteed return: 0%.

b. The expected return equals the possible returns, weighted by their probabilities: (25%)(.5) + (–5%)(.5) = 10%.

c. The portfolio expected return equals the asset expected returns weighted by the portfolio fractions invested in each asset: $\mu = \alpha\mu_1 + (1 - \alpha)\,\mu_2$ = (0%)(.5) + (10%)(.5) = 5%.

d. The standard deviation of a safe asset is 0%.

e. The variance of the risky asset equals the squared deviations of the possible returns from the mean, weighted by the probabilities: $(25\% - 10\%)^2(.5) + (-5\% - 10\%)^2(.5) = 15\%^2$. The standard deviation is 15%.

f. With one risky asset with standard deviation σ and one safe asset with standard deviation 0, the portfolio standard deviation is $\alpha\sigma$ = (.5)(15%) = 7.5%.

After the imposition of the tax, the return on the first asset continues to have an expected value of 0% and a standard deviation of 0%. The return on the second asset now has an expected value of .8(10%) = 8% and a standard deviation of .8(15%) = 12%. The opportunity locus shrinks toward the origin. If the investor had a tangency before with a 50-50 division, the investor will continue to have a tangency at an expected return of 5% and a standard deviation of 7.5%. In order to achieve this expected return and standard deviation, the investor now invests 5%/8% = 62.5% (instead of 50%) in the risky asset.

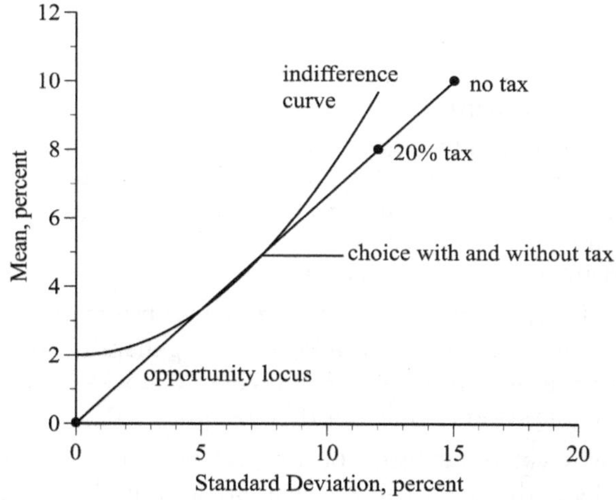

14

CAPM and Other Factor Models

14.1 Explain why this intermediate microeconomics textbook's explanation of a stock's beta coefficient is misleading:

> This is the ratio of the variability in the return of the common stock of the firm to the variability in the average return on the common stocks of all firms.... A beta coefficient of 1 means that the variability in returns on the common stock of the firm is the same as the variability in the returns on all stocks.

14.2 Explain why you either agree or disagree with this Motley Fool explanation of beta: "A stock with a beta of 1.0 generally rises and falls in sync with the overall market. More volatile stocks have betas greater than 1.0, while steadier ones sport betas under 1.0."

14.3 Explain why you either agree or disagree with this CAPM advice from the founder of the American Association of Individual Investors: "If the market was expected to rise, an investor should increase the R-square of the portfolio. If the market was expected to decline, a portfolio with a low R-square would be appropriate."

14.4 Answer this question: "Isn't it inconsistent to measure risk by the standard deviation in mean-variance analysis and by the beta coefficient in the capital asset pricing model?"

14.5 The Value Line investment advisory service used to run an investment contest periodically. In the 1972 contest, each entrant picked a hypothetical portfolio of 25 stocks out of more than 1000 eligible stocks. After 6 months, those entrants with the best-performing portfolios won prizes, while the losers were encouraged to subscribe to Value Line. Two academics entered two portfolios, one containing the 25 stocks with the highest beta coefficients and the other containing the 25 stocks with the lowest beta coefficients (some negative, many near zero).

a. What do you suppose was their reasoning?

b. The low-beta portfolio beat the high-beta portfolio and was among the top 2.3% of the entries. What do you think happened to the stock market during this period?

c. For its 1985 contest, Value Line divided 1,650 eligible stocks into 10 categories, each with 165 stocks. Each entrant elected a portfolio of 10 stocks, one from each category. Why do you think Value Line did this, and how do you suppose they chose the stocks to put in each category?

DOI: 10.1201/9781003630166-14

14.6 In 1989, the American Association of Individual Investors omitted beta coefficients from its descriptions of precious-metal mutual funds in its widely read mutual-fund guide. The director of research explained: "Our fear was people would look just at the beta and say here is an investment with very low risk." How could a mutual fund with a low beta coefficient be risky?

14.7 It has been argued that conglomerates benefit shareholders because the merger of dozens of unrelated companies diversifies away idiosyncratic risk, leaving only macro risk. Explain why you agree or disagree.

14.8 Which (if any) of these assumptions are made by CAPM?

a. All investors use mean-variance analysis.

b. All investors agree on the Markowitz frontier.

c. All investors are risk-averse.

d. All investors can borrow and lend at the Treasury-bill rate.

14.9 Historical plots of the rates of return on two stocks and on the market as a whole are in the figure below. During this period, which of these two firms' returns had the higher

a. average return?

b. standard deviation?

c. beta coefficient?

d. R-squared?

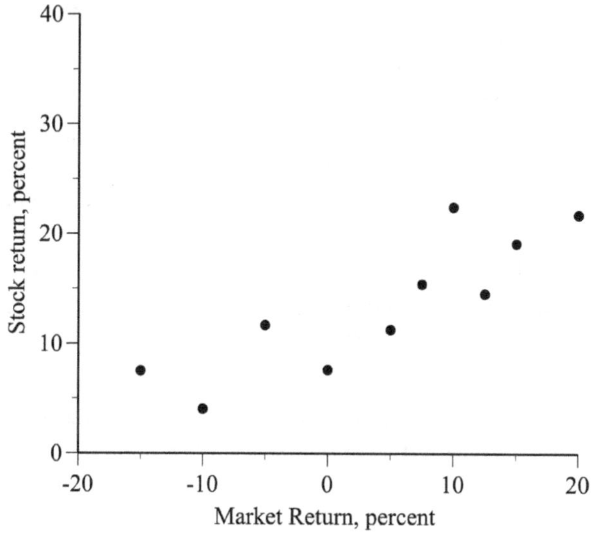

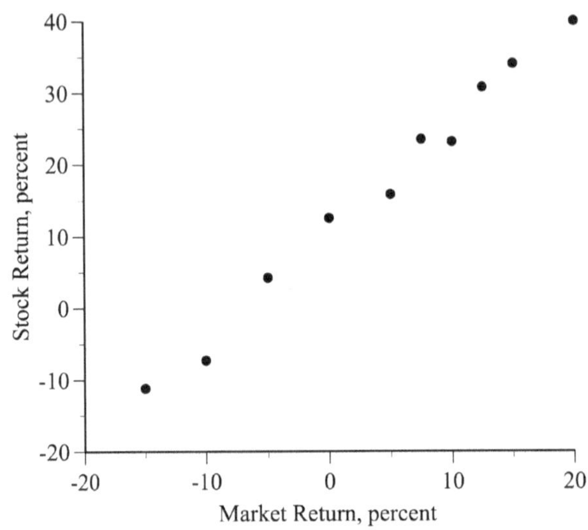

14.10 Value Line recommends that an investor who owns fewer than 15 stocks gauge riskiness by looking at Value Line's "safety ratings" for these stocks, and that an investor who owns more than 15 stocks instead calculate the average beta. Why are the safety ratings not identical to the beta coefficients, and why does the appropriate risk measure depend on the number of stocks an investor holds?

14.11 The standard deviation is an appealing and useful measure of risk, but financial analysts argue that beta is even better. What is their reasoning?

14.12 CAPM assumes that investors use mean-variance analysis to choose portfolios. If so, and investors are risk averse, explain why assets with relatively high variances either are or are not priced to have relatively high expected returns.

14.13 Many investors look at the beta coefficients provided by investment advisors. Explain why this advice is misleading: "A stock with a low beta is safer than a high-beta stock, because the lower beta is, the less the stock's price fluctuates."

14.14 In a stock picking contest, a student picked stock X and wrote that, "X has a beta of .90 which means it is a very stable stock." Explain why this logic is either true or is not true.

14.15 Is there any portfolio that has a beta of 1 and an R-squared of 1, too?

14.16 Explain why you either agree or disagree with this assertion: "According to the capital asset pricing model, zero-beta stocks have a zero expected return."

14.17 In the CAPM model, when, if ever, would someone buy an asset with a negative expected return?

14.18 A friend tells you about a gold mining stock that typically goes down when the stock market rises and goes up when the market falls (she estimates its beta to be –.2). Treasury bills currently return 5%, and the consensus opinion is that the expected return on the stock market is 10%. If the stock of the mining company is priced according to CAPM, what is the expected value of its return? Explain clearly and persuasively why this expected value is less than 5%.

14.19 A study of the determinants of price-earnings ratios asked 17 professional security analysts for the following data on 178 well-known stocks:

P/E = price/normal earnings, adjusted for temporary events

g = anticipated growth rate

d = anticipated dividends/earnings

b = beta coefficient

After averaging these data, the following cross-section equation was estimated to explain the variation in price-earnings ratios among firms:

$$P/E = 3.47 + 2.57g + 7.17d - .84b$$

Interpret the coefficients of the three explanatory variables and identify which, if any, have "wrong" signs.

14.20 Some new MBAs have just incorporated and raised $10 million by selling stock. What will the beta of this stock be if they

a. buy $10 million of assets with a beta of 1.2?

b. buy $8 million of assets with a beta of 1.2 and invest $2 million in Treasury bills?

c. borrow $4 million and buy $14 million of assets with a beta of 1.2?

14.21 A and B are two companies, identical in all respects, except that A has no debt and B is 50% debt-financed. For each of the following financial statistics, indicate whether you expect the value of the statistic to be higher for company A or B. Briefly explain your reasoning.

a. expected return on assets

b. standard deviation of return on stock

c. beta coefficient of stock

d. shareholders' required return on stock

14.22 Consider the following data on the value of a market index and the price of stock B:

	January 1, 2005	January 1, 2025
Market	5000	10000
Stock B	50	200

Explain why the estimated beta for this stock is not necessarily 2. In particular, show how the estimated beta could be negative.

14.23 In 2010, a fund manager wrote that he liked to focus on investments with substantial idiosyncratic risks.

a. What are idiosyncratic risks? Give two examples.

b. Why would a fund manager be attracted to investments with substantial idiosyncratic risks?

14.24 In a traditional index fund, the amount of money invested in each stock is proportional to its market value (number of shares times price per share). Robert Arnott advocates fundamental indexing, with relatively more money allocated to stocks that have high dividend/price and low price/earnings ratios. Which approach do you suppose

a. gives heavier weight to growth stocks?

b. is more vulnerable to speculative bubbles?

14.25 A researcher reported the following estimated equation using daily data:

$$\underset{[.29]}{R = .0002} + \underset{[12.69]}{1.212M} + \underset{[8.79]}{1.40S} + \underset{[3.00]}{.58H}, \quad R^2 = .05$$

where the t-values are in brackets and

R = return on Hemisphere Fund capital shares minus return on T-bills
M = return on S&P 500 minus return on T-bills
S = size factor
H = book-to-market factor

a. Is it possible for coefficients to be statistically significant when the R^2 is so low?

b. Why is the coefficient of M larger than 1?

c. Why do you think that the coefficient of H is positive?

d. What does the intercept measure?

14.26 Part of a case study prepared by the Tuck School of Business at Dartmouth analyzed the performance of the Legg-Mason Value Prime fund during a period when the fund earned an annual return of 27.3%, compared to the market's 21.6%. Monthly data were used to estimate the Fama-French 3-factor model,

$$R_i - R_0 = .22 + .99(R_M - R_0) + .36SMB + .22HML$$

where R_i is the fund's return, R_0 is the risk-free rate, R_M is the market return, SMB is the average return that month for the smallest 30% of stocks minus the average return for the largest 30%, and HML is the average return that month for the 50% of stocks with the highest book/

market ratio minus the average return for the 50% of stocks with the lowest book/market ratio. All returns are percentages.

The case study concludes that, "The relatively low t-statistic of 1.1, however, undermines her claim and indicates that … the high returns are associated with the fund's exposure to size and value risk rather than the skill of the manager. Finally, the [0.92] R^2 tells us that the three factors explain all but 8% of the variation in historical returns, further lending credence to the findings."

a. Which estimated parameter has a t-value of 1.1?
b. Why is 1.1 considered low?
c. What is an alternative explanation to "the high returns are associated with the fund's exposure to size and value risk rather than the skill of the manager"?

14.27 Shown below are 4 assets, the Markowitz Frontier, and CAPM's market portfolio. Which asset has the higher beta coefficient, 2 or 3? Explain your reasoning.

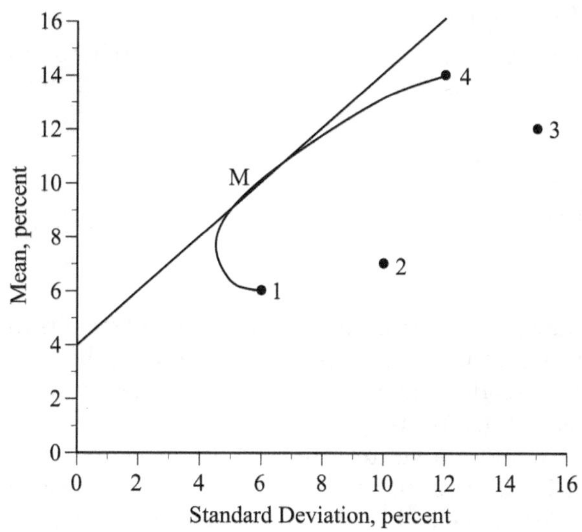

14.28 A savings and loan (S&L) named Far West Financial began trading on the NYSE in 1964. Using monthly data, its beta coefficient was .08 for the first 5 years and 1.51 for the next 10 years. Explain why we might expect an S&L to have a relatively low beta during some historical periods and a relatively high beta during other periods. What might we use instead of CAPM's beta to measure the systematic risk of S&Ls?

14.29 The CAPM model has been criticized for being overly simplistic in that the relationship between the return on the overall stock market and the return on an individual stock depends on the cause of fluctuations in the return on the overall market; for example, whether the market went up because of unexpected changes in economic activity, interest rates, taxes, or animal spirits. Consider, for example, a low-dividend, high-growth stock and a high-dividend, low-growth stock. Which intrinsic value would be affected more by an unexpected increase in interest rates?

14.30 The following factor-model equations were estimated

$$R_1 = 80 - 3U - 10Y$$
$$R_2 = 10 + 1U - 2Y$$

where R_1 and R_2 are the respective percentage rates of return on assets 1 and 2, U is the percentage unemployment rate, and Y is the percentage yield to maturity on 10-year Treasury bonds.

a. Interpret the coefficient –10.
b. Show how an investor could construct a portfolio consisting of only these two assets with a portfolio return that would not be sensitive to the unemployment rate.
c. What is the expected return for the portfolio in (b) if the 10-year Treasury yield is 5%?

Answers

14.1 This quotation makes it seem that the beta coefficient is the ratio of two variances. Instead, it is a measure of the amount by which the return on the stock tends to increase when the market return increases by 1 percentage point. (Formally, it is the ratio of the covariance between the stock return and market return to the variance of the market return.) A beta of 1 indicates that a 1 percentage point increase in the market return increases the expected value of the stock return by 1%. The variance of the stock need not equal the variance of the market portfolio.

14.2 If the return on the market is x% larger (or smaller) than expected, the expected return on a stock is beta(x%) larger (or smaller) than expected. However, the return on the stock will not be exactly beta(x%) larger (or smaller) than expected, unless the R-squared is 1. A stock's volatility also depends on its idiosyncratic risk. A stock can have a low beta and still be very volatile.

14.3 If the investor were confident that stock prices were going up, a high-beta portfolio would be appropriate. A high R-squared would also be nice, since the investor could then be confident that firm-specific risk has been diversified away, but a high beta is paramount. A high R-squared with a low or negative beta would be exactly the wrong portfolio.

14.4 No, it is not inconsistent. CAPM assumes that investors use mean-variance analysis and gauge risk by the standard deviation of their portfolio return. The insight provided by CAPM is that a well-diversified portfolio will eliminate idiosyncratic risk, leaving only systematic risk—which is measured by beta coefficients.

14.5 CAPM had been developed in the 1960s but was not yet widely understood.

a. The professors reasoned that their high-beta portfolio would do very well if the stock market went up and their low-beta portfolio would do relatively well if the market went down.

b. The market went down and the low-beta portfolio did well.

c. Value Line put the 165 highest-beta stocks in Category 1, the 165 stocks with the next highest betas in Category 2, and so on, so that no one could use the professors' strategy.

14.6 Beta gauges risk as part of a larger diversified portfolio. Because a gold fund is not very diversified, its return could have a very large standard deviation and a very low, even negative, beta coefficient.

14.7 If they want to, shareholders can diversify idiosyncratic risk without a merger by buying shares in unrelated companies. A merger is, in fact, harmful in that it reduces shareholder flexibility in choosing how much to invest in each company.

14.8 CAPM makes all of these assumptions.

14.9 Call the stock on the left A and the stock on the right B.

a. Looking at the heights of the data, B had the higher average return.

b. Looking at the dispersion in the heights of the data, B had the higher standard deviation.

c. Looking at the slope of a line fit to the data, B had the higher beta coefficient.

d. Looking at how close the points are to a line fit to the data, B had the higher R-squared.

14.10 The individual safety ratings are analogous to the standard deviations of individual stock returns. In a well-diversified portfolio (and 15 stocks may be sufficient), the idiosyncratic risk will be largely diversified away, leaving only systematic risk, which is gauged by beta coefficients.

14.11 The standard deviation is a useful measure of risk for a portfolio, or for a single stock if only one stock is held. But in a diversified portfolio, much of the risk is diversified away, and only systematic macro risk, as gauged by a stock's beta, contributes to the portfolio standard deviation.

14.12 According to CAPM, it is not the asset's variance that matters, but rather the macro risk that cannot be diversified away. This macro risk is gauged by the asset's beta.

14.13 The return on a stock depends on how well the overall market does and on factors specific to this particular company; the stock's beta coefficient measures the extent to which its return moves with the return on all stocks. A low-beta stock is not very sensitive to overall market movements, but still may be very volatile. While beta is not a good measure of risk for an individual stock, it may be a good gauge for a diversified portfolio, since the firm-specific risks will probably cancel each other out.

14.14 Beta measures the slope of the linear relationship between the stock return and the market return and is a measure of the stock's systematic risk. The stock itself could have a very high standard deviation.

14.15 The market portfolio has a beta of 1 and an R-squared of 1.

14.16 According to CAPM, zero-beta stocks have an expected return equal to the return on the safe asset:

$$\begin{aligned} E_i &= R_0 + \beta_i(E_M - R_0) \\ &= R_0 \text{ if } \beta_i = 0 \end{aligned}$$

14.17 If the beta coefficient is sufficiently low. Specifically, assuming $E_M - R_0 > 0$, CAPM gives

$$\begin{aligned} E_i &= R_0 + \beta_i(E_M - R_0) \\ 0 &> R_0 + \beta_i(E_M - R_0) \\ \beta_i &< \frac{-R_0}{E_M - R_0} \end{aligned}$$

14.18 The CAPM equation $E = R_0 + b(E_M - R_0)$ gives a 4% expected return:

$$\begin{aligned} E_i &= R_0 + \beta_i(E_M - R_0) \\ &= 5 - .2(10 - 5) = 4 \end{aligned}$$

Investors are willing to settle for an expected return on this risky stock that is less than the 5% guaranteed return on Treasury bills because the negative beta coefficient makes this stock very valuable in reducing the systematic, macro risk of a well-diversified portfolio.

14.19 All of the signs make sense. (Remember that each coefficient is ceteris paribus). For a given payout policy and beta, growth is good for a stock's price. For a given growth rate and beta, a high payout ratio is good for a stock's price. For a given growth rate and payout policy, a high beta requires a higher expected return and, therefore, a lower price.

14.20 a. 1.2

b. .8(1.2) + .2(.0) = .96

c. 1.4(1.2) + (−.4)(.0) = 1.68

14.21 a. The expected return on assets is the same.

b. Leverage increases the standard deviation of stock B's return.

c. Leverage increases stock B's beta coefficient.

d. The higher beta coefficient increases the shareholders' required return on stock B.

14.22 The market and stock did not necessarily increase monotonically over this time period. Perhaps the market rose above 10,000 and then fell back to 10,000, while Stock B fell and then rose to 200; if so, the estimated beta coefficient would be negative. In the illustrative graph below, both prices have been scaled to equal 1 on January 1, 2005. The beta is −2.24, with $R^2 = .49$.

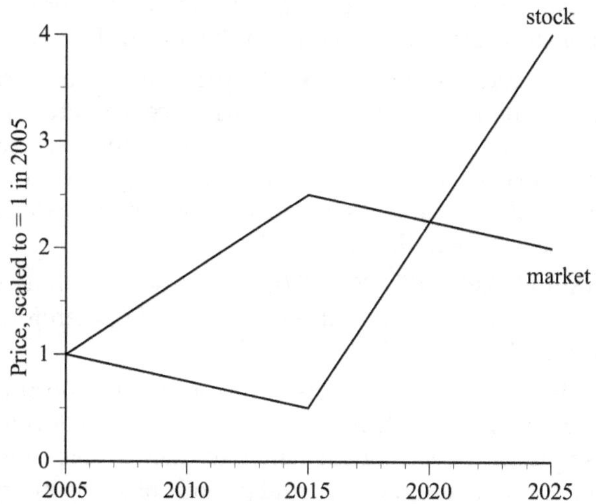

14.23 a. Idiosyncratic risks are risks specific to an investment that can be diversified away, for example, whether a technology company's patent infringement lawsuit will be successful, or whether a pharmaceutical company's drug application will be approved by the FDA.

b. Perhaps this manager feels that the fund can analyze idiosyncratic uncertainties better than macroeconomic uncertainties like interest rates and the overall economic outlook.

14.24 a. Traditional index funds give more weight to growth stocks since they have relatively high market prices relative to their dividends and earnings.

b. Traditional index funds are more vulnerable speculative to bubbles since stocks whose prices are soaring automatically become a larger part of their portfolios.

14.25 a. Yes, as here, we can reject the null hypothesis that a coefficient is equal to zero even if the model only explains a small part of the variation in the dependent variable.

b. Dual-purpose fund capital shares have considerable leverage.

c. The positive coefficient of H reflects the positive returns from value strategies, with low ratios of stock prices to dividends, earnings, and assets.

d. The intercept ("alpha") measures the extent to which the asset or portfolio gives an above-average, risk-adjusted return.

14.26 a. Alpha is the estimate of excess return beyond that explained by the model, so one question is whether it is statistically significant.

b. The t-value needs to be above (approximately) 2 for the usual criteria of statistically significance at the 5% level.

c. The case study is interpreting the three factors as various risks, so that alpha is risk-adjusted performance. An alternative explanation is that some types of stocks systematically beat the market because of market inefficiencies. Legg-Mason apparently achieved its above-average return by having relatively large investments in small, value stocks.

14.27 According to CAPM, $E_i - R_0 = \beta_i(E_M - R_0)$, so that an asset's expected return is positively related to its beta coefficient. Therefore, Asset 3 has a higher beta than Asset 2.

14.28 S&Ls traditionally borrow short-term from their depositors in order to make long-term, fixed-rate mortgages. Their (highly levered) net worth has consequently been more sensitive to interest rate movements than that of the average company. During periods of stable interest rates (like the 1960s), S&Ls had low betas. During periods with big interest rate movements (like the 1970s), S&Ls had high betas. Instead of the single index model, we might use a factor model with interest rates as one of the factors.

14.29 The high-growth stock has a longer duration, so it would be affected more.

14.30 a. If the yield to maturity on 10-year Treasury bonds increases by 1 percentage point, holding constant the unemployment rate, the rate of return on Asset 1 is predicted to fall by 10%.

b. If 1/4 of the portfolio is invested in Asset 1 and 3/4 is invested in Asset 2, then the portfolio return R_P is

$$\begin{aligned} R_P &= .25R_1 + .75R_2 \\ &= .25(80 - 3U - 10Y) + .75(10 + U - 2Y) \\ &= 27.5 - 4Y \end{aligned}$$

c. Substituting Y = 5 into the portfolio return equation in Part (b), the expected return is 27.5 – 4(5) = 7.5%.

15

Derivatives

15.1 Identify the most important error in this Motley Fool reasoning:

> If FishTop is selling for $50 per share and you expect it to rise, you could buy 'October $55' calls.... If, just before your option expires, FishTop is selling for $75 per share, you ... make $20, right? Not exactly. That option wasn't free. Let's say the premium you paid was $6 per share. That means your profit is down to $14. Which would be OK, but remember—if you had just bought shares of FishTop instead of spending money on options, you would have made a much better profit.

15.2 On December 14, 2012, an S&P 500 futures contract expiring on December 13, 2013, closed at 1386.40, 1.9% below the 1413.58 value of the S&P 500 on December 14, 2012. Explain why you either agree or disagree with this market analyst's reasoning: "If we trust markets, and I do, the stock market is telling us that the experts' best guess is that stock prices will be 1.9% lower a year from now than they are today."

15.3 Which of the following futures contracts would you expect to have the larger percentage cost of carry: A bond selling for par or the S&P 500? Explain carefully.

15.4 Alice Handy recalled when she was managing the endowment for the University of Virginia (UVA):

a. In the late 1990s, UVA had invested in several technology start-ups whose value increased greatly. In 1999, UVA was concerned about the dot-com bubble popping, but UVA was not permitted to sell its technology shares until a mandatory holding period ended. The Virginia State Legislature was persuaded to change a state law that did not allow state institutions to invest in derivatives, and Handy locked in the technology gains by using futures on the tech-heavy NASDAQ Index. Did UVA buy or sell these futures?

b. In early 2007, UVA couldn't find any attractively priced stocks, so UVA used options that would make money if the S&P 500 fell substantially. Do you think UVA bought calls, sold calls, bought puts, or sold puts?

15.5 Many savings and loan associations (S&Ls) have short-term deposits and long-term mortgages. Will their net worth (the market value of their assets minus the market value of their liabilities) decline if interest

DOI: 10.1201/9781003630166-15

rates go up or if they go down? Explain which of the following actions are appropriate and which are inappropriate if they want to insulate their net worth from the effects of changes in interest rates:

a. Buy 30-year zero-coupon bonds.
b. Buy bond futures.
c. Buy call options on Treasury bonds.
d. Buy put options on Treasury bonds.
e. Swap fixed-rate liabilities for variable-rate liabilities.

15.6 In 1997, many pension funds grew increasingly nervous about their stock portfolios as price-earnings ratios approached all-time highs. Which of the following could they have purchased, and which could they have sold to protect themselves from a collapse in stock prices:

a. stock-index call options
b. stock-index put options
c. stock-index futures

15.7 After Iraq invaded Kuwait in 1990, crude oil prices increased by more than 50%. As the market price neared $30 a barrel, the managers of Royal Caribbean Cruise Lines felt fortunate that they had locked in a price of $18.41 a barrel.

a. To protect itself against an increase in oil prices, should a company buy or sell oil futures?
b. Why might such a company be protected even if the delivery dates for its futures contracts do not coincide with its need for oil?
c. Which do you expect to be higher, the price of crude oil or the price of crude oil futures?
d. A 1990 *Wall Street Journal* article on companies using oil futures to protect against an increase in oil prices noted that, "The purpose of hedging isn't to minimize cost but to minimize risk." Explain their reasoning.

15.8 A major home builder is financing a residential construction project with a $47 million loan at an interest rate equal to the 1-year Treasury-bill rate plus 2 percentage points. The CEO is concerned that interest rates might increase sharply.

a. Identify two distinct reasons why a jump in interest rates would be bad financially for this company.
b. Which, if any, of these actions is an appropriate hedge: buy Treasury bond futures; sell Treasury bond futures, buy Treasury bond puts; buy Treasury bond calls.

15.9 In 1992, MG Corp, a U.S. subsidiary of the German giant Metallgesellschaft AG, contracted to sell gasoline, heating oil, and diesel fuel at fixed prices for the next 10 years. MG tried to hedge by purchasing short-term oil futures. An added bonus was that energy futures were "backward" at the time, with futures prices below spot prices. However, oil prices fell by more than $4 a barrel in 1993 and MG lost $1 billion on its futures contracts, threatening bankruptcy and prompting MG to wind down its fuel contracts and its hedging program.

a. Should MG have bought or sold oil futures to hedge their gasoline, heating oil, and diesel fuel contracts? Explain your reasoning.
b. Explain how crude-oil futures protect, but not perfectly, against fluctuations in the price of refined gasoline.
c. Explain why oil futures prices are usually above the current spot price for oil.
d. Ignoring its fuel contracts, if spot prices had been constant, would MG have made profits or losses on its oil futures? Explain.
e. Explain why Nobel laureate Merton Miller was confident that, in the long run, MG would have made back the $1 billion they lost in 1993.

15.10 During the dot-com bubble, it was argued that the value of technology stocks is positively related to interest rates because technology companies represent an option on future ventures that may prove extremely profitable, and option values are positively related to interest rates. Does this argument characterize technology companies as put or call options? Explain why the value of such an option is positively related to interest rates.

15.11 Most corporate bonds have call provisions that allow the firm to repurchase the bond at a set price before maturity. Interpret the position of the firm *and* the bondholders using the language of puts and calls; e.g., "the bondholders have implicitly bought a bond and written a put; the corporation has implicitly sold a put and a call."

15.12 In an efficient market, can the price of a put ever exceed the price of a call? When?

15.13 E.G. Capital Management, an investment management company, bought high-dividend stocks and wrote call options against these stocks. *The New York Times* said that this fund has done very well in sluggish markets, but "in surging markets …. will almost always underperform market indexes." Explain why this is so.

15.14 Investors who had been following a stock options strategy touted by brokers as a sure thing lost hundreds of millions of dollars when the Dow dropped 508 points on October 19, 1987. Were they buying calls, selling calls, buying puts, or selling puts? Explain your reasoning.

15.15 In 1989, the vice president of options and futures at Alex, Brown & Sons recommended that investors consider protecting their portfolios by purchasing put options, arguing that "The worst thing that can happen is the value of your portfolio goes up." Why does something bad happen when your portfolio goes up? Is this really the worst possible outcome?

15.16 Suppose that an investor who expects the S&P 500 to increase by 20% over the coming year could buy the S&P 500 today for 6000 or could buy a 1-year S&P 500 futures contract for 6000. Which would you recommend?

15.17 Finish this sentence from an annual report of the Templeton Emerging Markets Income Fund: "Unlike futures contracts, buyers of options are not required to deposit funds in a margin account because ..."

15.18 Some technical analysts follow the daily put-call ratio—the number of put options bought that day divided by the number of call options bought that day. A high ratio is considered a buy signal. Do you interpret this indicator as following market sentiment or being contrarian? Do you see any logical flaws in this indicator?

15.19 An investment advisory service argued that warrants are less speculative than stock: In 1956, General Tire sold at $53, while warrants that could be exercised at $70 until 1959 sold for $4.50. One hundred shares of stock cost $5,300 and 588 warrants cost half that, $2,350. If the stock doubled to $106 (giving a $5,300 profit on the stock), the warrants would be worth at least $36 (for a profit of $18,518). On the downside, if the stock's price is halved to $26.50 (a $2,650 loss), the warrants, even if worthless, would have a loss of only $2,350. Thus,

> Inescapable Conclusion: When an investment in the Warrant only one-half the size of the investment in the common, produces 3 1/2 times as much profit as the common on the upside and cannot possibly show any greater percentage loss on the downside even if it goes to zero, the Warrant must by definition be much less speculative than the common stock.

Do you agree?

15.20 An investment advisory service argued that the GSR (the ratio of the price of gold to the price of silver) always returns to the range between 34-to-1 and 38-to-1. Suppose that a gold futures contract with a delivery date 1 year from today is selling for $2400/ounce and a silver futures contract with the same delivery date is selling for $30/ounce.

a. If you want to bet that the GSR will be in its historical range on the delivery date, should you buy gold futures and sell silver futures, or do the reverse?

b. What ratio of gold contracts to silver contracts should you use to ensure you will make a profit if the GSR is less than 2400/30 on the delivery date?

15.21 A mutual fund that is fully invested in stocks with an average beta of 2 is concerned that the stock market may collapse, yet, because of capital gains taxes and transaction costs, doesn't want to sell any stocks. To hedge its $400 million portfolio completely, should it buy or sell index futures with an aggregate value of $200 million, $400 million, or $800 million?

15.22 Mortgage lenders often allow homebuyers to "lock in" a mortgage rate on loans. For example, on April 10, 2000, LoansDirect agreed (for a $400 fee) to loan $400,000 at a 7.75% interest rate on May 10, 2000. Loans Direct planned to sell this loan on May 10 to an insurance company, pension fund, or other investor at a price that depends on the May 10 level of mortgage rates. Would LoansDirect be hurt most by an increase or decrease in interest rates between April 10 and May 10? Should they hedge this risk by buying or selling Treasury-bond futures? If interest rates do move in this unprofitable way, will the hedge be less successful if the spread between mortgage rates and T-bond rates widens or narrows?

15.23 How do you explain the fact that futures prices for stocks are determined by the cost of carry, yet changes in futures prices before the stock market opens are often a good predictor of changes in market prices that day?

15.24 "Stock futures rose sharply today, indicating that investors are increasingly optimistic about the stock market." What is an alternative explanation?

15.25 Which would you expect to be higher, the price of gold or the price of 6-month gold futures? Does this spread widen or narrow if T-bill rates increase?

15.26 Do you think that the price of 3-month S&P 500 futures is currently above or below the value of the S&P 500? Explain your reasoning.

15.27 The prices of S&P 500 index futures are usually above the value of the S&P 500 index. Under what circumstances would you expect this to be so? On October 19, 1987, however, the S&P 500 futures price was, on average, 10% below the value of the index. How could an arbitrager have exploited this difference? (In practice, this arbitrage was difficult because trading in many securities was suspended temporarily.)

15.28 In 2017, a German-Russian citizen was accused of bombing the team bus carrying the Borussia Dortmund soccer team to a Champions League match. German investigators reported that he had borrowed "several tens of thousands of euros" and made "suspicious options purchases" on the day of the attack for shares of Borussia Dortmund, the only top-league German club listed on the stock exchange. Do you think he bought puts or calls? Explain your reasoning.

15.29 In 2017, a prominent monetarist economist argued that the ratio of the price of oil to the price of gold is a "golden constant."

> I developed a model. It employs the price of gold as a long-term benchmark for the price of oil. The idea being that, if the price of oil changes dramatically, the oil-gold price ratio will change and move away from its long-term value. Forces will then be set in motion to move supply and demand so that the price of oil changes and the long-term oil-gold price ratio is reestablished. This represents nothing more than a reversion to the mean. It explains why spot prices of gold and crude are parallel to each other and why the oil-gold price ratio hovers around .0721.

This argument suggests a convergence trade when the oil/gold ratio wanders away from .0721. In 2022, the ratio dropped to .05.

a. Should those betting a return to the golden ratio have bought gold futures and sold oil futures, or vice versa?
b. Why are you skeptical of this strategy?
c. Is this proposed convergence to a golden ratio an example of regression toward the mean?

15.30 Graph the profits as a function of the stock price at expiration for this butterfly strategy: simultaneously buy one call option for $10 with an exercise price of $100, sell two calls for $5 each with an exercise price of $110, and buy one call for $2.50 with an exercise price of $120. How would you describe this strategy (for example, a bet that the stock price will go up)?

15.31 Bernie Madoff told investors he was earning 15% a year, year after year, using a "split-strike conversion" strategy, which involves the purchase of stock and the simultaneous purchase of out-of-the-money put options and the sale of out-of-the-money call options. He used the S&P 100 index, but we can illustrate with Apple stock. On November 27, 2009, Apple stock closed at 200.59, while January 16, 2010, put options with an exercise price of 190 closed at 5.20, and January 16, 2010, call options with an exercise price of 210 closed at 5.90. Draw the profit picture for a split-strike conversion strategy as a function of the price of Apple stock on January 16, 2010. How would you describe this strategy (for example, a bet that the stock price will go up)?

15.32 An investment advisor recommended the following "absurdly easy" way to make money. On July 29, 1988, with the S&P 500 index at 272.02, a December put option on the S&P 500 with a striking price of 260 sold for $8 while a December call option with a 290 striking price sold for $1. Show the dollar gains and losses from selling the put and the call simultaneously, as a function of the value of the S&P 500 index when the options expire in December. How would you describe this strategy (for example, a bet that the S&P 500 will go up)?

15.33 A *Wall Street Journal* article extolled the virtues of "buy-write" funds:

> A few years back there was a flurry of interest in mutual funds that use a so-called buy-write strategy, in which a fund manager buys stock and sells stock options to generate income. It has the added benefit of smoothing out the stock market's ups and downs.... Buy-write mutual funds are working as advertised, and it's surprising that more traditional funds don't offer this strategy.

Does a buy-write fund manager sell put or call options? Use a graph of the profits as a function of the stock price on the expiration date to show how this strategy smooths out the market's ups and downs.

15.34 Draw the profit picture (as a function of the price of the stock on the exercise date) for this strategy: pay $10 for a call option with an exercise price of 100; sell a put option for $5 with an exercise price of $100. Identify a simple strategy that is equivalent to this mixed strategy.

15.35 A *Business Insider* story revealed how a middle-school "math teacher earned $114,000 trading stocks with a low-risk strategy." This teacher noticed that blog posts often talked about how people lost money buying short-term call options. So, he sold call options and bought the underlying stock to protect himself if the stock price soared. Use a graph of the profits as a function of the stock price on the expiration date to show how this strategy makes money and the downside, if any.

15.36 In September of 1997, The *Wall Street Journal* reported that corporate insiders were using "collars" to hedge their holdings in their company's stock without actually selling the stock. In a typical collar, the insider simultaneously sells a call and buys a put at a lower strike price, with the price of the put approximately equal to the price of the call. For example, on December 4, 1997, Microsoft stock traded for 142.5625, an April 1998 call with an exercise price of 150 traded for 3, and an April 1998 put with an exercise price of 135 traded for 2.125. Show the profits on the April exercise date for an investor who buys one share of Microsoft, sells one call, and buys one put.

15.37 In November 1989, an article in *The Wall Street Journal* reported that during periods of wildly gyrating stock prices, shrewd investors were using a cautious strategy known as a covered strangle: buy a stock and sell both a call and a put option against this stock. Assume that the price of the call is $10 and the price of the put is $5, and that the strike prices for the put and the call are equal to the current price of the stock, $100. Draw a graph showing the profits from a strangle strategy as a function of the price of the stock on the exercise date.

15.38 After Qualcomm closed at $50.14 on November 1, 2011, Goldman Sachs' options trading team suggested buying a $49/$52.50 Qualcomm "strangle" by simultaneously purchasing a call option with an exercise price of $52.50 and buying a put option with an exercise price of $49, both expiring on November 24, 2011. The total cost of this strangle was $3.04. Describe this strategy's implicit wager.

15.39 A prominent investment advisor recommended that an investor who is considering buying stock should consider instead buying a call and selling a put. Assuming the exercise prices are equal to the current stock price, compare the potential profits from these two strategies.

15.40 In theory, will an increase in interest rates raise or lower the price of a call option? Of a put option? Explain, without using equations, why this is so.

Answers

15.1 It is true that you would have made a $25 profit on the stock, as compared to a $14 profit on the options, but the former is only a 50% return, compared to 233% on the option.

15.2 Because of arbitrage, the difference between the current and futures price depends on the cost of carry, the difference between the 1-year T-bill rate and the dividend yield. On December 12, 2012, the T-bill rate was evidently 1.9% lower than the anticipated dividend yield over the coming year.

15.3 The cost of carry equals the interest on a safe investment (such as T-bills) minus the cash flow from the asset—dividends from stock, coupons from bonds. For a bond selling for par, the coupon rate equals the bond's yield to maturity. Because bond yields are now usually higher than dividend yields, stocks have a higher cost of carry.

15.4 a. They sold futures that would make capital gains if stock prices fell.

b. They bought puts that would make capital gains if stock prices fell.

15.5 They want to better match the duration of their assets and liabilities and/or take positions that will make money if interest rates rise, thereby offsetting the losses on their fixed-rate mortgages.

a. Inappropriate, because these will lose money if bond prices fall (interest rates rise).

b. Inappropriate, because these will lose money if bond prices fall (interest rates rise).

c. Inappropriate, because these will lose money if bond prices fall (interest rates rise).

d. Appropriate, because these will make money if bond prices fall (interest rates rise).

e. Inappropriate, because their assets are already longer duration than are their liabilities.

15.6 They want to profit from these derivatives if stock prices go down.

a. Sell stock-index call options.

b. Buy stock-index put options.

c. Sell stock-index futures.

15.7 a. A company could buy oil futures because the value of these futures increases as the price of oil increases.

b. Even if the delivery date doesn't coincide with the company's need for oil, an increase in the price of oil will generally raise the price of oil and oil futures on nearby dates.

c. The price of crude-oil futures should be higher than the price of crude oil because the cost of carry (storage expenses plus lost interest) is positive.

d. Neglecting commissions and other expenses, futures are a zero-sum game—gains by some require losses by others. Those who buy futures to hedge their positions cannot reasonably expect to make profits consistently, while those who sell futures consistently have losses. Taking commissions and other expenses into account, the average profit of buyers and sellers is negative. Unless the company consistently beats the market, the purchase of futures contracts will increase its average costs. Such hedges do reduce risk by effectively locking in the price of oil, insulating this cost from fluctuations—up or down—in the market price.

15.8 a. The interest paid on the loan would increase and the demand for homes would decrease.

b. The CEO wants to take actions that will be profitable if interest rates rise (and bond prices fall): sell Treasury bond futures and buy Treasury bond puts.

15.9 a. They should have bought futures (as they did). They would lose money on their contracts to deliver fuel at fixed prices if fuel prices increase. By buying futures, they make money on these futures if oil prices increase, in theory offsetting the losses on their delivery contracts.

b. To the extent crude oil and refined gasoline prices are related, an increase in the price of oil should be accompanied by an increase in the price of gasoline.

c. The difference between the futures price and the current spot price should reflect the cost of carry, which for oil is lost interest and storage costs. Thus, people wanting oil in the future would normally pay more for a futures contract than for current delivery, in order to earn interest and avoid storage expenses. Similarly, a company with a large oil inventory could sell at the current spot price and buy futures to replenish its inventory in the future, in the meantime, earning interest and avoiding storage expenses

d. MG would make a profit on its futures if the spot price on the delivery date is above the futures price they paid for the contract. Because the futures price was backward (below the spot price at the time of purchase), MG would have made profits on its futures if spot prices had been constant.

e. In the long run, MG should have made \$1 billion in profits on its contracts to deliver fuel at what are now above-market prices. (If spot prices rise before the contracts come due, MG should make \$1 billion on a continuing policy of rolling over oil futures. However, there were questions about whether the parties who had agreed to buy fuel from MG at fixed prices would have honored these contracts.)

15.10 This argument characterizes technology companies as call options that can make profitable investments in the future for a relatively low cost. The value of a call option is positively related to interest rates because the low price of a call option relative to the price of the underlying asset allows the investor to invest the difference in the interim.

15.11 The bondholders have implicitly bought a bond and sold a call; a corporation that issues a callable bond has sold a bond and purchased a call.

15.12 In theory, the price P_C of a call option and the price P_P of a put on the same stock with the same strike price E and exercise date are related by the put-call parity equation,

$$P_c = P_p = P - \frac{E}{1+R}$$

where R is the safe return on a Treasury bill that matures on the exercise date. As the price of the stock falls, the put becomes more valuable and the call less so. If the price of the stock is sufficiently far below the strike price, the no-arbitrage price of the put is larger than the price of the call.

15.13 In sluggish markets, the large dividends plus the call premiums will beat funds hoping for capital gains. However, in surging markets, E.G.'s stocks will be called away, limiting their capital gains.

15.14 Selling puts is the only one of these four strategies that could have catastrophic losses.

15.15 The bad thing when the portfolio goes up is that the price paid for the put is wasted, and this reduces your profits. However, a worse outcome would be a decline in the portfolio, leading to a loss equal to the cost of the put.

15.16 If you pay 6,000 for the S&P 500 now, you get a d% dividend yield over the coming year; if you pay 6,000 for an S&P 500 futures contract, you can invest 6,000 in a 1-year T-bill for an r% rate of return; choose the S&P 500 if $d > r$; choose the futures contract if $r > d$.

15.17 Templeton's answer: "Their risk of loss is limited to the premiums paid for the option."

15.18 Investors buy puts when they think the market is going down and buy calls when they think it is going up. An imbalance of put buying suggests that investors are bearish; so, buying at such a time is a contrarian strategy. One logical problem is that options are sold as well as bought. A large number of puts traded could just as well be interpreted as large sales (bullish) as large purchases (bearish). Also, many investors use puts and calls as part of an overall portfolio strategy, not just a simple bet on the direction of the market.

15.19 No; this argument focuses on the extremes and ignores the middle area where the stock does better than this warrant strategy. If the price of the stock is in the range \$53 to \$70, for example, the warrants are worthless while the stock investment has made a profit.

15.20 The current GSR = 2400/30 = 80.

a. Because the price of gold is historically high relative to the price of silver, you should sell gold and buy silver.

b. Let Pg be the price of gold and Ps be the price of silver on the delivery date. If you buy 80 silver contracts for every 1 gold contract, your net profit will be

$$80(\text{Ps}-30)+(2400-\text{Pg}) = 80\text{Ps}-\text{Pg}$$

If the price of gold is still 80 times the price of silver, you will have no profit. You will make money if the price of gold is less than 80 times the price of silver.

15.21 Sell futures (which will go down in price and be increasingly profitable if stock prices fall) with a value of \$800 million (because the \$400 million portfolio with a beta of 2 should fluctuate 2-for-1 with the market).

15.22 Loans Direct will be hurt by rising mortgage rates that reduce the market value of the monthly loan payments due on a \$400,000 loan at 7.75%. They can hedge this risk by selling Treasury bond futures, which will be profitable if interest rates rise and bond prices fall. Mortgage rates are above T-bond rates because of the greater default risk, and this hedge will be less successful if mortgage rates rise more than T-bond rates, widening the spread.

15.23 The cost of carry equation is: futures price = spot price + lost interest – dividends received. If the spot price is expected to open higher or lower than the closing price of the previous trading day, then the futures price will change in the same direction.

15.24 Maybe interest rates rose, which increased the cost of carry for stock futures.

15.25 The cost of carry from buying gold now depends on T-bill rates (lost interest) and storage costs. Since the cost of carry is positive, gold futures should cost more than gold, and this spread widens as T-bill rates increase.

15.26 Because of arbitrage possibilities, the price of S&P futures is equal to the spot price plus the cost of carry: the interest rate on 3-month T-bills minus the dividend yield. When the T-bill rate is higher than dividend yields, the cost of carry is positive, and the futures price is above the spot price.

15.27 The cost of carry for the S&P 500 is the T-bill rate (lost interest) minus the dividend yield. The futures price should be above the index value if the T-bill rate exceeds the dividend yield. On October 19, 1987, an arbitrager would want to sell stocks and buy futures.

15.28 He bought puts because these can make large profits if the stock price falls.

15.29 a. The appropriate convergence trade is a wager that the price of oil will rise relative to the price of gold—so buy oil futures and sell gold futures.

b. The prices of oil and gold both tend to increase over time, but neither has anything to do with the other, and there is no reason why the ratio of their prices should be .0721, or any other constant.

c. The appeal to "reversion to the mean" is misplaced. The regression-toward-the-mean principle says that when something is measured imperfectly, measurements that are far from the mean overstate how far the trait being measured is from the mean; for example, the winning score in a golf tournament probability overstates how far the golfer's ability is from the mean, so the golfer's score in the next tournament will probably be closer to the mean. This principle is important but has nothing to do with the ratio of the price of oil to the price of gold.

In practice, the ratio of the price of oil to the price of gold did not converge to .0721. It dropped to .04 in 2023 and below .03 in 2024.

15.30 This strategy is a bet against volatility:

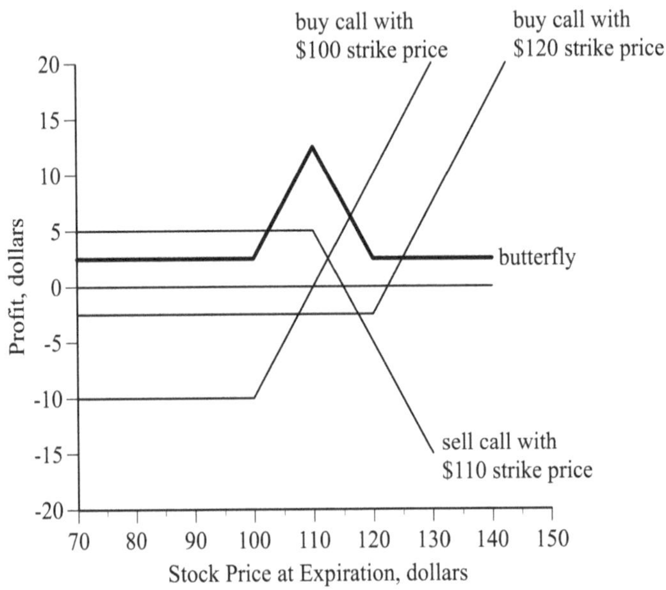

15.31 This strategy is a bet that the price of Apple stock will go up, with gains and losses both limited.

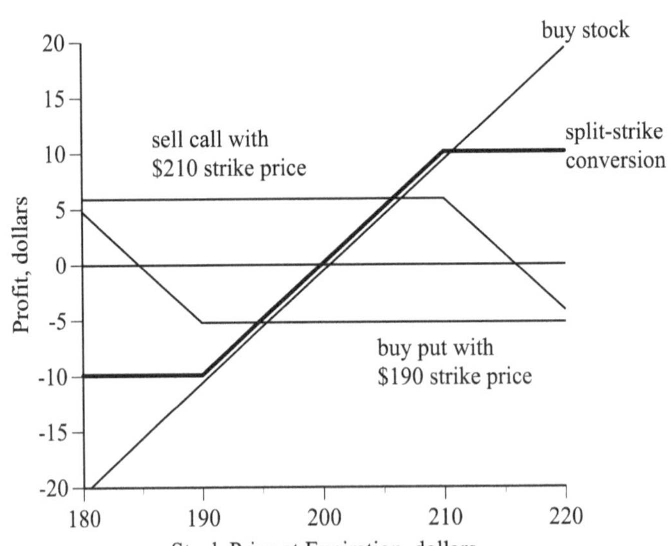

15.32 This is a bet against volatility:

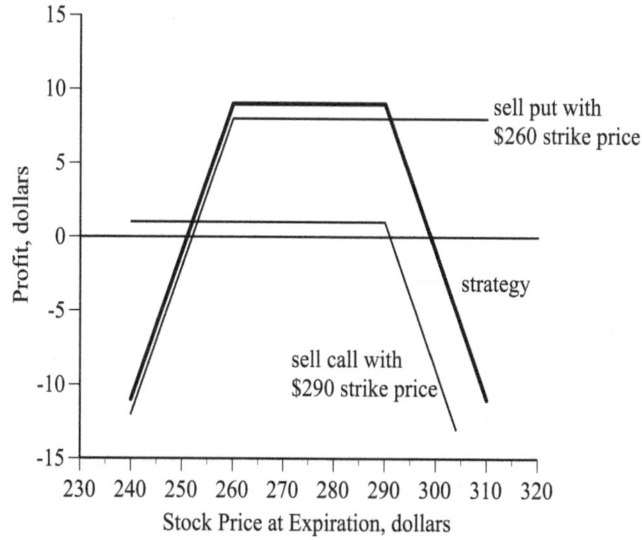

15.33 A buy-write fund sells call options, which generate extra income. This smooths out the market's ups and downs because it limits the upside potential of the fund while cushioning the downside.

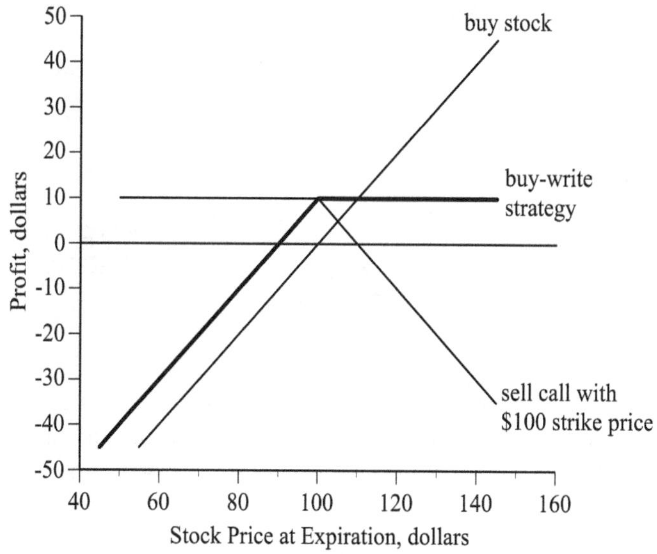

15.34 This strategy is equivalent to buying the stock for 105:

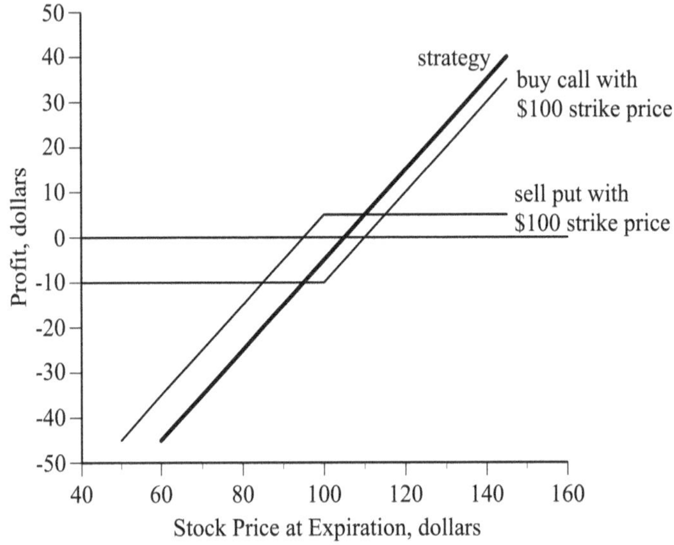

15.35 This covered-call strategy makes money on the price of the call, the stock's dividends, and any appreciation in the price of the stock up to the strike price. However, it loses money if the stock price drops by more than the option price, and it misses out on any price increase above the strike price.

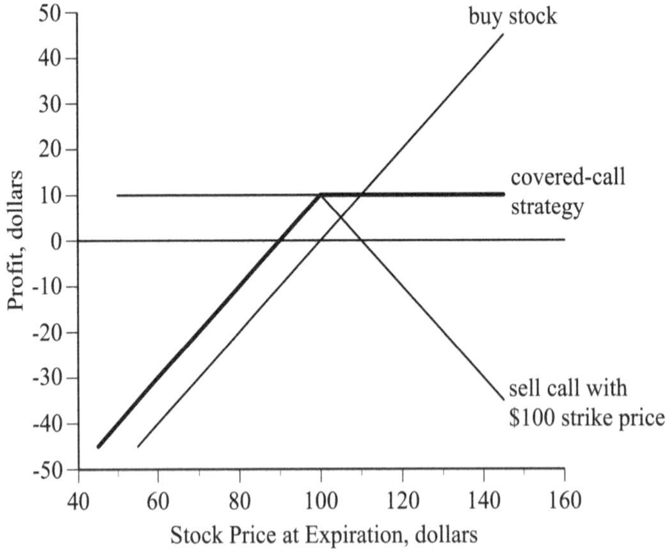

15.36 This strategy is a bet that the price of Microsoft stock will go up, with gains and losses both limited.

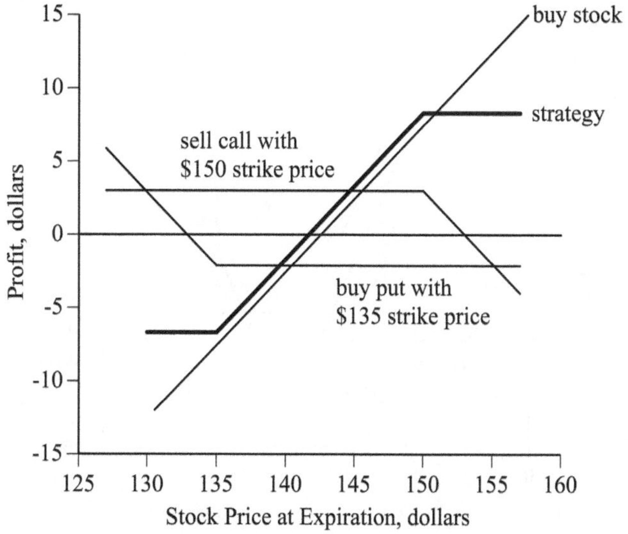

15.37 This strategy earns additional income from the sale of the call and the put, does not make additional profits if the price of the stock rises, and loses $2 for every $1 drop in the price of the stock:

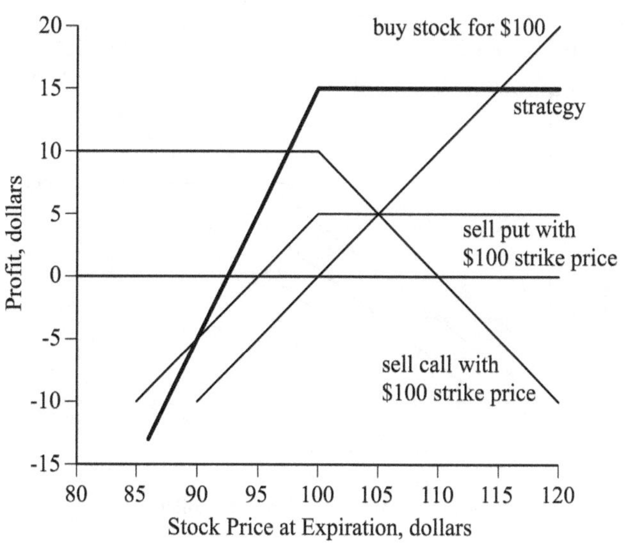

15.38 This strategy is a bet on volatility, in that the strategy is profitable if Qualcomm's price on the expiration day is above $52.50 + $3.04 = $55.54 or below $49.00 – $3.04 = $45.96.

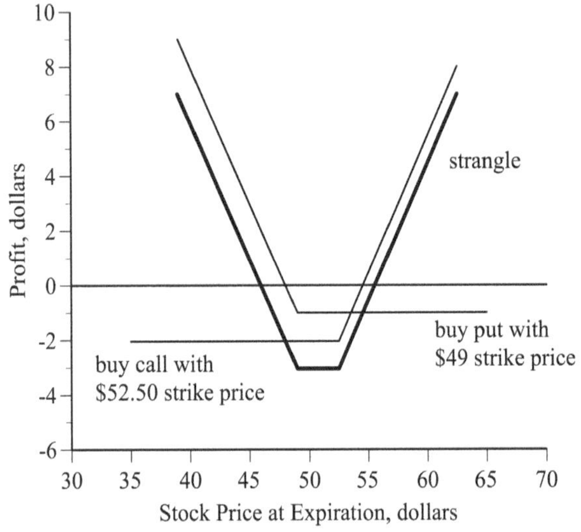

15.39 Consider a stock selling for $100, a call option with a strike price of $100 selling for $10; and a put option with a strike price of $100 selling for $5. The profit picture on the options' expiration date is identical to buying the stock, but lower by an amount equal to the difference between the prices of the call and put:

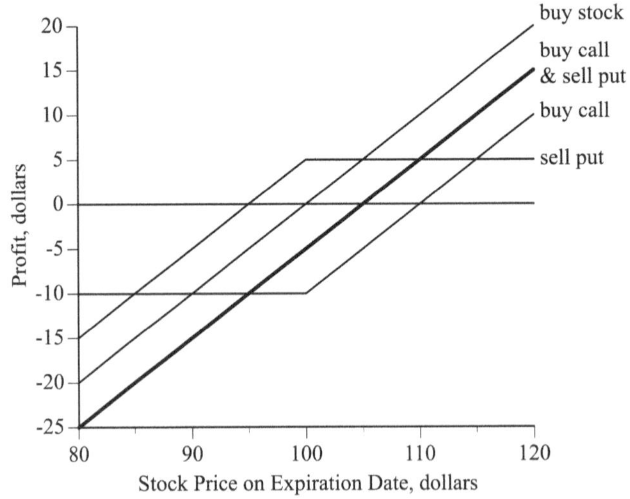

The stock purchase requires a much larger investment (in our example, \$100 versus \$5). Arbitrage can establish put-call parity where the difference in the percentage returns is equal to the risk-free rate of return.

15.40 If you want to buy a stock and buy a call option instead of buying the stock immediately, you pay a relatively small amount for the call and pay the rest later when you exercise the call—which allows you to invest the difference until the expiration date. Thus, higher interest rates make the call option more valuable. If you want to sell a stock and buy a put option instead of selling the stock immediately, you lose the interest you could have earned on the proceeds from the stock sale. Thus, an increase in interest rates makes the put option less valuable.

16

Miscellaneous

16.1 Briefly explain the practical implications of each of these Warren Buffett quotations. For example, for the quotation, "The rearview mirror is always clearer than the windshield," the answer might be: It is always easier to see what has happened in the past than to see what lies ahead.

a. Our favorite holding period is forever.

b. Be fearful when others are greedy and greedy only when others are fearful.

c. The term "institutional investor" is becoming one of those self-contradictions called an oxymoron, comparable to "jumbo shrimp," "lady mud wrestler," and "inexpensive lawyer."

d. May you live until Berkshire splits.

e. A stock is a disguised bond.

16.2 "Full retirement age" for Social Security benefits is 67 for anyone born in 1960 or later. Delaying the start of benefits past age 67 increases the size of the benefits by 8% for every year benefits are delayed up until age 70. For example, a person might have the option of receiving $2,000 a month in benefits beginning at age 67 or 1.08($2,000) = $2,160 a month in benefits beginning at age 68. (Either way, Social Security benefits are indexed for inflation after they begin.) Explain why you either agree or disagree with this advice from Laurence Kotlikoff, an economist who is most well-known for the financial advice he gives households:

> That's a safe real return of 8 percent. You can't get anything close to that in the market.

16.3 In 1997, Warren Buffett wrote that "Our portfolio shows little change. We continue to make more money when snoring than when active." One consequence of this inactivity is that the most successful investments will, over time, become an increasingly large proportion of the portfolio. Yet Buffett cautioned against selling these investments in order to diversify: "To suggest that an investor should sell off portions of his most successful investments simply because they have come to dominate his portfolio is akin to suggesting that the Bulls trade Michael Jordan because he has become so important to the team." Why is no stock really akin to Michael Jordan?

16.4 Critically evaluate this excerpt from Wikipedia: "If the stock does not currently pay a dividend, like many growth stocks, more general versions of

 DOI: 10.1201/9781003630166-16

the discounted dividend model must be used to value the stock. One common technique is to assume that the Miller-Modigliani hypothesis of dividend irrelevance is true, and therefore replace the stock's dividend D with E earnings per share. However, this requires the use of earnings growth rather than dividend growth, which might be different."

16.5 A Harvard Business School professor noted that, over a 50-year period, the average real return on Treasury bonds was 1%. He concluded that an 11% Treasury rate in 1984 "suggests .... inflation expectations close to 10%." What is the flaw in his reasoning?

16.6 Explain margin buying and explain why you would be cautious about following this advice from Consumers Digest's *Get Rich Investment Guide*: "Margin buying is an excellent way to buy shares, when you are sure a stock has reached its bottom, or nearly its bottom."

16.7 Explain why this observation is almost, but not quite right:

> Half of the professionally managed mutual funds consistently beat the market, while the other half consistently underperform the market.

16.8 A financial columnist offered several tips to investors who want protection from a bear market, while "allowing yourself room to make money if the bull is still alive." Explain to a novice investor how each action accomplishes the stated objective, and the drawbacks (if any).

a. Enter stop-loss orders.

b. Buy put options.

c. Sell stocks that are overvalued.

d. Sell stocks short.

e. Invest in mutual funds with proven track records.

16.9 Explain why you either agree or disagree with this plan: "I have a $500,000, 3% mortgage on my million-dollar house and $2 million in my IRA. I am going to use some of my IRA money to pay off my mortgage."

16.10 Suppose a company has 10 million shares outstanding that are currently trading for $20 a share. The company's board of directors unexpectedly gives the chief executive officer a bonus by allowing her to purchase 1 million new shares at $10, and she immediately does so. Simultaneously, the company sterilizes this new issue by repurchasing 1 million shares from the company's shareholders at $20/share. Assuming no change in the company's operations, what is the theoretical new value of the company's shares?

16.11 On April 30, 1985, Atlantic Richfield (Arco), the nation's sixth largest oil company, unveiled a massive restructuring plan "designed to confront what it sees as weakening oil markets." The company announced that it would: repurchase $4 billion of its stock; increase its dividend by a third; sell all of its refining and marketing operations east of the Mississippi; and reduce its investment spending to about $2.8 billion annually, down from a previously budgeted $3.6 billion. The day this program was announced, Arco was the most actively traded stock on the New York Stock Exchange, and its price jumped from $53.00 to $58.25. How could the stock price rise so much, when Arco seemed to be in so much trouble?

16.12 On October 19, 2017, Hewlett-Packard Enterprises announced that it would repurchase $2 billion of its own stock. Why might this repurchase benefit shareholders more than

a. investing $2 billion to expand its business?

b. retiring $2 billion of its debt?

c. paying $2 billion out in dividends?

16.13 The Great Recession from December 2007 to June 2009 was accompanied by a sharp decline in short-term interest rates and a modest decline in long-term interest rates.

a. Do you suppose that bond and stock prices were positively correlated, negatively correlated, or essentially uncorrelated during this period? Explain your reasoning.

b. Provide a logical explanation for the fact that short-term interest rates fell so much more than long-term rates.

16.14 In 1986, the managing director of the Bond Portfolio Analysis Group at Salomon Brothers argued that the duration of a portfolio of bonds and stocks may be much larger than the duration of the bonds alone. How is this possible?

16.15 Answer the question at the end of this quotation from a well-known financial consultant:

> Market efficiency is uneven at best. At times investors become overly pessimistic and the price-earnings ratio of the averages plummets; at other times they are overly optimistic and the price-earnings ratio skyrockets. Yet, in the course of the six-month period from August 1982 through February 1983, the overall market advanced roughly 60% even though the economy continued to plow through heavy water. The reduction in interest rates and the perception that there would be light at the end of the recession's tunnel was enough to buoy prices. Was the market efficient at 780 on the Dow Jones Industrial Average and inefficient at 1,240 six months later, vice versa, both, or neither?

16.16 A successful realtor said that paying $30,000 above market value on a $400,000 home is of little concern if the buyer will live in the house for 30 years, since this averages out to only an extra $30,000/360 = $83 a month. Explain why you either do or do not find this argument persuasive.

16.17 A realtor put her home on the market for $1.3 million, explaining that she had priced it at 50% more per square foot than comparable properties because, when she bought the house 20 years ago, she paid 50%

more per square foot than comparable properties. Is this argument persuasive?

16.18 A 2022 Motley Fool article pointed out how insurance companies have been one of the keys to Berkshire Hathaway's long-term success and recommended that investors follow Berkshire's strategy by buying stocks in a large reputable insurance company.

a. Explain why insurance companies have been one of the keys to Berkshire Hathaway's long-term success.

b. Explain why buying stocks in insurance companies won't replicate Berkshire's strategy.

16.19 Give brief, logical explanations for each of these *Wall Street Journal* headlines:

a. "Fears of Stronger Economy Hit 30-Year Bond" [October 3, 1993].

b. "Industrials Rise Despite Bond Drop" [October 19, 1993].

c. "Bond Slump Sends Stocks Tumbling" [November 23, 1993].

16.20 An advertisement for a penny stock report was headlined "5500% profit" and explained:

> EXAMPLE: On Sept. 1983 if you had purchased 25,000 shares of MAX AXAM at .25 a share ($6250), you could have sold on Feb. 1986 at $14.00 per share and pocketed $350,000. Imagine a gain of 5500%!

Why is this example unpersuasive?

16.21 Students in an introductory class for quantitative finance majors at the Stevens Institute of Technology create mock portfolios at the beginning of the semester. Any student whose portfolio beats the S&P 500 for the semester is given an automatic A grade on the final exam. If you were teaching this course, what problems would you see with this feature?

16.22 Vanguard founder John Bogle used historical data to rank-order three types of financial assets (stocks, long-term bonds, and Treasury bills) by the criteria shown in the table below (1 is best, 2 next best, and 3 worst; the two N/As represent not applicable). Fill in the blanks in this table, putting 1, 2, and 3 in the appropriate places in each column. For example, if you believe that common stocks have had the highest total return, long-term bonds the next highest, and Treasury bills the lowest, then in the Total Return column, you would write 1, 2, and 3 in that order. In the two columns with NAs, just put 1 and 2 in the right order.

	Total Return	Principal Stability	Current Income	Income growth	Income Stability
Stocks					
Bonds					
Bills			N/A	N/A	

16.23 The fine print in an advertisement for a municipal bond fund said, "not suitable for retirement plans." Why not?

16.24 A business professor estimated the intrinsic value of a stock by discounting the projected real dividends by a real required rate of return, which he assumed is equal to zero because the average interest rate on highly rated corporate bonds over the past 30 years had been approximately equal to the average rate of inflation. What problems do you see with his model?

16.25 If Congress were to make dividends a tax-deductible expense for corporations, what effects, if any, would you expect to see on corporate leverage?

16.26 Critically evaluate this investment advisor commentary:

> If you've followed the market and the economy over the last few years, you've probably got a rough understanding that the Federal Reserve is propping up stocks. Maybe you're not sure exactly how it works, but the idea is just sort of out there....
>
> Technically, the Fed isn't directly helping the stock market. It's buying long-term government bonds and mortgage securities. But by lowering the cost of credit for corporations, it's helped dump trillions into stocks as CEOs have leveraged up their balance sheet by issuing debt cheaply and using that money to repurchase their own shares.

16.27 In December 2008, Henry Blodget wrote this

> Consider, for instance, the late 1950s, when a tried-and-true 'sell signal' started flashing on Wall Street. For the first time in years, stock prices had risen so high that the dividend yield on stocks had fallen below the coupon yield on bonds. To anyone who had been around for a while, this seemed ridiculous: stocks are riskier than bonds, so a rational buyer must be paid more to own them. Wise, experienced investors sold their stocks and waited for the obvious mispricing to correct itself. They're still waiting.

a. What does Blodget mean by "a rational buyer must be paid more to own them"?

b. What rational reason is there for an investor to believe that she will get a better long-run return from stocks than from bonds if the dividend yield is less than the coupon yield?

c. What does Blodget mean by "They're still waiting"?

16.28 U.S. companies hold a trillion dollars in cash overseas in order to escape U.S. taxes. If there were a temporary zero tax rate (a "tax holiday") for cash brought back to the United States, it is expected that companies will use most of the money they bring back to repurchase stock. Why would they do this instead of

a. paying dividends?

b. paying off their debts?

c. investing in new plant and equipment?

16.29 An article in The *Wall Street Journal* reported that "many companies are using excess cash to buy their own shares rather than build new plants."

a. The *Journal* observed that, "Of course, that cash could go into dividend increases. But corporate finance officers find some compelling arguments in favor of stock repurchases." Identify one compelling argument.

b. Explain the *Journal*'s observation that share repurchases substantially boosted the prices of some stocks, but had little or no effect on the prices of other stocks.

16.30 Assuming a 6% required return for each asset, identify the asset with the longer duration:

a. A 10-year Treasury zero with a 2% yield or a 10-year Treasury bond with 2% coupons?

b. A 30-year Treasury bond with a 4% coupon or a 30-year amortized mortgage with a 4% APR?

c. A stock paying a \$2 annual dividend that will grow by 2% a year or a stock paying a \$1 annual dividend that will grow by 3% a year?

d. A 30-year amortized mortgage with a 4% APR or a perpetuity with a 3% yield?

e. An apartment building with rent and price growing by 3% a year forever or a perpetuity with a 3% yield?

16.31 For each of the following pairs, identify the asset with the longer duration:

a. a conventional 30-year mortgage at 8% or a 15-year zero with an 8% yield to maturity?

b. a 5-year zero with a 5% yield to maturity or a 10-year zero with a 10% yield to maturity?

c. a 10-year 7%-coupon bond with a 5% yield to maturity or a 10-year zero with a 6% yield to maturity?

d. a consol bond with a \$10 quarterly coupon or a no-growth stock that will pay a \$5 quarterly dividend forever, each priced to give a 10% required return?

16.32 For each of the following pairs, identify the asset with the longer duration:

a. a 5-year zero with a 10% yield to maturity or a 10-year zero with a 5% yield to maturity?

b. a 10-year zero with a 5% yield to maturity or a 10-year zero with a 15% yield to maturity?

c. a 30-year amortized $800,000 mortgage at 8% or a 30-year $400,000 zero with an 8% yield to maturity?

d. a 10-year 2%-coupon bond with a 2% yield to maturity or a 10-year 4%-coupon bond with a 4% yield?

e. a stock with a dividend that will always equal $1 or a stock with a dividend that is currently $1 and will grow by 5% a year?

16.33 In 1986, the Korea Fund, a closed-end investment company that invests in Korean stocks, had 5 million shares outstanding with a net asset value (NAV) of $18/share and a market price of $32/share, a 78% premium over NAV. The Korea Fund then sold 1.2 million new shares at $32, raising $38.4 million. Did this sale increase or reduce the fund's NAV? By how much?

16.34 A Yale economics professor and graduate student looked at bitcoin prices from January 1, 2011, to May 31, 2018 (as far back as there are reliable data). Explain why these conclusions they reached are far-fetched:

1. Bitcoin doesn't generate cash or pay dividends, so they created a proxy, the number of Bitcoin Wallet users (essentially the number of people owning Bitcoin), and then calculated a dividend-price ratio by comparing Bitcoin prices to the number of Bitcoin Wallet users.
2. Bitcoin's price increased from $.30 to $7,530.55, an annual return of 292%. They concluded that, "If you as an investor believe that bitcoin will perform as well as it has historically, then you should hold 6% of your portfolio in bitcoin."

16.35 Explain the biggest logical error in this September 10, 2001, calculation by a widely respected investment adviser: "The number of S&P500 shares outstanding has increased 3 billion, or 34%, to 9 billion over the past ten years. EPS [Earnings per share] over the past four quarters through the second quarter was $47.1 per share. If the number of shares outstanding remained at roughly the 7 billion level of 10 years ago, the EPS would have been $60 per share."

16.36 Dual-purpose mutual funds have two classes of shareholders: one receives all the dividends from the fund's portfolio; the other receives all the capital gains. Explain what is misleading about this analysis:

> Say that Widow A, who has $1,000 and wants all the income she can get from it, and Executive B, who also has $1,000 and wants all the growth he can get, join forces. The result is $2,000, which is duly invested and, in a year's time, has produced a not-unreasonable 5% in dividends and 10% in capital gains. Five percent of $2,000 is $100, and that would go to the widow, who finds that she has received a 10% return on her $1,000 investment. The 10% in capital gains amounts to $200, and that goes to the executive, who

discovers he's blessed with a 20% return. Almost miraculously, both are making twice as much as they would if the fund hadn't brought them together.

16.37 Firm A's stock was selling for $20/share, and Firm B's stock was selling for $40/share. Then Firm A offered to acquire Firm B by exchanging 2.5 shares of Firm A stock for each share of Firm B stock. The price of Firm A stock immediately fell to $18/share while the price of Firm B stock rose to $44/share.

a. Explain how the price of Firm A stock could go down while the price of Firm B stock could go up.

b. How could an investor bet that this acquisition will occur at a 2.5 exchange ratio, without incurring any market risk; that is, the investor will make a profit regardless of whether stock prices go up or down, as long as the acquisition occurs at a 2.5 exchange ratio?

c. Show that the investor in Part (b) will make a profit if A's stock price rises to $20 and B's price rises to $50.

d. Show that the investor in Part (b) will make a profit if A's stock price falls to $16 and B's price falls to $40.

16.38 Smith is considering buying a $1 million life insurance policy that will be in effect until his son Cory is 25. If Smith dies, he wants the $1 million proceeds from the policy to be invested at the prevailing Treasury interest rate R, with a constant amount X given to Cory each year for n years until Cory is 25. For example, if Smith dies when Cory is 15, the $1 million will be invested at R, and Cory will be paid a constant amount X each year for n = 10 years. The value of X should be set so that the last payment to Cory exhausts the insurance proceeds plus interest. An advisor says that X = R($1,000,000) + $1,000,000/n.

a. Explain why the advisor's formula does not accomplish Smith's objectives. Does the fund run out of money or have money left over when Cory reaches age 25?

b. What formula would you use to determine the value of X? Be specific.

16.39 Company BIG has 20 million shares outstanding with a market price of $10/share. It has a Games division that has a book value of $40 million and $10 million in earnings this year; it also has a Liquid Assets division that holds $50 million in Treasury bills that earned $2 million this year. Big spins off the Liquid Assets division by creating two new companies, Games and Liquid Assets. Each Big shareholder receives 1 share of Games and 1 share of Liquid Assets in exchange for 2 shares of BIG, which no longer exists. The spinoff will have no effect on the earnings of either the Games division or the Liquid Assets division. Predict the prices of each company's shares.

16.40 Here are some data for a hypothetical company that has no debt, has constant annual earnings, and pays out all of its earnings as dividends:

Replacement cost of assets per share: $100

Annual earnings per share: $12

Market price of stock: $150

a. What is the shareholders' required rate of return?
b. What is this firm's leverage?
c. What is the value of Tobin's q?
d. Identify two very different actions this company could take that would make its shareholders better off.

Answers

16.1 a. Don't buy a stock because you hope to sell it soon after for a profit. The purchase should be justified by the cash flow if you never sell.

b. The time to buy stocks is when the fears of others have caused prices to collapse; the time not to buy is when the greed of others has caused prices to soar.

c. Institutions are generally speculators, not investors. If you want to be an investor, don't imitate institutions.

d. Stock splits are nonevents, except for the wasteful transaction costs.

e. You should value a stock the same way you value a bond, by discounting the anticipated cash flow.

16.2 This advice is commonplace but wrong. You are not foregoing $2,000 in order to get $2,160. You are forgoing $2,000 in order to get $2,160 instead of $2,000. So, the first 2 years you give up 12($2,000) + 12($2,000) = $48,000 in order to get 12($2,160) = $25,920 a year later. Add in the time value of money, and the loss is even bigger. If you live long enough, the delay will pay off, but the payoff is not 8%.

16.3 Michael Jordan in his prime could be expected to perform far better than the average basketball player year after year. In the stock market, past performance is no guarantee of future performance.

16.4 Earnings are a means to an end, not the end itself. If the earnings are retained and invested in money-losing projects, they may as well have never been earned in the first place. (It is odd that the Wikipedia entry talks about dividend growth when there are no dividends.)

16.5 He (incorrectly) assumed that the real interest rate on Treasury bonds is *always* 1% because the average value was 1%.

16.6 Margin buying is when investors borrow money to purchase stock, thereby creating leverage that magnifies gains and losses. The problem with this advice is that investors cannot be sure that a stock has reached its bottom and will soon go higher. Why are people selling the stock if its price is sure to go up?

16.7 It is consistently the case that half (or more) of the mutual funds underperform the market, but it is not consistently the same funds.

16.8 a. A stop-loss order becomes an order to sell at the best available price if the price drops to (or below) the stop-loss price. A primary drawback is that stop-loss orders will be activated frequently in a seesaw market, so that the investor incurs lots of transaction costs (including the difference between the sale and repurchase prices), protecting the portfolio from crashes that never occur.

b. A put option gives the owner the right to sell the stock at a fixed price. A drawback is that if, as usually happens, the stock price doesn't fall below the exercise price, the put expires worthless and the investor is out the price of the put. It can be expensive to maintain them continuously.

c. If you sell an overvalued stock, you get out before the price collapses. The drawback is that it is not easy to identify overvalued stocks. How do you know that it is overvalued, while those who buy the stock from you think it is a good buy?

d. If you sell borrowed stock and replace it after the price has declined, you make a profit. As with (c), it is not easy to identify stocks that will decline in price. If you short a stock that goes up, you lose money.

e. Past performance is not a reliable guide to future performance.

16.9 This is seldom a good idea. The mortgage interest is usually tax-deductible, and the IRA returns are tax-deferred. The after-tax return on the IRA is likely to be substantially higher than the after-tax mortgage rate.

16.10 The total value is initially (10 million)($20) = $200 million. The company receives $10 million from the CEO and spends $20 million repurchasing shares. Its total assets drop to $190 million and its value per share falls to ($190 million)/(10 million) = $19.

16.11 Investors were happy to see Arco cut back on what were evidently insufficiently profitable operations.

16.12 a. The profit rate from an expansion might be less than the shareholders' required return.

b. Debt is a tax shield.

c. If the firm pays dividends, shareholders must pay taxes on their dividends. If the firm repurchases stock, shareholders can choose to hold onto their stock and avoid a taxable event.

16.13 a. The modest decline in long-term interest rates increased bond prices and also had a positive effect on stock prices, which was more than offset by the collapsing economy. So, bond prices went up, while stock prices went down.

b. Short-term rates fell to near zero as the Fed tried to keep the Great Recession from turning into a second Great Depression. The term structure was strongly upward sloping because investors expected the economy to improve and the Fed to allow short-term interest rates to rise to keep inflation in check once the recession was over.

16.14 The duration of a portfolio is an average of the durations of the assets in the portfolio. If the stocks have a longer duration that the bonds, then the inclusion of stocks in the portfolio will increase the portfolio's duration.

16.15 A reduction in interest rates and an anticipated end to an economic recession could be rational explanations for why prices jumped 60%. Regardless, the most sensible form of the efficient markets hypothesis does not claim that people are rational, only that market prices reflect available information, so that it is not possible to beat the market consistently by trading on information.

16.16 I'd rather have $30,000 to spend on something else than overpay for a house. This calculation also ignores the time value of money. Paying an extra $30,000 is only equal to $83/month for 30 years if the required rate of return is zero. At a 5% required return, paying an extra $30,000 is equal to paying an extra $159/month for 30 years.

16.17 No, the market value of the house depends on what it is worth to people now, not what she paid for it.

16.18 a. Insurance company premiums generate float that can be invested until the policies pay off. The premiums assume a very low rate of return (e.g., from investing in Treasury bonds) but the float can be invested in assets like stocks with higher rates of return. Berkshire is essentially borrowing at a low rate in order to invest at a higher rate.

b. Buying insurance company stocks doesn't give investors access to insurance-company float.

16.19 a. A stronger economy could increase the rate of inflation; a higher inflation rate raises nominal interest rates, reducing bond prices. (The news story noted that short-term yields had risen more than long-term yields.)

b. The Dow Jones Industrial index rose even while bond prices were falling (and interest rates rising), perhaps because of good news about the economy.

c. Stock prices fell because bond prices were falling (and interest rates rising), perhaps because there was no good news about the economy.

16.20 It is always possible, after the fact, the find an investment that would have been very profitable to buy if only we had known ahead of time that its price would soar.

16.21 There is a lot of luck in short-term stock price movements and there is a big incentive to make very risky investments (like derivatives), because there is a reward for beating the S&P 500, but no penalty for underperforming—no matter how badly.

16.22 Here is the completed table:

	Total Return	Principal Stability	Current Income	Income growth	Income Stability
Stocks	1	3	2	1	2
Bonds	2	2	1	2	1
Bills	3	1	N/A	N/A	3

16.23 No taxes are paid while an investment is inside an IRA, and there is no distinction between municipal bonds and other bonds when funds are withdrawn from an IRA. So, you want the highest possible returns, which are from corporate and federal bonds, not municipal bonds.

16.24 The fact that the average real interest rate was zero does not mean that the real interest rate is *always* zero. The professor should also have considered a risk premium for the stock.

16.25 Treating dividends and interest equally would remove the tax-shield advantage of corporate debt. Less debt means less leverage.

16.26 In theory, share repurchases are a nonevent, although substituting debt for equity does create a tax shield. A stronger and more relevant effect is that lower interest rates increase the present value of the profits and dividends generated by corporations.

16.27 a. A risk-averse buyer will not buy a riskier asset unless the expected return is sufficiently high.

b. Dividends increase over time, but coupons don't.

c. Dividend-yields have been below coupon yields for 50 years now.

16.28 a. Shareholders must pay taxes on dividends, but only pay taxes on stock repurchases if they sell (and, then, only on their capital gains).

b. Debt creates a tax shield.

c. They may not have any sufficiently profitable projects.

16.29 This is a conservation-of-value question.

a. The *Journal* explained: "if cash dries up, companies can halt a repurchase program easily and more quietly than they can cut a dividend, which often results in much publicity and a big drop in stock price. What's more, dividends are taxable; a successful buy-back program creates capital gains taxed at a lower rate." [The second explanation is more general.]

b. The former may have abandoned insufficiently profitable operations or planned investments, while the latter were dispersing surplus cash (a financial nonevent).

16.30 The duration is the present-value weighted average wait until receiving the cash flow; here, the asset with the longer duration is

a. a 10-year Treasury zero.

b. a 30-year Treasury bond.

c. a stock paying a $1 annual dividend that will grow by 3% a year.

d. a perpetuity.

e. an apartment building with rent and price growing by 3% a year forever.

16.31 The duration is the present-value weighted average wait until receiving the cash flow; here, the asset with the longer duration is

a. a 15-year zero with an 8% yield to maturity.

b. a 10-year zero with a 10% yield to maturity.

c. a 10-year zero with a 6% yield to maturity.

d. equal, because both are no-growth with no maturation date.

16.32 The duration is the present-value weighted average wait until receiving the cash flow; here, the asset with the longer duration is

a. 10-year zero with a 5% yield to maturity.

b. neither. They are equal.

c. 30-year $400,000 zero with an 8% yield to maturity.

d. 10-year 2%-coupon bond with a 2% yield to maturity.

e. the second stock because a growth stock has a longer duration than a no-growth stock.

16.33 Before the 1986 sale of additional shares, the Korea Fund's assets were $18 (5 million) = $90 million. After the sale of 1.2 million new shares, the fund had 6.2 million shares and assets of $90 + $38.4 = $128.4 million, for a NAV of $128.4/6.2 = $20.70/share, a 15% increase over the $18 NAV before the sale. Selling shares at a premium over NAV always raises a fund's NAV, just as does redeeming shares at a discount from NAV.

16.34 a. The number of bitcoin wallet users has nothing to do with cash paid to investors and, so, is a worthless proxy.

b. It is farfetched to think that bitcoin prices will quadruple every year because this is an unsustainable compound growth rate; after 10 years, the price would be more than \$6 billion.

16.35 The 34% increase in the number of shares during this 10-year period gave firms additional cash. To the extent this cash was used to purchase assets or pay down debt, it increased the firms' aggregate earnings. We should not assume, as does the quotation, that the money raised by these stock sales had no effect on earnings.

16.36 Their total returns have not doubled. If they had invested directly, they would have each earned 15%. Now, one earns 10% and the other 20%, an average of 15%. The widow gets an extra 5% in dividends, but gives up 10% in capital gains; the executive gets an extra 10% in capital gains and gives up 5% in dividends.

16.37 a. Evidently, the market feels that this merger will not create enough value to justify the 25% premium.

b. An investor can buy 1 share of B for \$44 and sell 2.5 shares of A short for \$18/share. This is a perfect hedge in that the investor can use the 2.5 shares of A she receives for the 1 share of B to cover the short.

c. The position in Part (b) gives the investor a profit of 2.5(\$18 – \$20) + (\$50 – \$44) = \$1.

d. The position in Part (b) gives the investor a profit of 2.5(\$18 – \$16) + (\$40 – \$44) = \$1.

16.38 If n = 10 years and R = 5%, the advisor's formula gives X = R(\$1,000,000) + \$1,000,000/n = .05(\$1,000,000) + \$1,000,000/10 = \$150,000.

a. The fund doesn't earn R(\$1,000,000) each year, since the fund's balance is declining each year. The value of X is too large and the fund runs out of money before n years (in 8 years if n = 10 years and R = 5%).

b. The correct value of X is determined by the fact that the present value of the n payments of X should equal \$1,000,000. So, solve this equation for X:

$$\$1,000,000 = \sum_{t=1}^{n} \frac{X}{(1+R)^t}$$

Using a mathematical simplification

$$\$1,000,000 = \frac{X}{R}\left(1 - \frac{1}{(1+R)^n}\right)$$

$$X = \frac{R(\$1,000,000)}{\left(1 - \frac{1}{(1+R)^n}\right)}$$

If $n = 10$ years and $R = 5\%$, the correct value of X is \$129,505.

16.39 We can use the conservation of value principle because the spinoff has no effect on earnings. Company BIG has a total market value of $10(20 million) = $200 million. Liquid Assets should be valued at $50 million because this is the market value of its assets. Games should consequently be valued at $150 million. Therefore, the price per share should be ($150 million)/(10 million) = $15.00 for Games stock and ($50 million)/(10 million) = $5.00 for Liquid Assets. This makes sense because each shareholder traded 2 shares of Big worth a total of $20 for 1 share of Games and 1 share of Liquid assets, which are worth a total of $20.

16.40 a. Using the perpetuity formula: P = D/R, shareholders' required return is R = D/P = $12/$150 = .08 (8%)

b. With no debt, there is no leverage: 1/1

c. Tobin's q = market price/replacement cost = $150/$100 = 1.5

d. Retain some earnings to expand since q > 1 (ρ > R) or borrow some money to create a tax shield.

17

Longer Exercises

These exercises can be assigned as solo or group projects with the results presented in class. Some are relatively short and can be done in class; for example, part of the class time can be devoted to working on the exercises and the remaining time spent presenting the results. Longer exercises can be done outside class with the results presented in class.

Some of the intended lessons, in addition to the financial principles, are that we often have to make assumptions and that uncertainty can be handled by considering a variety of plausible assumptions. Most of these questions do not have "correct" numerical answers but, rather, reasonable approaches.

I often use two-person teams and assign an exercise to two teams. Two-person teams seem to work well for bonding with minimal free riding. Two teams working on the same exercise allows a comparison of answers; more than two teams can become repetitive if they agree on the answer.

1. Present Value

1.1 In a 2020 divorce case, a 55-year-old woman had to choose between (a) $500,000 now or (b) $2,000/month for the next 10 years and, then, $5,000/month for the rest of her life. What would you advise? Explain your reasoning.

1.2 Smith has decided to install solar panels on a rental property—both to help the environment and to reduce the tenants' utility bills. One company (BE) will install the panels for $15,422, to be paid either in cash or in a monthly amortized 10-year loan at a 5.99% APR. Another company (GC) will install the panels for $17,326, to be paid either in cash or in a monthly amortized 20-year loan at a 4.99% APR. Which do you recommend?

1.3 Mr. Smith just turned 67, and his job pays far more than his living expenses. The Social Security Administration estimates that Mr. Smith will receive $3,822 in monthly Social Security benefits if he begins collecting, now, at age 67 and $4,815 in monthly benefits if he begins collecting benefits when he turns 70. (Each of these estimates is in current dollars; Social Security benefits are fully indexed for inflation. If, for

DOI: 10.1201/9781003630166-17

example, the CPI increases by 3%, Social Security benefits will increase by 3%.)

Would you advise Smith to begin receiving Social Security benefits at age 67 or 70? Either way, he will continue working, and this will not reduce his benefits. Also, ignore the possibility that Smith may have to pay taxes on some of his Social Security benefits.

1.4 Consider an individual who has no initial wealth and whose annual income starts at $50,000 and grows by 5% a year. If this person saves 25% of each year's income and earns a 10% after-tax annual rate of return on their savings, what is the crossover point—the year at which the annual income from accumulated saving is larger than the annual income from working? Larger than annual spending?

1.5 Charlie just turned 76 years old, and his wife Gloria just turned 79. They paid $108,000 for a qualified longevity annuity contract (QLAC) that will pay them $1,330 a month starting when Charlie turns 85 and continuing as long as either of them is still alive. If they both die before receiving $108,000 in benefits, their heirs will receive $108,000, minus any payments that have been made to Charlie and Gloria. Estimate the rate of return if the surviving spouse lives to 90. Lives to 100. Assume that the last payment is made the month before turning 90 or 100.

1.6 Employees and their employers pay Social Security taxes on the employee's income up to a cap level, which increases each year. This datafile (https://economics-files.pomona.edu/GarySmith/SocialSecurityTaxes.txt) shows Mr. Smith's income that was subject to Social Security taxes each year that he worked from 1963 through 2010, the annual Social Security tax rate, and the total Social Security taxes he and his employer paid each year.

In 2011, at age 66, Smith retired and began receiving $2,365 in monthly Social Security benefits, an annual amount of $28,380. Social Security benefits are annually indexed for inflation. If, for example, the CPI increases by 3%, Social Security benefits increase by 3%.

What was the rate of return on Smith's Social Security contributions? That is, if he had invested the money he and his employers paid to Social Security, what rate of return would he have had to earn to generate the benefits he will get from Social Security? (Work with annual data and assume that no taxes are paid on Smith's Social Security benefits.)

1.7 Cameron bought a car for $38,000 cash. He could have leased the car by making an initial payment of $3,000 and then five annual payments of $5,000 (beginning 1 year after the beginning of the lease), plus a final residual payment of $16,000 at the end of 5 years (at which time he becomes the legal owner of the car). Either way, he has to pay insurance, repairs, maintenance, and other operating expenses out of his own pocket. Should he have leased instead?

The dealer also offered Cameron an alternative lease plan: an initial payment of $0 and then five annual payments of $1400, plus a final residual payment of $41,000 at the end of 5 years. Is this more or less attractive than the initial leasing plan?

1.8 A recent court case involved a 59-year-old single woman with $663,369 in investable funds. Your task is to estimate a judicious, sustainable, constant monthly level of real, inflation-adjusted spending using withdrawals from her prudently invested portfolio for the remainder of her life.

2. The Term Structure

2.1 It has been argued that interest rates move up and down in lockstep with the rate of inflation—an x% increase or decrease in the rate of inflation causes an x% increase or decrease in interest rates. Test this theory by using annual data to estimate the model, $R = \alpha + \beta P + \varepsilon$, where R is the interest rate on one-year Treasury bonds and P is the annual rate of inflation.

2.2 Are future interest rates better predicted by current interest rates or by the current rate of inflation? Use annual data to estimate these two models, $Y = \alpha_1 + \beta_1 X + \varepsilon_1$, and $Y = \alpha_2 + \beta_2 P + \varepsilon_2$, where Y is the interest rate on 1-year Treasury bonds, S is the interest rate the previous year and P is the annual rate of inflation the previous year.

2.3 Are current interest rates or the current rate of inflation more important for predicting future interest rates? Use annual data to estimate the model, $R = \alpha + \beta_1 S + \beta_2 P + \varepsilon$, where R is the interest rate on 1-year Treasury bonds, S is the interest rate of the previous year, and P is the annual rate of inflation the previous year.

2.4 [The FRED database (https://fred.stlouisfed.org/) has monthly data on: (a) the Market Yield on U.S. Treasury Securities at 1-Month Constant Maturity, Quoted on an Investment Basis (DGS1MO); and (b) Consumer Price Index for All Urban Consumers: All Items in U.S. City Average (CPIAUCSL). The "EDIT GRAPH" button can be used to see monthly rate data and the percent change in the CPI, which can then be annualized.]

Over the last 50 years, have the monthly returns on U. S. Treasury-bills been closely related to the rate of inflation over the same horizon, giving a roughly constant short-term real interest rate? Estimate the equation $R = \alpha + \beta P + \varepsilon$, where R is the market yield on 1-month securities and P is the monthly rate of inflation. How close is α to 0 and β to 1?

Also, calculate the (exact) real rate of return each month and see if this has been roughly constant. Use a histogram and/or boxplot to display your real rates of return.

2.5 [FRED has TIPS real interest rate data for maturities of 5 years (https://fred.stlouisfed.org/series/DFII5), 10 years (https://fred.stlouisfed.org/series/DFII10), 20 years (https://fred.stlouisfed.org/series/DFII20), and 30 years (https://fred.stlouisfed.org/series/DFII30). Students might be asked to construct time series graphs, boxplots, and/or histograms for individual or pairs of maturities; perhaps different teams looking at different maturities and/or figures. Warning: a time-series graph with all four maturities is very crowded.]

It has been argued that interest rates move in lockstep with the rate of inflation, keeping real interest rates (approximately) constant. One way to investigate this hypothesis is to look at the interest rates on Treasury Inflation-Protected Securities (TIPS), which, because the coupons and maturation value are indexed to inflation, are real interest rates. Use a time series graph and side-by-side boxplots to look at the monthly interest rates on 5-year and 30-year TIPS. What conclusions do you draw?

2.6 [FRED (https://fred.stlouisfed.org/release/tables?eid=212994&rid=354) is one source of current interest rates on Treasury zero-coupon bonds of various maturities.]

According to the expectations hypothesis, what is the anticipated 1-year Treasury rate 1 year from now? The five-year rate 5 years from now? The ten-year rate 10 years from now?

2.7 The first two columns of this data file (https://economics-files.pomona.edu/GarySmith/termstructuredata.txt) show the date; for example, year = 1946 and month = 12 is December 1946. The other columns show the interest rates on zeros maturing immediately and 1, 2, 3, … months in the future; e.g., in December 1946, a zero maturing in 12 months (in December 1947) had an interest rate of .72%.

Use these data to determine the average term structure over the 40-year period (1947–1986). Show your results in a table and a graph.

Now estimate the annual risk premia π_n for 2, 3, 4, 5, and 10-year zeros from the difference between the average interest rates on an n-year zero and a 1-year zero:

$$\pi_n = \bar{R}_n - \bar{R}_1$$

A justification for this procedure is here (https://economics-files.pomona.edu/GarySmith/termstructureriskpremia.pdf).

2.8 Find historical data on the interest rates on highly rated and lower-rated corporate bonds. Has the spread between these rates been (approximately) constant? If not, how would you explain any substantial widening or narrowing of the spread?

2.9 The Fama bond strategy asserts that future interest rates can be predicted better by current interest rates than by the implicit forward rates embedded in the term structure. For example, if the current yields are 1% on 1-year zeros and 2% on 2-year zeros, the forward rate on 1-year zeros one year from now is (approximately) 3%. Fama's strategy says that a better predictor is the current 1% rate on 1-year zeros. Test this theory by using these FRED data on the yields on 1-year (https://fred.stlouisfed.org/series/THREEFY1) and 2-year (https://fred.stlouisfed.org/series/THREEFY2) Treasury zeros.

3. Amortized Loans

3.1 In the early 1980s, a Houston homeowner had to sell her home in order to take a job in California. She had two offers on her house. The first was $160,000 cash. The second was $180,000, of which $30,000 was cash and the remaining $150,000 was an owner-financed, 30-year mortgage with an 8% loan rate. Which offer was the more financially attractive? Does your answer depend on whether the loan is paid off early?

3.2 A college loaned a professor a total of $375,000 to buy a house: $255,000 at 7% and an additional $120,000 at 12%. Both loans were conventional 30-year mortgages with constant monthly payments. For simplicity, the college business office combined these two loans into one 30-year mortgage with a single interest rate. What is the appropriate interest rate?

At the time, mortgage rates averaged around 18%. What is the value of this loan to the professor if she would otherwise have to borrow at substantially higher interest rates? (Do not consider the possibility that she might pay off her mortgage before 30 years.)

3.3 The owners of a new restaurant called First Street Bar and Grill have used almost all of their available cash to establish their restaurant and are now considering a bank loan to raise more money. One imaginative owner suggested that First Street instead issue a Gold Card for $3,000 that would enable the purchaser to have their next $5,000 in meals at First Street for free. Does this Gold Card make good financial sense? If they do issue a Gold Card, which of the following deals is more financially advantageous to First Street: a card that costs $3,000 and can be used for $5,000 in meals or a card that costs $6,000 and can be used for $10,000 in meals? One owner suggested a $500 monthly limit on the use of the Gold card. Why might such a limit be financially advantageous for First Street?

You have been hired as a financial consultant to First Street. You will have to make some assumptions, including the owners' presumption that the food is so good that the Gold Card holder would have eaten at First Street anyway and that the restaurant does not go out of business prematurely.

3.4 In 2021, Ms. Jackson bought a small Seattle condo for $450,000 and needed to decide between two payment options:

a. a $135,000 cash down payment and a $315,000 loan at 2.25% interest rate

b. a $90,000 cash down payment and a $360,000 loan at 3.00% interest rate

Both loans were conventional mortgages amortized over 30 years with monthly payments. Neither loan had points or any differences other than the size of the loan and the annual interest rate. Assuming that she will pay off each mortgage as scheduled over 30 years, what is the implicit interest rate on the additional $45,000 borrowed with Option (b)? What if she sells her condo and pays off her mortgage after 5 years? Which loan would you advise her to take?

3.5 Critically evaluate this analysis of a Reverse Annuity Mortgage by the owner of a Washington, D.C. real estate firm, "showing the real problem with RAMs from the homeowner's point of view":

> Assume Laura owns her house valued at $100,000 and has no mortgage. An 80% loan on the house would be $80,000. Bountiful Bank will give Laura a 10-year payout of monthly payments. With current mortgage rates of 16%, we have a little reverse figuring to do.
>
> What we have to do is find the payment per month on the 16% page of the amortization table in the 10 year column that, when multiplied by 120 payments (10 years x 12 months), equals $80,000. Let's pick a payment for two 10-year loans at 16%:
>
> $50,000 loan gives $838/month at 16%
> $40,000 loan gives $667/month at 16%
>
> From these monthly payments we can determine the total amount of money paid to Laura:
>
> $838/month x 120 payments = $100,560
> $667/month x 120 payments = $80,040
>
> Therefore, in effect, $40,000 is the amount the bank is willing to give Laura over 10 years, $333/month ($40,000/120 payments)!
>
> In effect, Laura sold her $100,000 house for $40,000. And don't forget Sad Lot S&L has inflation working for it now. The $333/month payment won't actually be worth $333 as time progresses.

3.6 [This problem can be simplified with additional assumptions; for example, assume that the mortgage interest is not an itemized deduction.]

Financial advisor Suze Orman has often recommended paying down a mortgage instead of putting money in an IRA (also taking money out of an IRA to pay down a mortgage). Consider this scenario:

Cory is 35 years old, and he expects his combined federal and state income tax rate to be 30% for his entire life. He is about to take out an amortized 30-year $300,000 mortgage with a 6% APR. Cory is considering two options:

a. Put $10,000 of his current salary in an IRA. After 30 years, Cory will withdraw this money and pay taxes on the full amount, the $10,000 plus what it has earned for 30 years.

b. Pay a 30% income tax on this $10,000 and use $7,000 to pay down the size of his initial mortgage to $293,000. The saving in monthly mortgage payments for the next 30 years will be invested in an ordinary non-IRA account.

What do you recommend?

4. Bonds

4.1 Select five financial assets that have very different timing of their cash flows, for example, one might be a 30-year mortgage with a 4% interest rate, and another might be a 5-year Treasury zero with a 4% interest rate. For each of these five assets, compare the duration, modified duration, and actual percentage change in present value resulting from a one-percentage-point change in the required return.

4.2 Austin is 25 years old and pays a 25% combined federal and state income tax. She is considering two investment options:

a. Put $10,000 of her current salary in an IRA. After 30 years, Austin will withdraw this money and pay taxes on the full amount, the $10,000 plus what it has earned for 30 years.

b. Pay a 25% income tax on this $10,000 and invest $7,500 in a non-IRA brokerage account. Assume an effective tax rate of 10% on the annual returns. Assume that the same investments will be made with either strategy. Compare the future values after 30 years, considering possible annual returns of 0% to 15% and possible tax rates of 15%, 25%, and 35% on IRA withdrawals after 30 years.

4.3 Your client wants to invest $1,000 of her income either in 30-year Corporate AAA bonds paying 3.8% or 30-year California AAA bonds paying 3.1%. Assume that the bonds pay 3.8% (or 3.1%) each year and that the after-tax income is reinvested to earn the same interest rate. For example, an investment of $1 will be worth $1(1+r) after 1 year and $1(1+r)^2 after 2 years, where r is the after-tax interest rate on the bond.

There are three ways to make this investment:

a. A conventional account. Pay an income tax rate t on the $1,000 and invest the remainder (1 – t)$1,000 in bonds, paying income taxes every year on the interest.
b. Traditional IRA. Invest $1,000 in bonds and pay no taxes until the money is withdrawn. When the money is withdrawn, pay taxes on every dollar withdrawn, both interest and principal.
c. Roth IRA. Pay an income tax rate t on the $1,000 and invest the remainder (1 – t)$1,000 in bonds. No additional taxes will ever be paid.

In each case, the coupons will be reinvested in the account, and she does not anticipate needing the money until she retires 30 years from now. What do you recommend?

Specifically, for each account, which bond do you recommend? Which account do you recommend? How much difference does it make?

4.4 Suppose that the term structure is flat with 5% interest rates on Treasury bonds with maturities ranging from 1 to 30 years. You pay $100 for a 20-year Treasury bond selling for par, immediately after which the interest rates on all Treasury bonds fall to 4%. Assume that the coupons are paid annually and that, each year, you reinvest the coupons in 1-year bonds with a 4% interest rate. Calculate the realized rate of return on your investment for holding periods from 1 to 20 years. Repeat this exercise, assuming (a) that the interest rate stays at 5% and (b) immediately after purchasing the bond, all interest rates increase to 6%. What is your conclusion?

5. Stock Exchanges

5.1 [Can assign one company to each team.] From the largest U.S. IPOs in history, look at an IPO that happened at least 10 years ago. Present a brief report on the company and its stock performance compared to the S&P 500.

Deutsche Telekom	11/18/1996
Alstom	6/22/1998
Conoco	10/22/1998
Goldman Sachs Group	5/3/1999
Enel spA	11/2/1999
United Parcel Service	11/9/1999

Infineon	3/13/2000
China Unicom Ltd	6/21/2000
Visa	3/18/2008
Agere Systems	3/27/2001
Kraft Foods	6/12/2001
CIT Group	7/1/2002
Blackstone Group L.P.	6/21/2007
General Motors	11/18/2010
HCA Holdings	3/10/2011
Alibaba	9/18/2014

5.2 A January 1, 2020, Yahoo Finance story quoted Lending Tree Chief Economist Tendayi Kapfidze's view of bitcoin: "It's a pyramid scheme.... You only make money based on people who enter after you." A blogger responded:

> Isn't this how the entire stock market works? You buy a stock at a price, and the stock you buy only increases in value based on people after you buying the same stock? The more people who buy the stock the higher the stock increases in value? That is what causes the stock to increase in value. Otherwise no one would invest in the stock market.

Who do you agree with?

Use historical S&P 500 index data on dividends, earnings, and prices to compare: (a) S&P 500 dividends and prices over time; and (b) S&P 500 earnings and prices over time.

5.3 Suppose that at age 25, you invest $1,000 in each of 10 stocks that do not pay dividends. Each year for 50 years, the change in each stock's price is given by a normal distribution with a mean of 10% and a standard deviation of 20%. Use Monte Carlo simulations to compare these two strategies:

a. Buy-and-hold your original 10 stocks for the entire period.
b. At the end of each year, sell any stock whose price is lower than its purchase price; receive a 30% tax refund on the realized capital loss; and invest what is left over after selling this stock and getting a tax refund in a new stock with an annual return given by a normal distribution with a mean of 10% and standard deviation of 20%. (Ignore limits on deductible capital losses and rules on wash sales.)

Redo your simulations, this time assuming that the returns on the selected stocks have a mean of 10% and a standard deviation of 40%.

5.4 Suppose that at age 25, you invest $1,000 in each of 10 stocks that do not pay dividends. Each year for 50 years, the change in each stock's price is given by a normal distribution with a mean of 10% and a standard deviation of 20%. Use Monte Carlo simulations to compare these three strategies

a. Buy-and-hold your original 10 stocks for the entire period.

b. At the end of each year, sell any stock whose price is higher than its purchase price; pay a 15% tax on the realized capital gain; and invest what is left over after selling this stock and paying the tax in a new stock with an annual return given by a normal distribution with a mean of 10% and standard deviation of 20%.

c. At the end of each year, sell any stock whose price is lower than its purchase price; receive a 30% tax refund on the realized capital loss; and invest what is left over after selling this stock and getting a tax refund in a new stock with an annual return given by a normal distribution with a mean of 10% and standard deviation of 20%. (Ignore limits on deductible capital losses and rules on wash sales.)

5.5 [Can do the same exercise with Berkshire Hathaway or any other stock that has decades of data.]

Use historical data on the S&P 500 index to compare the cumulative total returns (dividends plus capital gains) for these three strategies for an investor who invests $1,000 on the first day of the first year of your data:

a. Buy-and-hold the S&P 500 for the entire period.

b. At the end of each year, sell the S&P 500 if its price level is higher than its purchase price; pay a 15% tax on the realized capital gain; and repurchase the S&P 500 immediately.

c. At the end of each year, sell the S&P 500 if its price level is lower than its purchase price; get a tax refund equal to 30% of the realized capital loss; and repurchase the S&P 500 immediately. (Ignore limits on deductible capital losses and rules on wash sales.)

6. Dividend-Discount Models

6.1 Consider an investment paying $1 annually, that will begin 1 year from today and grow at a rate g forever. What fraction of its present value consists of the cash flow during the first 50 years?

6.2 Stocks, like bonds, should be valued by discounting the cash flow by a term structure of required returns. As John Burr Williams wrote, "A constant rate is wrong, and can only lead to wrong results."

To investigate the consequences of using a constant required return, consider this term structure of required returns, R_i that can be used to value a stock that pays an annual dividend that will be $1 a year from now and then grow at a rate g. (The first-year dividend is discounted by the first-year required return; the second-year dividend by the second-year required return; and so on.)

Year	R_i, percent	Year	R_i, percent
1	6.00	11	8.375
2	6.25	12	8.50
3	6.50	13	8.625
4	6.75	14	8.750
5	7.00	15	8.875
6	7.25	16	9.00
7	7.50	17	9.125
8	7.75	18	9.25
9	8.00	19	9.375
10	8.25	≥ 20	9.50

Compare the intrinsic values of this stock if the dividends are discounted by: (a) the term structure of required returns; (b) the 1-year rate (6.00%); (c) the 5-year rate (7.00%); (d) the 10-year rate (8.25%; (e) the 20-year rate (9.50%); and (f) John Burr Williams' yield to perpetuity π, where

$$\frac{1}{\pi}=\frac{1}{(1+R_1)}+\frac{1}{(1+R_2)^2}+\frac{1}{(1+R_3)^3}+\ldots$$

Consider the cases g = 0 and g = .03.

6.3 Critically evaluate: "We gauge whether the overall stock market is cheap or expensive by using the dividend-discount model P = D/(R – g). Since our average holding period is 3 months, we use the 3-month Treasury bill rate plus a 3% risk premium as our required return." Do you agree with this logic? Does it make much difference? Compare the valuations using g = .04 and (a) the current 3-month Treasury bill rate plus a 3% risk premium; and (b) the current term structure of interest rates plus a 3% risk premium.

6.4 In 2013, an InvestorPlace Assistant Editor wrote that,

> If you plan to buy and hold Walt Disney (NYSE:DIS) stock in perpetuity, why not glom on to Disney's 7.55% Coupon 2093 Maturity long-term note? The price of this offer is now well above par (the $100 mark), but its 3.56% yield to maturity is a nice return, fully 2 percentage points better than Disney's current dividend yield.

Why might a Warren Buffett disciple buy Disney stock instead of Disney bonds? Use a simple dividend discount model with a continuing 1.5% dividend yield, constant 3.56% interest rates, and a constant required return to compare these alternative investments over an 80-year horizon.

6.5 In 1986, dividends were taxed as ordinary income (with the highest tax rate being 50%) while long-term capital gains were taxed at a 20% rate. (Both tax rates were reduced to 15% in 2003.) The Smith Barney brokerage firm argued in 1986 that while the elimination of the favorable tax treatment of capital gains would favor "yield-oriented" (i.e., high dividend/price ratio) stocks, the Federal Reserve might have to lower interest rates to bolster the economy and the "Declining interest rates would benefit the faster growing companies more, in terms of changing valuation, than they would help yield-oriented stocks."

Why does the taxation of capital gains at the same rate as dividends (instead of a lower rate) favor high-yield stocks? Why are low interest rates especially favorable for growth stocks? Use the constant-growth dividend discount model to support and quantify your arguments. Assume a 50% tax on dividends, that the tax rate on capital gains is increased from 20% to 50%, and that all capital gains are realized annually.)

7. Earnings and Assets

7.1 Pick a random starting date and compare the performance of these three strategies over a 50-year horizon: 100% S&P 500, 100% 10-year Treasury bonds, 60/40 (60% stocks and 40% 10-year Treasury bonds). Summarize these strategies for a potential client.

7.2 When two people (call them Casey and Charlie) had their divorce finalized on January 1, 2013, each person got $7 million in stocks and cash. Casey also got the mortgage-free house they had lived in, and Charlie got the family business. There was no spousal support or child support (their children were grown and gone) and each seemed set for life.

Casey was 47 years old at the time and had seen friends lose money day-trading stocks, so Casey sold all the stocks and put $7 million in a checking account, where it earned no interest but seemed perfectly safe. Casey spent a total of approximately $2 million over the next 9 years, an average of about $220,000 a year. Casey still had $5 million safely parked in checking accounts, but now realized that the money would run out in another 23 years or so, even sooner with inflation. Casey went back to court in 2022, asking for spousal support because Charlie's business was thriving and the original settlement was not sufficient to maintain Casey's lifestyle.

Acting as Charlie's lawyer, provide estimates of how much wealth Casey would have had on December 31, 2021, if Casey had invested 100% in: (a) S&P 500; (b) 10-year Treasury bonds; or (c) a checking account.

7.3 [This website (https://www.multpl.com/s-p-500-historical-prices/table/by-year) has data on the S&P 500 on January 1 of every year going back to 1871. This website (https://www.multpl.com/s-p-500-earnings-yield) has data on the S&P 500 earnings yield on January 1 of every year going back to 1871. This website (https://www.multpl.com/s-p-500-dividend-yield/table/by-year) has data on the S&P 500 dividend yield on December 31 of every year going back to 1871.]

How well is the percentage change in the S&P 500 each year predicted by the earnings yield and dividend yield at the start of that year?

7.4 Legendary fund manager Peter Lynch popularized the PEG ratio (the ratio of a stock's P/E to its percentage growth rate) as a way of gauging whether a stock is cheap or expensive. Lynch argued that a fairly priced stock has a PEG of 1, while a stock with a PEG greater than 1 is overpriced and a stock with a PEG less than 1 is underpriced. For example, a company with a 20% growth rate that is selling for 10 times earnings would have a PEG of .5, "a very attractive ratio that would make the company an immediate buy." Explain the general logic of comparing the price-earning ratio to the growth rate. Then use the constant-growth model to show a specific hypothetical example of a company with a PEG ratio of (approximately) .5 that is not an "immediate buy."

7.5 [Can assign, say, 5, 6, or 10 stocks to a team.]

Legendary fund manager Peter Lynch popularized the PEG ratio (the ratio of a stock's P/E to its percentage growth rate) as a way of gauging whether a stock is cheap or expensive. Lynch argued that a fairly priced stock has a PEG of 1, while a stock with a PEG greater than 1 is overpriced and a stock with a PEG less than 1 is underpriced. For example, a company with a 20% growth rate that is selling for 10 times earnings would have a PEG of .5, "a very attractive ratio that would make the company an immediate buy."

Test this theory with stocks from the Dow Jones Industrial Average on December 31, 2009: 3M (MMM) 12.5%, Alcoa (AA) 15%, American Express (AXP) 11.5%, AT&T (T) 5%, Bank of America (BAC) 5%, Boeing (BA) 8.5%, Caterpillar (CAT) 10%, Chevron Corporation (CVX) 7%, Cisco Systems (CSCO) 10%, Coca-Cola (KO) 9%, E.I. du Pont de Nemours (DD) 5.5%, Exxon Mobil (XOM) -2.8%, General Electric (GE) 8.5%, Hewlett-Packard (HPQ) 11%, Home Depot (HD) 9.5%, Intel (INTC) 10%, International Business Machines (IBM) 10%, Johnson & Johnson (JNJ) 7%, JPMorgan Chase (JPM) 8%, Kraft Foods (KFT) 9.1%, McDonald's

(MCD) 9%, Merck (MRK) 5%, Microsoft (MSFT) 11%, Pfizer (PFE) 1.9%, Procter & Gamble (PG) 10%, Travelers Companies (TRV) 7%, United Technologies (UTX) 10%, Verizon (VZ) 4%, Wal-Mart (WMT) 11%, Walt Disney (DIS) 5%.

The percentage numbers given in this list are the median forecasts of stock analysts of the long-run growth of earnings for each company. For each stock you analyze, find the closing price on December 31, 2009, the per-share earnings for the preceding 12 months, and the stock's rate of return since then. Compare the P/Es with the projected growth rate of earnings, and compare the PEGs with each stock's subsequent return.

7.6 Legendary fund manager Peter Lynch popularized the PEG ratio (the ratio of a stock's P/E to its percentage growth rate) as a way of gauging whether a stock is cheap or expensive. Lynch argued that a fairly priced stock has a PEG of 1, while a stock with a PEG greater than 1 is overpriced and a stock with a PEG less than 1 is underpriced. For example, a company with a 20% growth rate that is selling for 10 times earnings would have a PEG of .5, "a very attractive ratio that would make the company an immediate buy."

Here are the January 2014 PEGs of the 30 Dow stocks. See if there is a relationship between the PEG and the subsequent return on the stock from January 1, 2014, through the most recently available data:

	PEG		PEG
AT&T, Inc.	3.80	Johnson & Johnson	3.32
American Express	1.73	JPMorgan Chase	2.24
The Boeing	2.23	McDonald's	2.13
Caterpillar	1.73	Merck	14.39
Cisco Systems	1.44	Microsoft	1.88
Chevron	1.46	3M	1.92
Coca-Cola	2.85	Nike	1.99
du Pont	1.60	Pfizer	2.88
Walt Disney	1.53	Procter & Gamble	2.45
Exxon Mobil	5.71	Travelers	1.35
General Electric	2.24	United Health Group	1.90
Goldman Sachs	1.95	United Technologies	1.35
Home Depot	1.29	Verizon	6.14
IBM	1.22	Visa	1.56
Intel	2.76	Wal-Mart	1.74

7.7 [Can assign different starting dates to different teams.]

This website http://www.dogsofthedow.com/ ranks the 30 Dow stocks each December 31 by dividend yield. Click the 2010 tab to find the ten Dow Jones industrial stocks with the highest dividend yields on

December 31, 2009. From a historical list of the Dow stocks on December 31, 2009, you can identify the 20 stocks in the Dow Jones Industrial Average with the lowest dividend yields. Compare the returns during the subsequent 10 years (January 1, 2010–December 31, 2019) for these two investment strategies:

1. (Dogs of the Dow). Invest an equal amount in each of the 10 Dow stocks with the highest dividend yields on December 31, 2009.
2. Invest an equal amount in each of the 20 Dow stocks with the lowest dividend yields on December 31, 2009.

7.8 [Can assign different starting dates to different teams.]

This website http://www.dogsofthedow.com/ ranks the 30 Dow stocks each December 31 by dividend yield. Click the 2010 tab to find the ten Dow Jones industrial stocks with the highest dividend yields on December 31, 2009. From a historical list of the Dow stocks on December 31, 2009, you can identify the 20 other stocks in the Dow Jones Industrial Average. Compare the returns during the subsequent 10 years (January 1, 2010–December 31, 2019) for these two investment strategies:

1. (Motley Fool's Foolish Four).
   a. On December 31, 2009, identify the 10 stocks in the Dow Jones Industrial Average with the highest dividend yields.
   b. Of these 10 stocks, choose the 5 stocks with the lowest price per share.
   c. Of these 5 stocks, cross out the stock with the lowest price.
   d. Invest 40% of your wealth in the stock with the next lowest price.
   e. Invest 20% of your wealth in each of the other three stocks.
2. On December 31, 2009, identify the 26 stocks in the Dow Jones Industrial Average that are not included in the Foolish Four Strategy. Invest an equal amount in each of these 26 stocks.

8. Real Assets

8.1 You own a house with a cost basis of $1 million and no mortgage. You can sell it now for $1.8 million net of sale expenses, giving a capital gain of $800,000. Since this was your family's primary residence for 2 of the last 5 years (the minimum occupancy requirement) and your tax status is married filing jointly, $500,000 of this $800,000 capital gain is tax exempt. Alternatively, you can rent the home for several years before selling and receive net after-tax rental income of $100,000 a year, but you would then lose the $500,000 capital gains tax exemption. Show how you would decide between these two alternatives.

8.2 Explain why you are wary of the following analysis. Be specific!

We projected the cash flow (millions of dollars) for these two alternative 10-year projects and chose the one with the higher IRR:

Year	Project A	Project B
0	−100	100
1	10	−20
2	15	−20
3	20	−15
4	25	−10
5	30	−10
6	35	−10
7	30	−10
8	20	−10
9	10	−10
10	−40	−5

8.3 Trammel Crow analyzed the construction of an office building adjacent to a prestigious golf course. One option was to buy 5 acres for $650,000 and construct one 30,000 square foot building. A second possibility was to purchase 8.75 acres for $1,000,000 and build two 30,000 square foot buildings. Each building would cost $3,000,000 to construct and would take 1 year to be ready for occupancy. The second option would cost less per square foot of building area to develop and would eventually yield double the rental income of the first option. However, due to the softness of the office leasing market, it would be necessary to offer 2 years of free rent in order to lease the second building. (The first building would be entirely pre-leased.) Detailed cash flow projections indicated that (except for the 2 years of free rent) each building would yield $440,000 a year forever, beginning 1 year after the purchase of the property. Assume that the construction costs are paid at the same time that the land is purchased. What is your recommendation?

8.4 The internal rate of return (IRR) is the discount rate that makes the net present value (NPV) of an investment's positive or negative cash flow X_t equal to zero.

$$0 = X_0 + \frac{X_1}{(1+\text{IRR})^1} + \frac{X_2}{(1+\text{IRR})^2} + \ldots$$

Calculate the IRRs for each of these three independent projects. In each case, do you recommend doing the project?

a.

Year	Cash
0	1,000,000
1	−100,000
2	−100,000
⋮	⋮

b.

Year	Cash
0	−35,000,000
1	90,000,000
2	−50,000,000

c.

Year	Cash
0	−42,000,000
1	90,000,000
2	−50,000,000

8.5 An international commercial construction company bought 300 acres in the Central Valley for $4,000 an acre in 2004. It financed the purchase with $200,000 cash and a $1,000,000 loan at 6%. The unpaid balance on this loan is currently $836,858. Now the company is deciding between two options:

a. Build a residential community with 900 homes. The company will spend $180 million in the first year to build the community and will sell the homes for $225 million in the second year. There will be no additional income or expenses after the second year.

b. Construct a quarry that will produce crushed rock and sand ("aggregate") used in construction projects. The quarry will cost $106 million in the first year to develop, then generate annual profits (revenue net of all wages, taxes, and other expenses) of $11.5 million in the next year, growing at 3% annually for 50 years, after which the quarry site will be closed and have no commercial value.

Which option do you recommend?

8.6 A real estate developer is choosing between constructing a 10-story or a 20-story office building. The 10-story building will cost $200 million to construct and yield net rental income of $30 million a year. The 20-story building will cost $500 million to construct and yield net rental income of $50 million a year. In either case, net rental income is projected to increase by 3% a year. Which is more financially attractive? Assume that the total construction costs are paid at a single point in time and that the rental income is paid annually, beginning one year after the construction costs are paid.

8.7 A town is considering two real estate development proposals for a large parcel of vacant land. One developer proposes constructing a shopping center that is predicted to generate net tax revenue that would be $128,000 one year from today and then grow at 1% a year forever. The second proposal is for residential homes developed in three stages. The net tax revenue from the first stage would be $29,000 one year from today and then grow at 2% a year forever. The net tax revenue from the second stage would begin at $36,000 six years from today and then grow at 2% a year forever. The net tax revenue from the third stage would begin at $41,000 eleven years from today and then grow at 2% a year forever.

The city will give each developer an immediate $2 million subsidy, and all tax revenue projections are real, inflation-adjusted, and net of all expenses that the city might incur. Which project has the higher IRR for the city? If the city's required real rate of return is between 3% and 4%, which project has the more attractive tax projections?

8.8 Pick a single-family home in a city that interests you (perhaps your hometown or where you plan on living in the future) and use data from RealEstate.com, ZipRealty.com, Zillow.com and/or other sources to determine whether buying this home to live in is an attractive financial investment.

8.9 Use either RealEstate.com, ZipRealty.com, or Zillow.com to find the prices for houses that are for sale in your hometown or where you plan to live in the future. Specify a plausible multiple-regression model for explaining these prices and use a random sample of at least 60 houses to estimate your model's parameters.

8.10 Much of Southern California's growth has been fueled by households looking for affordable homes and developers looking for relatively inexpensive land where they can build affordable homes. This Southern California sprawl has enveloped the Inland Empire and has now moved into the San Bernardino high desert. For example, many people who work in Fontana, Rancho Cucamonga, and Ontario choose to live 35–45 miles away in Victorville and other high desert communities where homes are more affordable. Estimate how much cheaper homes would have to be in Victorville to cover the cost of the round-trip commute. Assume that the time spent commuting can be ignored because commuters listen to informative economics podcasts.

9. Conservation of Value

9.1 [Can assign subsets to different teams; for example, one merger per team.]

From the largest U.S. mergers and acquisitions (M&A) in history, you will look at a M&A that happened at least 10 years ago. Compare the rates of return on the stocks involved before and after the M&A with the overall market. Present a brief report on the companies and stock performance.

America Online and Time Warner on January 11, 2001

Pfizer and Warner-Lambert on June 19, 2000

AT&T and BellSouth on June 19, 2000

Exxon and Mobil on November 30, 1999

Glaxo Wellcome PLC and SmithKline Beecham on December 26, 2000

Royal Dutch Petroleum and Shell Transport & Trading formed Royal Dutch Shell on July 20, 2005

Comcast purchased AT&T Broadband, a division of AT&T, and formed Comcast

Corporation on November 18, 2002

Citicorp and Travelers Group on October 7, 1998

Pfizer and Wyeth on October 15, 2009

Bell Atlantic and GTE on July 2, 2000

SBC Communications and Ameritech on October 8, 1999

Pfizer and Pharmacia on April 15, 2003

JP Morgan Chase and Bank One on June 30, 2004

9.2 [Can assign subsets to different teams; for example, one spinoff per team.]

Some of the biggest corporate spinoffs in history were: Hewlett-Packard and Agilent Technologies in 1999; BCE and Nortel in 2000; AT&T and Liberty Media in 2001; Viacom in 2006; Altria and Kraft Foods in 2007; Abbott Laboratories and AbbVie in 2013; Kraft Foods Group and Mondelez International in 2012; eBay and PayPal in 2015; Honeywell International and AdvanSix in 2016; the dissolution of DowDuPont in 2019; and IBM and Kyndryl in 2021. Compare the rates of return on the stocks involved before and after one of these spinoffs with the overall market. Present a brief report on the companies and stock performance.

9.3 Find 30 recent stock splits. Calculate the return on the stock minus the return on the S&P 500 on: (a) the day the split was announced (or the next trading day if the split was announced after the close of trading); and (b) on the day that the stock split took effect. Is the average value of this difference on either day (a) or (b) substantial and a statistically persuasive difference from zero?

10. Technical Analysis

10.1 An old Wall Street saying is, "As January goes, so goes the year." Use a simple regression model to see whether the February–December percentage change in the Dow Jones industrial average of stock prices is well predicted by the percentage change in January.

10.2 A former chairman of Goldman Sachs Asset Management wrote that,

> There's an odd little thing called the five-day rule.... The rule simply states that when the main U.S. stock-market indexes show a combined positive return after the first five days of trading, the year as a whole is very likely to be a good one....
>
> Jose Ursua, a former colleague of mine at Goldman Sachs, has run these numbers all the way back to 1928. He finds that when stocks rallied during the first five days, there was a 75.4 percent chance of a rally for the year. For the period since 1950, the probability rises to 82.9 percent. Few rules in finance are as unambiguous as that.

One problem with this evidence is that the market usually goes up. Another is that if the market goes up in the first five trading days of January, the market is already part way to being up for the year (and it is too late to go back and buy stocks on December 31 of the previous year). Test the more useful theory that if the market goes up during the first five trading days in January, then it is more likely to go up during the remainder of the year.

10.3 Use a simple regression model to see whether the annual percentage change in the Dow is well predicted by the percentage change in the preceding year.

10.4 Use a simple regression model to see whether the annual percentage-point change in the interest rate on 10-year Treasury bonds is well predicted by the change in the preceding year.

10.5 Collect daily data during 2 recent years for Y = the percentage price change in the S&P 500 and for 100 explanatory variables, each equal to the daily difference between the high and low temperatures in 100 diverse cities. Use the first year of your data to estimate 100 simple regression models, each using one of your 100 explanatory variables. Identify the five cities with the highest t-values and estimate a multiple regression model using only these five cities as explanatory variables. Finally, use the estimated coefficients for the multiple regression model you estimated with the first year's data to predict the daily percentage price changes in the S&P 500 during the second year. What is your conclusion?

10.6 Collect daily data during 2 recent years for Y = the percentage price change in the S&P 500 and for 100 explanatory variables, with the daily value of each explanatory variable equal to a randomly generated number. Use the first year of your data to estimate 100 simple regression models, each using one of your 100 explanatory variables. Identify the five variables with the highest t-values and estimate a multiple regression model using only these five explanatory variables. Finally, use the estimated coefficients for the multiple regression model you estimated with the first year's data to predict the daily percentage price changes in the S&P 500 during the second year. What is your conclusion?

10.7 Use a random number generator to create 500 observations for 101 variables. Let the first random variable be Y, the variable you want to predict and let the other 100 variables be the potential explanatory variables that will be used to predict Y. Use the first 250 observations to estimate a multiple regression model using the 100 explanatory variables to predict Y. (Alternatively, you can estimate five models with 20 explanatory variables.) Identify the five explanatory variables with the highest t-values. Reestimate your multiple regression model using these five explanatory variables and the first 250 observations to predict Y.

Now, use the estimated coefficients for the second multiple regression model that you estimated with the first 250 observations to predict the values of Y for the second 250 observations. What is your conclusion?

10.8 Select a 10-year period, such as 2015–2024. Estimate a multiple regression model using the following four explanatory variables, all recorded the year before the Super Bowl, to predict the Super Bowl score differential (AFC team score minus NFC team score) in the first 5 years of your data:

High temperature in London on June 30

Dow Jones Industrial Average on June 30

Average number of letters in the names of Physics Nobel Prize winner(s) that year

Number of points earned by the soccer team winning the Premier League in the season ending that May

How well does your model estimated from the first 5 years predict the Super Bowl score differential in the last 5 years of your data? What is your conclusion?

10.9 Use a multiple regression model with the high temperatures on election day in these ten cities as explanatory variables for predicting the Democratic Party candidate's percentage of the total two-party vote for President in the 11 presidential elections 1980–2020: Claremont, California; Bozeman, Montana; Broken Bow, Nebraska; Burlington, Vermont; Caribou, Maine; Cody, Wyoming; Dover, Delaware; Elkins, West Virginia; Fargo, North Dakota; and Pocatello, Idaho. Now use your estimated model to predict the Democratic Party candidate's percentage of the total two-party vote for President in 2024. What is your conclusion?

10.10 In 2000, the *American Economic Review* published an article reporting that, during the period January 1, 1967, to December 31, 1997, the average stock return on the first trading day (normally Monday) following a daylight saving time change was lower than on other Mondays. Test this theory using the daily S&P 500 returns for January 1, 1998–December 31, 2024. Be sure to distinguish between spring and fall daylight saving time changes.

10.11 A 1907 book titled *Friday the 13th* described a malicious stockbroker's attempt to cause a stock market crash on Friday the 13th. Almost 28,000 copies were sold in the first week, and the idea of a link between Friday the 13th and a bad stock market was born. Use daily S&P 500 returns for the period 1975–2024 to see whether the returns on Friday the 13th have differed systematically from the returns on other Fridays.

10.12 In 2002, the *American Economic Review* published an article reporting that a "sell in May and go away" strategy had been profitable during the period January 1970–August 1998. This strategy assumes that the stock market does better during the months of November–April than during the months of May–October. The authors estimated the model $R = \alpha + \beta S + \varepsilon$, where R is the monthly return and S is a dummy variable equal to 1 in months November–April and 0 in months May–October. Test this model using the monthly S&P 500 returns for January 1999–December 2024.

10.13 A Santa Claus rally describes a sustained increase in stock prices that occurs in the week leading up to December 25. However, there seems to be some disagreement over whether these rallies happen in the week leading up to Christmas, or if it's the week after Christmas. Test these two theories using daily data for either the Dow or the S&P 500.

10.14 Calculate the daily returns for either the Dow or the S&P 500 for at least two consecutive years. The first year(s) will be the in-sample period used to estimate a multiple-regression model for predicting daily stock returns. The remaining data will be the out-of-sample period used to test your model. Now select at least n = 30 explanatory variables that have daily data over the same time period and are clearly unrelated to stock returns. (Alternatively, you can use monthly data for the market return and your explanatory variables as long as you have at least 100 in-sample observations and 100 out-of-sample observations.)

Use a statistical package that can use a stepwise regression procedure to identify the explanatory variables that best predict the daily market returns during the in-sample period. Then use the explanatory variables you have chosen and the coefficients estimated with the in-sample data to predict stock returns in the in-sample and out-of-sample periods. Compare the in-sample and out-of-sample prediction accuracy.

11. The Efficient-Market Hypothesis

11.1 One way to test whether there is momentum or reaction in the stock market is to calculate the correlation between adjacent returns using least squares estimates of the model

$$Y = \alpha + \beta X + \varepsilon$$

where Y is the return during one period and X is the return during the previous period. Estimate this model using at least 1 year of daily observations on changes in either the Dow or the S&P 500. Is there a substantial and statistically persuasive empirical relationship?

11.2 A statistical run is a sequence of uninterrupted pluses or uninterrupted minuses. Collect data on the monthly returns for either the Dow or the S&P 500 over at least a 30-year period. Find the median monthly return and identify each monthly return as being above or below the median. Count the number of runs.

For instance, if we were only looking at 12 monthly returns and the median return was 1.0%, we would label the months when the return was above 1.0% with a plus sign and the months when the return was below 1.0% with a minus sign. The results might look like one of these patterns:

2 runs (momentum)	+	+	+	+	+	+	−	−	−	−	−	−
12 runs (reaction)	+	−	+	−	+	−	+	−	+	−	+	−
6 runs (random)	+	−	−	+	−	+	+	+	+	−	−	−

As indicated by these three patterns, stock prices will exhibit few runs if there is momentum in stock returns and many runs if there is reaction. You can use an Internet calculator to determine the expected value of the number of runs in your data and the statistical significance of your results.

11.3 Investigate how well mutual fund performance is predicted by past performance.

11.4 [This website (https://www.multpl.com/shiller-pe/table/by-year) has data on the Shiller PE ratio (CAPE) on January 1 of every year going back to 1872. This website (https://www.multpl.com/s-p-500-historical-prices/table/by-year) has data on the S&P 500 on January 1 of every year going back to 1871.]

Starting with January 1, 1872, how well does the CAPE ratio at the start of each year predict the percentage change in the S&P 500 that year?

11.5 This website (https://som.yale.edu/faculty-research-centers/centers-initiatives/international-center-for-finance/data/stock-market-confidence-indices/united-states-stock-market-confidence-indices) has data on the U.S. One-Year Confidence Index, the percentages of individual and institutional investors who expect the Dow Jones Industrial Average to be higher a year from the date of the survey. How accurate have these two surveys been in predicting whether the Dow Average would be higher 1 year after the date of the survey?

11.6 This website (https://som.yale.edu/faculty-research-centers/centers-initiatives/international-center-for-finance/data/stock-market-confidence-indices/united-states-stock-market-confidence-indices) gives data on the U.S. One-Year Confidence Index, the percentage of individual and institutional investors who expect the Dow Jones Industrial Average to be higher a year from the date of the survey. Is this Confidence Index positively or negatively related to the change in the Dow Average during the year *before* the date of the survey?

11.7 This website (https://som.yale.edu/faculty-research-centers/centers-initiatives/international-center-for-finance/data/stock-market-confidence-indices/japan-stock-market-confidence-indices) gives data on the Japan One-Year Confidence Index, the percentage of U.S. and Japan institutional investors who expect the Nikkei Stock Average to be higher a year from the date of the survey. How accurate have these two surveys been in predicting whether the Nikkei Average would be higher 1 year after the date of the survey?

11.8 This website (https://som.yale.edu/faculty-research-centers/centers-initiatives/international-center-for-finance/data/stock-market-confidence-indices/japan-stock-market-confidence-indices) gives data on the Japan One-Year Confidence Index, the percentage of U.S. and Japan institutional investors who expect the Nikkei Stock Average to be higher a year from the date of the survey. Is this Confidence Index positively or negatively related to the change in the Dow Average during the year *before* the date of the survey?

11.9 Mondays have a reputation on Wall Street for being wild and often downright nasty—a reputation that has been confirmed by several studies. For example, a calculation of daily percentage stock returns from 1963–1978 found that the overall average daily return was .0152%. Only Monday had a negative average—a staggering −33.5% on an annual basis. The researchers tried to find a reasonable explanation and came up empty, concluding that it is "an obvious anomaly."

Compare the average daily returns for each day of the week for either the Dow or the S&P 500 during a recent 10-year or 20-year period.

11.10 This site (https://www.multpl.com/s-p-500-price-to-book) has data on the ratio of the price to book value for the S&P 500. Starting with

December 31, 1999, look at the price-to-book ratio for the quarter ending on December 31 of each year and the rate of return for the S&P 500 during the subsequent year. Is the relationship positive or negative? Substantial and statistically persuasive?

11.11 Since 1983, *Fortune* magazine has published an annual list of the most-admired companies based on surveys of thousands of executives, directors, and securities analysts. Select a 5-year period (for example, 2015–2019) and identify the top 10 most-admired companies each year. Construct a most-admired portfolio consisting of an equal investment in each of the 10 most-admired companies in the first year of your data. Calculate the return on this portfolio from the day of the announcement of the first-year's top-10 until the announcement of the top-10 for the second year; then invest the portfolio equally in the second-year top-10 stocks. Continue this for all 5 years and compare the performance of the most-admired portfolio to the S&P 500.

12. The Human Factor in Investments

12.1 In the 1980s, Kahneman and Tversky asked students the following question: "Imagine that you have decided to see a play and paid the admission price of $10 per ticket. As you enter the theater, you discover that you have lost the ticket. The seat was not marked and the ticket cannot be recovered. Would you pay $10 for another ticket?" They asked a different group of students this question: "Imagine that you have decided to see a play where admission is $10 per ticket. As you enter the theater, you discover that you have lost a $10 bill. Would you still pay $10 for a ticket for the play?" Do this experiment with an updated ticket price and see if there is a substantial and statistically persuasive difference in the responses to these two questions. How might this relate to investing?

12.2 Ask a random sample of students the following question: "Your favorite singer is performing tonight and you paid $200 for a ticket to the concert. Unfortunately, you will have to drive 60 miles through a snowstorm to get to the concert. Will you go?" Ask another random sample of students this question: "Your favorite singer is performing tonight and you were given a free ticket to the concert. Unfortunately, you will have to drive 60 miles through a snowstorm to get to the concert. Will you go?" Is there a substantial and statistically persuasive difference in the responses to these two questions? How might this relate to investing?

12.3 Ask a random sample of students the following question: "Your favorite singer is performing tonight and a friend paid $200 for a ticket to the concert. Your friend is sick and gave you the ticket for free. Unfortunately, you will have to drive 60 miles through a snowstorm to get to the concert. Will you go?" Ask another random sample of students this question: "Your favorite singer is performing tonight and a friend got a free ticket to the concert. Your friend is sick and gave you the ticket. Unfortunately, you will have to drive 60 miles through a snowstorm to get to the concert. Will you go?" Is there a substantial and statistically persuasive difference in the responses to these two questions? How might this relate to investing?

12.4 Anchoring is a general human tendency to rely on a reference point when making decisions. For example, randomly selected people were asked one of these two questions:

> The population of Bolivia is 5 million.
> Estimate the population of Bulgaria.
>
> The population of Bolivia is 15 million.
> Estimate the population of Bulgaria.

Those who were told that Bolivia's population is 15 million tended to give higher answers than did those told that Bolivia's population is 5 million. Several similar questions confirmed this pattern. People use a known "fact" as an anchor for their guess. Redo this study using questions you make up. How might this relate to investing?

12.5 Anchoring is a general human tendency to rely on a reference point when making decisions. For example, randomly selected people were asked one of these two questions, each involving an unrelated "fact," for example,

> Annual per capita income in Bulgaria is $4,000.
> Estimate the population of Bulgaria.
>
> Annual per capita income in Bulgaria is $20,000.
> Estimate the population of Bulgaria.

Those who were told that Bolivia's per capita income is $20,000 tended to give higher answers than did those told that Bolivia's per capita income is $4,000. Several similar questions confirmed this pattern. People use a known "fact" as an anchor for their guess. Redo this study using questions you make up. How might this relate to investing?

12.6 Ask someone to shoot 10 basketball free throws, then ask them to shoot 2 free throws blindfolded, and then 10 more free throws not blindfolded. Repeat this experiment with several different people, but don't let anyone in your sample see your experiment with other people. For half the people in your sample, loudly cheer after each blindfolded shot and tell the person that they made the shot; for the other half, groan after each blindfolded shot and say they missed badly. Does the negative/positive reinforcement during the blindfolded shots have any effect on their performance when not blindfolded? How might this relate to investing?

12.7 Ask 50 female students these four questions: "Among female students at this school, is your height above average or below average?" "Is your weight above average or below average?" "Is your intelligence above average or below average?" "Is your physical attractiveness above average or below average?" Ask 50 male students these same questions (in comparison to male students). Try to design a survey procedure that will ensure candid answers. For each sex and each question, were the students equally likely to answer "above average" or "below average." Also, compare the male and female answers to each question. How might this relate to investing?

12.8 Stand in a place where a reasonable number of people walk by, but not in large groups. Stare at the sky and have a friend record the percentage of the people walking by who look up at the sky, too. Repeat this experiment at the same location with 5, 10, or 15 of your friends staring at the sky. Again, have a friend record the percentage of people walking by who look up at the sky. Is there a big difference in the results? How might this relate to investing?

12.9 For the two most recently completed major league baseball seasons, identify those players with at least 502 official times at bat in each season. Use the simple regression model to see how well each player's batting average in the most recent season is predicted by his batting average in the preceding season. Do these results exhibit regression toward the mean? How might this relate to investing?

12.10 For the three most recently completed major league baseball seasons, identify the 10 players with at least 502 official times at bat in the middle season that had the highest batting averages. How did these players to in the adjacent seasons? For example, you might identify the 10 players with at least 502 times at bat in 2023 who had the highest batting averages in 2023 and then look at their batting averages in 2022 and 2024. Do these data show regression toward the mean? How might this relate to investing?

12.11 Select a recent 10-year period, like 2015–2024, and identify the 30 stocks in the Dow Jones Industrial Average at the start of this period. Then use the first 5 years of the period to calculate some measure of profitability, like average return on assets, for each firm. Do the same for the last 5 years of your data. Now, use the first 5 years to divide the 30 firms into three groups: the ten firms with the highest average profits during the first 5 years, the ten firms with the next highest, and the ten lowest firms. Then compare the average profitability of the firms in each of these groups during the first 5 years with their average profitability during the last 5 years. Repeat these calculations, this time choosing your three groups of ten firms based on their profitability during the last 5 years.

What pattern(s) do you see? What is the implication for investors?

12.12 Use the monthly data collected by Robert Shiller on S&P 500 real dividends, real earnings, and real stock prices from 1950 to the present to estimate this equation for each of these three data: $\ln[Y] = \alpha + \beta X + \varepsilon$, where ln[Y] is the natural logarithm of dividends, earnings, or prices and X is the year: 1950, 1951, and so on. Which has the highest R^2? The lowest? What is the implication for investors?

12.13 Ask ChatGPT and/or other large language models (LLMs) (or several LLMS) these four financial questions. How well did they do?

1. I need to borrow $47,000 to buy a new car. Is it better to borrow for one year at a 9 percent APR or for 10 years at a 1 percent APR?
2. I have to sell my house and my two best offers are
   (A) $625,000 cash
   (B) $100,000 cash and an owner-financed $600,000 30-year conventional amortized loan at a 3 percent APR.

   Which offer is more financially attractive?
3. I am a 25-year-old white male in good health. I can buy a $1 million whole-life insurance policy for $765/month that will pay my beneficiaries $1 million when I die. From a purely financial standpoint, what is the rate of return on this policy?
4. I'm thinking about buying a new home. The house costs $1 million. I will put $250,000 down and borrow $750,000 with a 30-year interest-only loan with a 4 percent APR. The annual interest payments will be $30,000. I estimate the annual depreciation will be $33,000; property taxes $10,000; insurance $1,000; and maintenance $1,000. Please help me calculate the first-year rate of return.

12.14 The 2001 best-selling book, *Good to Great*, identified 11 stocks that had outperformed the overall stock market and were still improving 15 years after they made the leap from good to great:

Abbott Laboratories	Kimberly-Clark	Pitney Bowes
Circuit City	Kroger	Walgreens
Fannie Mae	Nucor	Wells Fargo
Gillette	Philip Morris	

Compare the performance of a portfolio of these 11 stocks with the S&P 500 since January 1, 2002.

12.15 In the early 1970s, the attention of institutional investors was focused on the Nifty 50—a small group of "one-decision" stocks that were so appealing that they should always be bought and never sold, no matter what the price. There is some uncertainty about the exact composition of the Nifty 50, with one *Forbes* article referring to a Morgan Guaranty Trust list and several other *Forbes* articles referring to a Kidder Peabody list. If any group of stocks is clearly the stocks of the Nifty 50 legend, it is the 24 stocks that appear on both lists:

	1972 P/E
Polaroid	90.7
McDonald's	85.7
MGIC Investment	83.3
Walt Disney	81.6
Baxter Travenol	78.5
Intl Flavors & Fragrances	75.8
Avon Products	65.4
Emery Air Freight	62.1
Johnson & Johnson	61.9
Digital Equipment	60.0
Kresge (now Kmart)	54.3
Simplicity Pattern	53.1
AMP	51.8
Black & Decker	50.5
Schering	50.4
American Hospital Supply	50.0
Schlumberger	49.5
Burroughs	48.8
Xerox	48.8
Eastman Kodak	48.2
Coca-Cola	47.6
Texas Instruments	46.3
Eli Lilly	46.0
Merck	45.9

Compare the performance of these 24 stocks with the performance of the S&P 500 since December 31, 1972. Is their post-1972 performance related to their price/earnings (P/E) ratios in December 1972?

13. Mean-Variance Analysis

13.1 Use mean-variance analysis to describe your assessment of the opportunities now available for investors dividing all of their wealth among these three asset classes: 1-year T-bills, 20-year Treasury zeros, and an

S&P 500 index fund. Ignore taxes and assume that the investments will be made for 1 year with no adjustments during the year.

			Correlations		
	Mean	**Std Dev.**	**T-bills**	**T-bonds**	**S&P 500**
T-bills					
T-bonds					
S&P 500					

Use an online Markowitz portfolio calculator to determine the Markowitz frontier. What is the (approximate) optimal portfolio with a mean of 4%?

13.2 Below are inflation-adjusted means, standard deviations, and correlations for U.S. cash (short-term bonds), Treasury bonds, and stocks. One set of data is historical; another set was assumed by David Swensen in 2000 when he managed Yale's endowment. Compare the mean-variance portfolios implied by these two sets of data. How would you characterize the difference in investment opportunities presented by the historical data and by Swensen?

	Historical		Swensen	
	Mean	**Std Dev**	**Mean**	**Std Dev**
Cash	−.4	4.1	.0	5.0
U.S. bonds	1.2	6.5	2.0	10.0
U.S. stocks	9.2	21.7	6.0	20.0

	Historical Correlations			Swensen Correlations		
	Cash	**Bonds**	**Stocks**	**Cash**	**Bonds**	**Stocks**
Cash	1.00	.70	−.09	1.00	.50	.00
U.S. bonds	.70	1.00	.06	.50	1.00	.45
U.S. stocks	−.09	.06	1.00	.00	.45	1.00

13.3 A recent court case involved an unmarried 65-year-old woman with $15 million in liquid assets, a home with no mortgage, and no other sources of income. Assuming that her portfolio invests in cash, Treasury bonds, and U.S. stocks, your task is to estimate a reasonable annual rate of return from a prudently invested portfolio over the next 20 years.

13.4 Calculate the value surplus VS for two of the stocks listed below,

$$VS = 100\left(\frac{V-P}{P}\right)$$

where P is the market price and V is the intrinsic value given by the constant-dividend-growth equation

$$V = \frac{D}{R - g}$$

with D = annual dividend, R = real required return, and g = real annual dividend growth rate.

	D	P	D/P
Coca-Cola (KO)	1.76	62	2.88%
Johnson & Johnson (JNJ)	4.52	177	2.57%
Unilever (UL)	1.80	49	3.73%
JPMorgan Chase (JPM)	4.00	135	3.01%
Pfizer (PFE)	1.60	49	3.32%
First American Financial (FAF)	2.08	56	3.95%

Assume that the constant real required return for each of your stocks is 4.5% and that the real dividend growth rates for each stock are independent and can each be described by a truncated normal distribution with a mean of 2% and a standard deviation of .5%:

$$g \sim N[.02, .005] \qquad .00 \le g \le .04$$

First, do 10,000 Monte Carlo simulations using a random number generator that simulates draws from a normal distribution with mean .020 and standard deviation .005.

In each of these 10,000 simulations, do two draws from a normal distribution in order to determine a value of g for your first stock and a value of g for your second stock. (If any values of g are below .00, set them equal to .00; if any values of g are above .04, set them equal to .04.) Use these two values of g to determine the value surplus VS_1 for your first stock, the value surplus VS_2 for your second stock, and the portfolio value surplus PVS = $\alpha VS_1 + (1 - \alpha)VS_2$ for 11 values α = .0, .1, .2, ... 1.0.

Your results will be 10,000 values of 13 variables: VS_1, VS_2, and PVS for 11 values of α.

Show your results with

1. A histogram of the values of VS_1 that also shows how often VS_1 was negative.
2. A histogram of the values of VS_2 that also shows how often VS_2 was negative.
3. A scatterplot with 11 points, one for each value of α. Each point should show the average value of PVS (vertical axis) and the frequency with which PVS was negative (horizontal axis).

14. CAPM and Other Factor Models

14.1 Choose 10 stocks and a recent 10-year period; for example, 2015–2024. Use monthly returns for these 10 stocks and the S&P 500 during the first 5 years of your 10-year period to estimate betas for each stock. Repeat this exercise using monthly returns for the last 5 years of your 10-year period. Are there any particularly large or small betas in either period? If so, how do you explain them? How closely correlated are the beta coefficients for these two 5-year periods? Are there any drastic changes in any of the betas from one period to the next? If so, what is your explanation?

14.2 Choose 10 stocks and a recent 10-year period; for example, 2015–2024. Use daily returns for these 10 stocks and the S&P 500 during the first 5 years of your 10-year period to estimate betas for each stock. Are there any particularly large or small betas in either period? If so, how do you explain them? Repeat this exercise using data for the last 5 years of your 10-year period. How closely correlated are the beta coefficients for these two 5-year periods? Are there any drastic changes in any of the betas from one period to the next? If so, what is your explanation?

14.3 Choose 10 stocks and a recent 10-year period. Use monthly data for the first 5 years to estimate the Fama-French three-factor model plus a momentum factor,

$$R = \alpha + \beta_1 MKT + \beta_2 SMB + \beta_3 HML + \beta_4 UMD + \varepsilon$$

where

R = return on an individual stock minus return on Treasury bills
MKT = market return minus return on Treasury bills
SMB = size factor (small minus big)
HML = value factor (high value minus low value)
UMD = momentum factor (up minus down)

Are any of the 4 factor betas for these 10 stocks markedly different from the factor betas for the other stocks? Are all of the p-values for the factor betas less than .05? Are the five R^2 values impressive?

Now repeat this exercise using monthly data for the last 5 years of your 10-year period. Did any of the betas change dramatically? For each of the 4 factors, make a scatterplot of the 10 betas estimated for these 5-year periods. Is there a close correlation?

14.4 Choose 10 stocks and a recent 10-year period. Use daily data for the first 5 years to estimate the Fama-French three-factor model plus a momentum factor:

$$R = \alpha + \beta_1 MKT + \beta_2 SMB + \beta_3 HML + \beta_4 UMD + \varepsilon$$

where

R = return on an individual stock minus return on Treasury bills
MKT = market return minus return on Treasury bills
SMB = size factor (small minus big)
HML = value factor (high value minus low value)
UMD = momentum factor (up minus down)

Are any of the 4 factor betas for these 10 stocks markedly different from the factor betas for the other stocks? Are all of the p-values for the factor betas less than .05? Are the five R^2 values impressive?

Now repeat this exercise using daily data for the last 5 years of your 10-year period. Did any of the betas change dramatically? For each of the 4 factors, make a scatterplot of the 10 betas estimated for these 5-year periods. Is there a close correlation?

14.5 In a stock picking contest, a student picked stock X. He wrote that, "X has a beta of 0.90 which means it is a very stable stock." Explain why this either is or is not true. Choose 20 stocks and, using either daily or monthly data for a recent 10-year period, estimate the beta coefficient and standard deviation of returns for each stock. How closely correlated are the estimated betas and standard deviations? Are there any outliers?

14.6 Here is list of dual-purpose mutual funds, with their starting and closing dates in parentheses: American Dual Vest (August 24, 1967–June 29, 1979), Hemisphere Fund (January 18, 1968–December 10, 1984), Income & Capital Shares (September 26, 1967–March 31, 1982), Leverage Fund of Boston January 3, 1968–December 31, 1981), Scudder Duo Vest (August 31, 1967–March 31, 1982), Gemini Fund (October 18, 1967–March 19, 1985), Gemini Fund II (February 19, 1985–February 19, 1997). Compare the mean and standard deviation of the daily returns from each of these dual-purpose fund's capital shares with the S&P 500. Then use the fund's daily returns to estimate the Fama-French three-factor model, augmented by a momentum factor.

15. Derivatives

15.1 Pick 5 well-known stocks and use Yahoo Finance or another website that gives the implied stock volatilities based on the Black-Scholes model for put and call options with the same expiration date but several different strike prices. Summarize your findings. (Warning: There is likely to be considerable noise in your data because many options are traded infrequently and in small lots, but the overall patterns should be clear.)

15.2 On November 13, 2024, with the spot price of gold at $2,662.74, futures contracts for gold with a February 25, 2025, delivery date sold for $2,697.30. One could also buy call options on the February gold futures contracts at the following prices:

Strike Price	Call Price
$2,650	$94.80
$2,675	$81.00
$2,725	$58.30
$2,750	$49.10

Show the dollar gains or losses from each of these strategies as a function of the price of the futures contract when the options expire in February. How would you describe each strategy? (For example, a call option is a wager that the stock price will increase.)

a. An investor buys the 2,650 and 2,750 calls and sells the 2,675 and 2,725 calls.

b. An investor buys the 2,675 and 2,725 calls and sells the 2,650 and 2,750 calls.

15.3 On December 13, 2024, Apple stock sold for $248.13/share; a March 21, 2025, call option with a strike price of $250 sold for $11.50, and a put option with the same expiration date and a $250 strike price sold for $10.46. Use a graph to compare the profit possibilities for these two strategies as a function of the price of Apple on the March expiration date: (a) buy 1 call and 1 put; and (b) buy 2 calls and 1 puts. How would you describe these strategies? (For example, a call option is a wager that the stock price will increase.)

15.4 On December 13, 2024, Apple stock sold for $248.13/share; a March 21, 2025, call option with a strike price of $250 sold for $11.50 and a put option with the same expiration date and a $250 strike price sold for $10.46. Use a graph to compare the profit possibilities for these two strategies as a function of the price of Apple on the March expiration date: (a) sell 1 call and 1 put; and (b) sell 2 calls and 1 put. How would you describe these strategies? (For example, a call option is a wager that the stock price will increase.)

15.5 On December 13, 2024, Apple stock sold for $248.13/share; a March 21, 2025, call option with a strike price of $250 sold for $11.50 and a put option with the same expiration date and a $250 strike price sold for $10.46. Use a graph to compare the profit possibilities for these two strategies as a function of the price of Apple on the March expiration date: (a) buy 1 call and 1 put; and (b) buy 1 call and 2 puts. How would you describe these strategies? (For example, a call option is a wager that the stock price will increase.)

15.6 On December 13, 2024, Apple stock sold for $248.13/share; a March 21, 2025, call option with a strike price of $250 sold for $11.50 and a put option with the same expiration date and a $250 strike price sold for $10.46. Use a graph to compare the profit possibilities for these two strategies as a function of the price of Apple on the March expiration date: (a) sell 1 call and 1 put; and (b) sell 1 call and 2 puts. How would you describe these strategies? (For example, a call option is a wager that the stock price will increase.)

15.7 On December 13, 2024, Apple stock sold for $248.13/share; a March 21, 2025, call option with a strike price of $260 sold for $6.92 and a put option with the same expiration date and a $240 strike price sold for $6.45. Use a graph to compare the profit possibilities for these two strategies as a function of the price of Apple on the March expiration date: (a) buy 1 share of Apple; and (b) buy 1 share of Apple, sell 1 call, and buy 1 put. How would you describe these strategies? (For example, a call option is a wager that the stock price will increase.)

15.8 Find the current spot price of gold and the prices of gold futures with various delivery dates. Assuming that the only cost of carry is lost interest, calculate the implied term structure of risk-free interest rates. How does this compare to the term structure of Treasury zeros?

15.9 Find the current value of the S&P 500 and the prices of an E-Mini S&P 500 futures with various delivery dates. Taking into account the cost of carry, calculate the implied term structure of risk-free interest rates. How does this compare to the term structure of Treasury zeros?

Index

FSC
www.fsc.org
MIX
Papier | Fördert gute Waldnutzung
FSC® C083411

Kolibri 360 GmbH
Ferdinand-Jühlke-Straße 7
99095 Erfurt, Deutschland
produktsicherheit@kolibri360.de